T0357508

MUNICH
AND THE BAVARIAN ALPS

MUNICH
AND THE BAVARIAN ALPS

CONTENTS

DISCOVER 6

EXPERIENCE MUNICH 48

EXPERIENCE THE BAVARIAN ALPS 162

NEED TO KNOW 298

Left: Flugelhorns used by a Bavarian brass band
Previous page: Mist descending over the Bavarian Alps
Front cover: The beautiful church at Ramsau

DISCOVER

Red roofs seen from above in Munich

WELCOME TO
MUNICH AND THE
BAVARIAN ALPS

Forested mountains, lakes the size of oceans and the world's biggest beer festival – Munich and the Bavarian Alps make for the perfect adventure. Whether you're seeking thriving culture, natural tranquillity or a mix of the two, this DK travel guide is the perfect companion.

1 Admiring the classics in Munich's Alte Pinakothek.

2 Gingerbread hearts, an Oktoberfest tradition.

3 Surfing the Eisbach wave in the Englischer Garten.

4 Sunset over Maria Gern church in Upper Bavaria.

Located in the southeast of Germany, Bavaria has a proud reputation. Think of the state and you'll likely picture opulent castles perched atop verdant mountains, half-timbered houses sitting snug in cobbled streets and locals donning lederhosen and dirndls. These grand landscapes and time-honoured traditions are certainly worth celebrating, but they're only a fraction of Bavaria's charm.

Nowhere is the state's invigorating variety more apparent than in the capital, Munich. Germany's third-largest city is a hotbed of dynamic culture and riotous creativity, a place of bustling beer halls, world-beating museums and vast urban parks. Visit in autumn for the world's biggest beer festival, Oktoberfest, when thousands of revellers gather to sample Bavaria's best brews. Away from the beer, intimate music venues, huge art galleries and some of Europe's heartiest cuisine make Munich an easy city to fall in love with. And when the urban bustle gets too much, that Alpine wonderland is just a short trip away.

With so much to see and those mountains beckoning, it can be hard to know where to start. We've broken Munich and the Bavarian Alps down into easily navigable chapters, with detailed itineraries, expert local knowledge and colourful, comprehensive maps to help you plan the perfect visit. Whether you're staying for a weekend, a week or longer, this DK guide will ensure that you make the most of all that the region has to offer. Enjoy the book, and enjoy Munich and the Bavarian Alps.

REASONS TO LOVE
MUNICH AND THE BAVARIAN ALPS

Masterpieces of European art. Folk festivals dating back centuries. Blissful walks under ancient forest canopies. There are so many reasons to love Munich and the Bavarian Alps. Here are just a few of them.

1 MUNICH'S MUSEUMS
There are more than 80 museums in Munich alone. Swoon over classical art at the Alte Pinakothek *(p132)* or marvel at scientific wonders displayed at the Deutsches Museum *(p102)*.

WALKING THE ISAR RIVER 2
Follow the idyllic Isar as it flows through the Englischer Garten *(p118)* and heads south of Munich. The river banks with pebble beaches offer fine Alpine views.

3 OKTOBERFEST
With rousing oompah music, food stalls and vast quantities of beer, it's little wonder the world's largest folk festival draws in around seven million visitors annually.

THE ZUGSPITZE 4

View Bavaria from above at the summit of the Zugspitze *(p249)*, Germany's highest mountain, which is accessible via a sublime cable-car journey or a rugged but unforgettable two-day hike.

NATIONAL PARK BAYERISCHER WALD 5

As Central Europe's biggest forest, the Bavarian Forest *(p204)* offers visitors an abundance of natural beauty. Look out for lynx and wolves as you take to the canopy trail.

HEARTY FOODS 6

Dumplings, schnitzel and so many sausages: Bavarian food is among the heartiest in Europe. Sample it at Munich's oldest market, the Viktualienmarkt *(p70)*.

LAKE COUNTRY 7

Lakes spread out across Bavaria like a shimmering mosaic. Chiemsee *(p227)* is fondly known as the Bavarian Sea, while Königssee *(p225)* offers fairy-tale beauty.

GRAND HISTORY 8

From ornate 14th-century palaces like the Residenz *(p82)* to stirring religious sites in Landsberg *(p238)*, here you can soak up Central Europe's rich and fascinating history.

9 THE BEER

Bavaria is a beer lover's haven. Here you can visit the oldest brewery in the world, Weihenstephan *(p186)*, sample Tilman's craft beers or kick back in a huge beer hall.

10 CAPTIVATING CASTLES

Bavaria's ambitious kings carved out a legacy in stone, designing some of the world's most ornate castles, like Schloss Neuschwanstein *(p270)* and Schloss Nymphenburg *(p150)*.

MODERN ARCHITECTURE 11

Munich might be famous for its older architecture, but it's home to spectacular modern designs, too. The Museum Brandhorst *(p142)* has 36,000 ceramic rods on its exterior.

CULTURAL TRADITIONS 12

Bavarians proudly celebrate their customs, from their lederhosen and dirndls to the storied folk festivals that have brought locals together for centuries.

EXPLORE
MUNICH AND THE
BAVARIAN ALPS

This guide divides Munich and the Bavarian Alps into seven colour-coded sightseeing areas, as shown on the map below. Find out more about each area on the following pages.

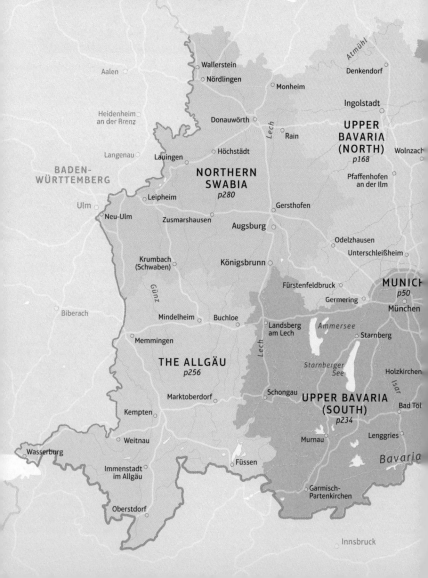

Aalen

Wallerstein

Nördlingen

Monheim

Denkendorf

Atmühl

Ingolstadt

Heidenheim
an der Brenz

Donauwörth

Lech

Rain

UPPER
BAVARIA
(NORTH)
p168

Wolnzach

Langenau

Lauingen

Höchstädt

NORTHERN
SWABIA
p280

BADEN-
WÜRTTEMBERG

Leipheim

Pfaffenhofen
an der Ilm

Ulm

Neu-Ulm

Zusmarshausen

Gersthofen

Odelzhausen

Augsburg

Unterschleißheim

Krumbach
(Schwaben)

Königsbrunn

Fürstenfeldbruck

MUNICH
p50

Germering

München

Biberach

Günz

Mindelheim

Buchloe

Landsberg
am Lech

Ammersee

Starnberg

Memmingen

Lech

Starnberger
See

Holzkirchen

THE ALLGÄU
p256

Marktoberdorf

Schongau

UPPER BAVARIA
(SOUTH)
p234

Isar

Bad Töl

Kempten

Lenggries

Weitnau

Murnau

Bavaria

Wasserburg

Füssen

Immenstadt
im Allgäu

Garmisch-
Partenkirchen

Oberstdorf

Innsbruck

NETHERLANDS

GERMANY

POLAND

BELGIUM

CZECH
REPUBLIC

SLOVAKIA

FRANCE

Munich ●

AUSTRIA

HUNGARY

SWITZERLAND

ITALY

Vils

Weiden in
der Oberpfalz

Amber

Schwandorf

Wernberg-Köblitz

Naab

Roding

CZECH

REPUBLIC

Regensburg

Viechtach

Zwiesel

Regen

Kelheim

Straubing

Bogen

Metten

Freyung

Abensberg

Plattling

Deggendorf

Danube (Donau)

Tittling

Abens

Dingolfing

LOWER BAVARIA
p190

Vilshofen

Obernzell

Ergolding

Isar

Passau

Landshut

Moosburg

Rott

Freising

Eggenfelden

Pfarrkirchen

Pocking

Zell an
der Pram

Erding

Inn

Dorfen

Mühldorf

Ried im
Innkreis

Haag

UPPER BAVARIA
(EAST)
p216

Ebersberg

Inn

Mattighofen

Rott am Inn

Alz

Altenmarkt
an der Alz

Traunreut

Seewalchen
am Attersee

Rosenheim

Salzburg

Freilassing

Miesbach

Raubling

Bernau

Anger

Strobl

Berchtesgaden

Alps

Hallstatt

AUSTRIA

0 kilometres   25

0 mile   25

N
↑

1 Central Marienplatz.

2 The sweeping lawns of the Englischer Garten.

3 The Crown of Bavaria in the Residenz.

4 The Hofbräuhaus.

From weekends exploring Munich's galleries to Alpine tours through southern Bavaria, this region offer endless options for exploration. These carefully curated itineraries ensure you'll see the very best of the city and the wider state.

24 HOURS
in Munich

Morning

Affectionately referred to as a "big village" by locals, Munich is a conveniently walkable city. It's fitting to begin your trip at Sendlinger Tor *(p72)*, one of Munich's three remaining Gothic town gates; here you can pop into one of the Glockenbach district's cafés for a Bavarian breakfast. Afterwards, head down Sendlinger Straße, where you'll come across the opulent Asamkirche on your left *(p62)*, a perfect introduction to Bavarian Baroque. Continue to Marienplatz and behold the city's main square and neo-Gothic town hall; you can rest a little as you soak up the atmosphere of Munich's bustling centre. When you're ready, head towards Germany's largest city palace, the Residenz *(p82)*, first built in the 14th century for the Wittelsbach dynasty. For lunch, stroll up to the University District, where you can choose from a range of excellent restaurants.

Afternoon

This afternoon, you'll swap grandeur for greenery. Head east until you reach the Englischer Garten *(p118)*, one of the world's largest urban parks. The park's Chinesischer Turm beer garden is a popular choice for a break and an afternoon brew; if you're lucky, you'll catch a brass band playing in the wooden tower. Slowly saunter south to the tip of the park, until you reach the Eisbach standing wave *(p119)*, where you can admire neoprene-clad surfers riding this landmark. Stop off at the Haus der Kunst *(p125)* next door to take in some art and end the afternoon with a coffee in the gallery's glorious Goldene Bar.

Evening

A trip to Munich wouldn't be complete without a beer hall, where locals have socialized for centuries. It's a 15-minute walk from the Haus der Kunst to the Hofbräuhaus *(p93)* where you can eat a hearty dinner and sing along with the music at the city's most famous watering hole. Alternatively, walk to Maxmonument, a grand statue commemorating King Maximilian II, and take tram 19 to Holzapfelstraße, where you'll find yourself outside the Augustiner brewery *(p93)*. If the weather's good, ask for a rooftop spot; otherwise, join locals at tables inside for some Bavarian revelry.

←

1 The grand façade of Schloss Nymphenburg.

2 The striking BMW Welt.

3 At the Augustiner-Keller beer garden.

4 Artwork at the Alte Pinakothek.

3 DAYS
in Munich and Beyond

Day 1

Today is all about immersing yourself in Munich's unique art and culture. Start in the proudly hip Schwabing district (p91), the epicentre of the city's bohemian movement in the early 20th century. As you stroll past the chic shops, galleries and boutiques of Hohenzollernstraße and Feilitzschstraße, you can channel the creative energy of famous residents, including artist Wassily Kandinsky. For a traditional Bavarian lunch, head to Schwabing's Restaurant ÖEINS (www.öeins.de), before making a stop at one of the traditional Wirtshäuser (pubs) to wash it down. In the afternoon, head south down Nordenstraße to the esteemed temples of visual art, the Pinakothek der Moderne (p136) and the Alte Pinakothek (p132). After spending a few hours marvelling at the masters, finish your day with some restorative vegan fare at Katzentempel (www.kaztentempel.de).

Day 2

It's time to head farther afield. Catch the 17 tram from Karlsplatz to Schloss Nymphenburg (p150), the Baroque summer residence of the Wittelsbach family's kings. Admire the opulence of the palace before strolling through the gardens, keeping an eye out for roaming deer. Spend an hour or two in the lovely botanical gardens next door; they have a butterfly exhibition in the winter. Afterwards, walk back through the palace gardens to Hirschgarten, to have lunch in the world's biggest beer garden (it seats 8,000). After lunch, hop on tram 12 and spend the afternoon at Olympiapark (p154), to see the site of the infamous 1972 Summer Olympics. The BMW Museum (p155) is located nearby; it's a fun and informative way to spend a couple of hours, especially if the weather's wet. Marvel at the futuristic architecture of BMW Welt, before returning to the city centre for dinner (we recommend Nürnberger sausages at Bratwurst Glöckl, www.bratwurst-gloeckl.de, next to the Frauenkirche).

Day 3

Grab some pretzels for breakfast before hopping on a suburban train (S-Bahn) at Hauptbahnhof, Munich's main train station, for a 20-minute journey to Starnberger See (p255). As you explore the lakeshore, enjoy freshly caught fish and an ice cream with a glorious panorama of the Bavarian Alps. For lunch, hop on a bus from Starnberg to Kloster Andechs (p242) at Ammersee, a lake farther west. Here, you can enjoy Bavarian dishes and beer brewed by Benedictine monks, all with spectacular views. It's a pleasant 45-minute walk to Herrsching (or a 15-minute bus ride), where you can take the suburban train back to Munich. Head to the Augustiner-Keller (www.augustinerkeller.de/en), within walking distance of the central station, to enjoy a beer-hall atmosphere at dinner.

5 DAYS
in the Bavarian Alps

Day 1

Bavarian Alpine road trips are every bit as beautiful as their Swiss or Austrian counterparts (and often a good deal cheaper). Begin your adventure by taking a leisurely 90-minute drive from Munich to Berchtesgaden *(p222)* close to the Austrian border; explorer Alexander Humboldt described the town as one of the most beautiful in the world. Base yourself here for a day of sublime Bavarian hiking. History buffs can spend an afternoon at Hitler's mountain retreat, the Eagle's Nest *(p222)* – the spot commands dizzying views across the southern Alps – while nature lovers will fall in love with Königssee *(p225)*, a mountain lake with gloriously clear waters. Listen to the eerie echoes as a boatsman sounds his trumpet on a slow trip across the lake, before stopping at the beer garden at St. Bartholomä for a well-deserved bite to eat.

Day 2

Today's destination is Tegernsee *(p253)*, but with so many beautiful sights en route, you'll be in no rush to arrive. It's worth stopping at Bavaria's largest lake, Chiemsee *(p227)*. Choose from a range of short lakeside walking trails, or hire mountain bikes *(www.fahrradverleih-chiemsee.de)* and cruise around the lake's cycle paths, looking across to Chiemsee's largest island, Herreninsel *(p226)*. Head back to the car and drive for an hour or so to reach the charming resort town of Tegernsee. A bastion of Bavarian tradition, here you can visit the charming monastery before kicking back at one of the town's many music festivals (summer only). Our suggestion? A hearty lakeside dinner at Bräustüberl, with its huge, leafy beer garden *(www.braustuberl.de)*.

Day 3

It's an hour's drive southwest from Tegernsee to Garmisch-Partenkirchen *(p249)* via Bad Tölz *(p253)*, a pretty Bavarian town on the banks of the Isar river. While in Bad Tölz, take a wander around Marktstraße to admire the unique 17th-century houses; many have trompe l'oeil wall paintings and striking stucco-

1. The landscapes of Berchtesgadener Land.

2. The quaint houses of Bad Tölz.

3. Canoeing on the Eibsee.

4. Schloss Neuschwanstein in winter.

work. Once you've settled in Garmisch-Partenkirchen, your itinerary will depend on the season. In winter, you're in one of Bavaria's finest Alpine ski resorts, and the pistes will keep you occupied all afternoon. In summer, head out to the Partnachklamm, a startlingly deep gorge with river rapids and waterfalls. Finish your day with a meal at Toni Alm (tonialm. de), which offers views of the Zugspitze, a tantalizing taste of tomorrow's activity.

Day 4

Germany's highest peak, the Zugspitze (p249), is your focus today. Drive for 15 minutes to the breathtaking, teal-coloured Eibsee (p248), where you can plunge into the lake's cool morning waters. Suitably reinvigorated, it's time to ascend. One option is to take the cable car up to the peak. Slowly climbing along the world's highest steel tramway, with a dense forest of pine, spruce and fir slowly falling away below, will be an experience you're unlikely to forget. Another route is to take the old cogwheel train part way up the Zugspitze from Garmisch-

Partenkirchen, before changing to the cable car. Intrepid hikers can also take a two-day hike to the summit. However you get there, the restaurant at the top, Panorama 2962, offers great Bavarian dishes and 360-degree views.

Day 5

It's an hour's drive west from Garmisch-Partenkirchen to Schloss Neuschwanstein (p270), the almost inconceivably grand palace built by King Ludwig II in the 19th century. On the way, stop at the Ettal Abbey (p247), a huge Benedictine monastery and Baroque church. Head on to Neuschwanstein; you'll want most of the afternoon to take in its opulent interior and explore its vast gardens. Once you've seen the palace inside and out, head to the Marienbrücke, a suspension bridge a 15-minute walk away, to enjoy the best views of the palace and surrounding mountains. One of the most beautiful outlooks in Bavaria, it's a fitting place to toast the end of your adventure (and there are plenty of beer gardens close by, for that final local beer).

Tasting Tours

The hardest part of eating your way around Bavaria is knowing where to start. Thankfully, food tours help you curate the perfect itinerary. Viktualienmarkt, Munich's central food market, has over 100 stands and a leafy beer garden - try the best of the region's cuisine at a market tasting tour *(www. forkandwalktoursmunich. com)*. Farther afield, sample Bavarian grub (with a nip of whisky to wash it down) at a tour of SLYRS distillery *(www.slyrs.com)*.

$\rightarrow$

Dining alfresco at Viktualienmarkt, Munich's central food market

MUNICH AND THE BAVARIAN ALPS FOR
FOODIES

Doughy pretzels, crispy pork knuckles and sausages galore: there are few cuisines as hearty as Bavaria's. Whether you snack on bratwurst or whip up your own dumplings, great food is sure to be a core part of your adventure.

Signature Sausages

When in Bavaria, it's important to know your bratwurst from your *gelbwurst*. The former was developed to ensure no meat scraps went to waste, and can now be enjoyed in beer halls across the state. *Gelbwurst* is typically made from minced veal and back bacon; many non-Bavarians are put off by its pale colouring, but looks can be deceiving. Pick it up fresh from Munich's esteemed butchers like Metzgerei Burzlaff *(Franziskanerstraße 11)*.

1,200

The number of types of sausage in Germany.

$\uparrow$ Hearty bratwurst on a grill at a food market in central Munich

TOP 4 BAVARIAN DISHES

Weißwurst
The classic breakfast is a pair of veal sausages, served with pretzels.

Schweinshaxe
A huge pork knuckle typically eaten with dumplings.

Kaiserschmarrn
A fluffy pancake, shredded and dusted with icing sugar.

Obatzda
A cheese spread served alongside pretzels.

Modern Innovations

Bavaria is famed for its meat-heavy dishes, but innovative vegan options are constantly improving, spearheaded by a new school of young chefs. Max Pett *(www.max-pett.de)* is a mainstay on Munich's vegan scene, serving up vegan schnitzel and other adaptations of Bavarian classics, many of which are proudly gluten free. SIGGIS *(www.siggis.jetzt)* is a new addition, with two vegan branches in the city centre.

←

Sliced schnitzel with roasted potatoes, a Bavarian classic

Cook Up A Storm

You've sampled it, now why not make it yourself? Wirtshaus in der Au *(www.wirtshausinderau.de)*, a charming Munich tavern, offers superb dumpling cookery classes. Close to the Austrian border, you can enjoy the quintessential Bavarian day out by combining Alpine hikes with lessons in rural cooking – learn to make traditional soft pretzels at a class in the beautiful village of Oberaudorf *(www.adventure-bavaria.com)*.

→

Learning to shape delicate pretzels before baking

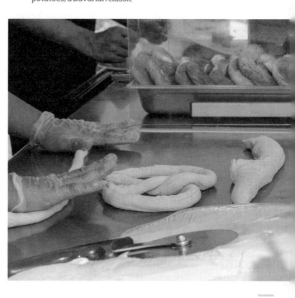

MUNICH AND THE
BAVARIAN ALPS FOR

NATURAL WONDERS

The Bavarian Alps offer some of Central Europe's most astounding landscapes. The region's mountain passes, pristine glacial lakes, ancient woodland and gentle meadows are as inspiring as they are invigorating.

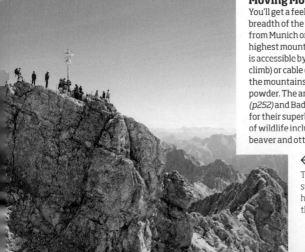

Moving Mountains

You'll get a feel for the expansive breadth of the Alps when looking south from Munich on a clear day. Germany's highest mountain, the Zugspitze (p249), is accessible by foot (it's a tough two day climb) or cable car. In the winter months, the mountains are dusted in soft, white powder. The areas around Schliersee (p252) and Bad Tölz (p253) are well known for their superb pistes and an assortment of wildlife including deer, European bison, beaver and otters.

 ←

The cross at the summit of Germany's highest mountain, the Zugspitze

Gorgeous Gorges

River rapids are formed from deep crevasses carved into rock, running with glacial water. They are abundant in southern Germany and throughout the Bavarian Alps, and can be explored via gorge walkways. The Partnachklamm, an hour's walk from Garmisch-Partenkirchen (p249), is the best known, but the Höllentallklamm (www.hoellentalklamm-info.de) offers stiff competition.

The Partnachklamm gorge walkway in Upper Bavaria

RETURN OF THE WOLF

Bavaria's last Eurasian wolf was killed in 1847, and for over a century the animal was extinct in Germany. Since 2006, they have been re-introduced, crossing the border from Poland and heading south. But as the wolf population has grown so has controversy, with farmers complaining about threats to their livestock. Wolves have become a vexed political issue, with some parties promising to cull their numbers.

Fabled Forests

The German term *waldeinsamkeit* has no direct translation, but is used to capture the feeling of being alone in the woods. And in Bavaria, you'll have the chance to experience it first hand. The Bayerischer Wald (p204) is among Central Europe's largest forest reserves. Smaller-scale forests are abundant, too, like the Perlacher Forst to the south of Munich.

Looking out over the canopy of the Bayerischer Wald

Wonderful Waterfalls

There are few better rewards at the end of a long hike than the sight of a roaring cascade of water, and Bavaria is home to many. One particularly stunning hike starts at the magical Königssee (p225) and ends at Germany's highest waterfall, the 470-m (1500-ft) Röthbachfall. Alternatively, you can add a scenic hike onto a trip to the enchanting Schloss Neuschwanstein to behold the roaring Lech waterfall in Füssen (p276).

Walking by a wild creek near the tall Röthbachfall

New Spots

Only Munich's "Big Six" breweries are permitted to serve beer at Oktoberfest: Hofbräuhaus, Löwenbräu, Augustinerbräu, Paulaner, Hacker-Pschorr and Spaten-Franziskaner. While they're solid choices, there are a great many younger breweries making alternatives to the classics. Our tip? Seek out Giesinger Bräu's unfiltered beers or try Tilman's pale ales at bars across Munich.

←

Löwenbräu Original, one of the brewery's signature beers

MUNICH AND THE BAVARIAN ALPS FOR
BEER LOVERS

With over 600 breweries (almost half of all those in Germany) and the world's largest hop-growing region, the Hallertau, it's safe to say beer and Bavaria go hand in hand. Here you can enjoy hops in their myriad varieties, whether at Oktoberfest or at a lesser-known monastic watering hole.

All Eyes on Oktoberfest

The globe's biggest celebration of beer, Oktoberfest is a two-week folk festival like no other. From the end of September, Munich welcomes hundreds of thousands of dirndl- and lederhosen-wearing revellers, there to enjoy beer served in litre glasses (a *Maß*). The tents each have their own atmosphere, from the downright debauched to the family-friendly. With seven million litres of beer poured during the festival, there's no greater tribute to brewing.

→

Inside the Hacker-Festhalle during Oktoberfest

The World's Oldest Breweries

Every glass of beer in Bavaria offers a small taste of history, and there are few experiences as definitively Bavarian as sitting in a monastery beer garden in summer. The Weihenstephan brewery in Freising *(p186)* is the world's oldest continuously operating brewery. Founded nearly a thousand years ago in 1040 on the site of a monastery, the brewery produces a range of lagers and wheat beers. Opened only a decade later, the beautiful Weltenburg Abbey *(p208)* brews the delicious but formidably strong Asam Bock, named after the Asam brothers *(p63)* and best enjoyed in a beer garden.

$\longrightarrow$
The Weihenstephan, brewing almost a millennium

Beer Hall Basics

Beer halls have been Bavaria's social hubs for centuries. The most popular is the Hofbräuhaus *(p93)*, a vast, echoing hall that can seat 3,500 guests at its long benches; it often hosts traditional brass band music. If you're keen to learn more about the history of the beer hall, head to the Bier- und Oktoberfestmuseum *(p71)*, just a stone's throw from the Hofbräuhaus.

$\longleftarrow$
Munich's oldest beer hall, the Hofbräuhaus

TOP 4 TYPES OF GERMAN BEER

Dunkel
A dark beer ranging from amber to red-brown in colour.

Helles
The most popular of Munich's beers, helles was introduced in 1894.

Eisbock
This strong beer is named for the process of freeze distilling.

Weissbier
A translucent lager, whose yeast content gives it a sweet flavour.

Perfect Paragliding

Paragliding offers perhaps the most exhilarating Alpine experience of all, as you soar with the birds high above glacial lakes, dense forests and sunlit valleys. The quaint town of Oberstdorf *(p277)* on the Austrian border is a haven for paragliders; you can arrange a tandem flight or sign up for a once-in-a-lifetime flight to see Neuschwanstein from above *(www.ok-bergbahnen.com/en)*.

→

A soaring descent over the snowy peaks near Oberstdorf

MUNICH AND THE BAVARIAN ALPS FOR
OUTDOOR ADVENTURES

On a clear day in Munich, the peaks of the Alps look close enough to touch. It's no surprise, then, that hikers are such a familiar sight in the city. Lovers of the outdoors come from far and wide to explore Bavaria's wilderness.

Wild Swimming

With so many limpid lakes and refreshing rivers, it's often tempting to take the plunge in Bavaria. Visit Bavaria's biggest lake, the Chiemsee *(p227)*, for plenty of sandbanks and jetties, or find a secluded spot at the Isar river in which to bathe.

→

Cooling off in a brisk lake near Füssen

Step by Step

Southern Germany is home to a rugged network of *Fernwanderwege*, or long-distance hiking routes, many of which are within reach of public transport. The mountains close to Tegernsee *(p253)* are a popular choice for day-trippers from Munich, while the Allgäu mountain trails tend to be more secluded and untamed.

 GREAT VIEW
Peak Reflections

Seeing the towering peak of the Zugspitze reflected in the teal-green and translucent Lake Eibsee *(p248)* makes for one of the most stunning Bavarian views.

↑ Hiking the rocky Alpine trails in the Allgäu

Climbing High

Pack your climbing shoes: Bavaria offers some of Europe's greatest ascents. The Brauneck is a particularly good climbing location in the summer months. Just an hour north of Munich, the Waldkletter-park Oberbayern *(www.waldkletter-park-oberbayern.de)* is a huge climbing park. But climbing can be found in the city, too: try ascending the roof of the Olympic Stadium *(www.olympiapark.de)*.

← A mountaineer scaling a rock face in the Bavarian Alps

On Two Wheels

Drifting through shaded forests, climbing undulating hills or circling glistening lakes, Bavaria's cycle paths are varied and extensive. The Bavarian Forest cycle trail *(p204)* travels through a folkloric arboreal landscape. For seasoned cyclists, the 440-km (270-m) Romantic Road *(p295)* makes for an excellent biking holiday.

→ Touring the cycling network in the lush Bavarian Forest

Happily Ever After

Bavaria is rightly famous for its fairy tale landscapes: the state's dense forests, mountain top palaces and resplendent, gilded halls are certain to fire up young imaginations. Behold Schloss Neuschwanstein *(p270)*, on which the Disney Sleeping Beauty castle is said to be based, spot wolves in the Bayerischer Wald *(p204)* and ride rollercoasters at the fairy tale-themed park Märchenwald Wolfratshausen *(www.maerchenwald-isartal.de)*, just south of Munich.

→

Taking in the views of Schloss Neuschwanstein

MUNICH AND THE BAVARIAN ALPS FOR
FAMILIES

A state so commonly described as "fairy tale" is sure to make children's dreams come true, and there are few places in Bavaria where young travellers aren't welcome – even beer gardens have playgrounds!

Perfect Playgrounds

Epic adventure playgrounds are a common fixture across Bavaria, with complex climbing structures and suspension bridges helping to develop children's motor skills. One of the largest is the great Altmühlsee Erlebnisspielplatz, in the Altmühl valley. Another full day can be spent at the Stadtpark Erding, just outside of Munich, where children can explore several playgrounds and visit a free petting zoo.

←

A pirate-themed adveture playground in Bavaria

TOP 3 FAMILY WALKS

Landsberg am Lech *(p238)*
You can walk from town to a nature park in just ten minutes, before taking a half-hour stroll through the park.

Schliersee *(p252)*
For a family-friendly Alpine hike, park at Spitzingsee, and take the flat path to the Albert-Link-Hütte.

Nördlingen *(p284)*
Here you can marvel at a meteorite crater while walking its perimeter.

Up, Up and Away!

With breathtaking cable-car trips and mountain train rides, the fun is often in the journey. For a taste of what locals call "Bavarian Canada", hop on one of the small forest trains in the Bayerischer Wald *(p204)* and enjoy one of Germany's most stunning train trips. Alternatively, take the old cogwheel train from Garmisch-Partenkirchen *(p249)* up to the Zugspitze, Germany's highest peak.

→

Ascending the cog rail with the Zugspitze in the distance

Inspiring Museums

Whatever they're into, kids can learn a lot at Bavaria's family-friendly museums. The Deutsches Museum *(p102)* is the biggest science museum in the world, and has been renovated to include a host of interactive elements. When the sun's out, head to the dinosaur museum at Altmühltal to see a T-Rex up close *(www.dinosauriermuseum.de)*.

←

Face to face with a dinosaur at Altmühltal

Rural Exhibitions

While the majority of Bavaria's museums are in Munich, there are some delightful cultural spots to explore across the state. The Buchheim Museum at Starnberger See *(p255)* displays the contemporary collection of Lothar-Günther Buchheim in a glorious lakeside setting, while another lakeside gallery, the Franz Marc Museum in Kochel am See *(p250)*, shows the Blaue Reiter artist's excellent lifework.

→

Exterior of the Buchheim Museum in Starnberger See

MUNICH AND THE BAVARIAN ALPS FOR
ART AND CULTURE

Berlin might hog Germany's cultural headlines, but Munich's abundance of institutions gives the capital a run for its money. Beyond the city, a selection of well-curated gems can be found throughout wider Bavaria.

Literary Munich

Once home to novelist Thomas Mann, children's author Erich Kästner and poet Rainer Maria Rilke, among others, Munich has a rich literary pedigree. These luminaries lived in the bohemian neighbourhood of Schwabing *(p91)*, but contemporary wordsmiths now make for the Literaturhaus *(p91)*, the base for Munich's annual literary festival.

←

Alfresco drinks outside Munich's Literaturhaus in summer

Urban Art

It isn't widely known beyond the city, but Munich is the birthplace of Germany's graffiti scene. Visit MUCA *(www.muca.eu)*, close to the Asamkirche, to see exhibitions from urban artists. For more public street art, head to the Bahnwärter Thiel project in Sendling *(p157)* to see artists in action.

Street art-inspired façade of the MUCA building

BLAUE REITER

At the turn of the 20th century, a group of artists led by Wassily Kandinsky and Franz Marc came together in Schwabing to form the Blaue Reiter (Blue Rider), a collective that would come to define modern German art. The artists rejected traditional painting and instead embraced an often abstract spirituality, commonly making use of the colour blue. The Lenbachhaus *(p140)* is home to the largest collection of their art.

Munich's Museums

From Rubens' esteemed oil paintings at the Alte Pinakothek *(p132)* to Damien Hirst's *Waste* at the Museum Brandhorst *(p142)*, Munich is home to art that spans the centuries. The city's most popular museums are the Haus der Kunst *(p125)*, the three Pinakothek galleries and the science-focused Deutsches Museum *(p102)*.

↑ Admiring art at the Alte Pinakothek

Winter Sports

The state's sporting scene comes alive in winter. Known as *Eisstockschießen*, Bavarian curling is one of Europe's oldest winter sports – you can find games played on Maisinger Lake near Starnberg *(p243)*. For faster thrills, hit up the pistes. They may not be as lavish as their French counterparts, but resorts like the Garmisch Classic *(p249)* offer fine runs.

The historic game of Bavarian curling, still popular in the state

MUNICH AND THE BAVARIAN ALPS FOR
SPORTS FANS

Home to one of the most famous football clubs in the world, Bayern Munich, Bavaria is a true haven for sports lovers. With an abundance of grounds and facilities – not to mention those Alpine pistes – you'll be well catered for, whether you want to cheer from the sidelines or play a starring role.

A Game of Two Halves

Football has a long and storied history in the Bavarian capital, from the earliest days of the Bundesliga to the opening game of the UEFA Euros in 2024. No football fan's visit would be complete without a trip to Bayern Munich's ground, the Allianz Arena *(p161)*. Tours provide a look around the stadium and tickets include entrance to the FC Bayern Museum. If you'd prefer to support the underdog, Munich's second team is TSV 1860; their games are just as thrilling (and tickets are a good deal easier to come by).

→

Bayern Munich playing a home game at the Allianz Arena

Pounding the Pavements

There are few athletic pastimes as simple as running, and Bavaria's running routes rival Europe's very best. Three rivers converge in Passau (p200), and the river banks make for a leafy, shaded run, complete with spectacular views of the city; the best routes start at the Dom St Stephan. In Munich, head out for a jog in the Englischer Garten (p118), one of the world's largest urban parks. You'll be in great company on weekend mornings.

$\rightarrow$

Jogging the green trails of the Englischer Garten

City Surfing

Surfing in the capital city of a landlocked state? You might think it impossible. But thanks to Munich's standing wave at the Eisbach tributary (p119), surfers gather in all weathers, in any season, to ride the iconic wave. Surfing started here in 1972, when authorities submerged concrete blocks to lull a current: overnight, the wave was born.

$\leftarrow$

Surfing on the Eisbach, which flows through the Englischer Garten

ALLIANZ ARENA

Opened in 2005 with a capacity of 75,000 spectators, the Allianz Arena is a stadium of superlatives. Before the stadium opened, Bayern Munich had played at Munich's 1972 Olympic Stadium, sharing the stadium with TSV 1860, but fans demanded a state-of-the-art, purpose-built construction befitting a team of global renown. Designed by architect duo Herzog/de Meuron, the stadium was built using plastic panels. It remains one of the most innovative stadiums in the world.

Abbeys and Monasteries

Bavarian Catholicism is writ large across the state, with a host of opulent churches. One of the most famous is the Ettal Abbey *(p247)*, a striking Benedictine monastery with Baroque elements and bright frescoes. Weltenburg Abbey *(p208)*, another Benedictine monastery, is also worth a day trip; with its own brewery and a gloriously spacious beer garden, it's a delight to visit in summer.

$\longrightarrow$

The Benedictine Ettal Abbey in Garmisch-Partenkirchen

MUNICH AND THE BAVARIAN ALPS FOR
HISTORY BUFFS

Narcissistic kings, powerful dynasties and an embarrassment of opulent castles: Bavaria's history is the stuff of legend. Thankfully, the past can be seen everywhere – prepare to be humbled by this archive of human history.

Industrial Bavaria

Following World War II, Bavaria fell under US occupation. In West Germany, capitalism reigned supreme, and heavy industry took off. Siemens relocated from Berlin to Munich in 1949 and BMW manufactured motorcycles en masse in its factory *(p155)*. Beyond Munich, Audi is based in Ingolstadt *(p176)*.

$\longrightarrow$

The vast lobby of the Audi Forum in Ingolstadt

Did You Know?

Munich is known as the "German Silicon Valley" for its industrial innovations.

World War II Sites

Indelibly associated with the Nazis, the early 20th century was a dark time for Bavaria. Rather than covering up this history, the state has made a concerted effort to reckon with it, turning former Nazi strongholds into affecting museums. Built on the site of the former Brown House, the Nazi Party headquarters, the NS-Dokumentationszentrum, or nsdoku (p143), is a large museum reflecting on the legacy of European fascism, while the Dachau concentration camp (p189) offers a sobering reminder of Nazi atrocities.

← The Mortal Agony of Christ Chapel at Dachau

THE REIGN OF THE WITTELSBACHS

From 1180 to 1918, Bavaria was ruled by the Wittelsbach family. Perhaps the most famous Wittelsbach monarch was the reclusive, poetic Ludwig II (1845–1886), whose 22-year rule left behind a legacy of outlandish tales (some, but not all, apocryphal) as well as a host of magnificent castles. After 738 years of Wittelsbach rule, in 1918 the revolutionary socialist Kurt Eisner proclaimed Bavaria a "free state". Eisner was assassinated just a year later by a right-wing nationalist.

Bavarian Castles

The picture-postcard view of Schloss Neuschwanstein (p270) is synonymous with Bavaria, but the state boasts plenty of august palaces, many of them built by "Mad King" Ludwig II. The Bavarian Rococo Schloss Linderhof (p246) was built at his demand, while Schloss Herrenchiemsee (p226), intended as a private island retreat on Bavaria's largest lake, was his most expensive project.

↑ The lavish Rococo interior of Schloss Linderhof

Top of the Pops

Munich's live music offerings are not confined to opera or traditional brass bands. The city has been attracting some of the biggest names in pop, including global star Adele who performed a summer-long residency in 2024. International stars, such as The Rolling Stones and Taylor Swift, play at the Olympiastadion (p154), the site of the 1972 Olympics. Up-and-coming bands play at the Muffathalle (p108) or Backstage (close to the Hirschgarten).

$\rightarrow$

The Rolling Stones performing at the Olympiastadion

MUNICH AND THE BAVARIAN ALPS
AFTER DARK

Bavaria's capital takes on a new dimension when the sun goes down. From lazy nights in beer gardens to sophisticated evenings at the ballet or opera, Munich caters for every night owl.

Opera and Ballet

With a history as grand as Bavaria's, it makes sense that opera would have found a home here. Munich's opera house, the Nationaltheater (p87), was where Richard Strauss's last opera, *Capriccio*, premiered in 1942. Snap up tickets to the ballet or opera at the box office. For contemporary classics, head to Munich's concert hall, the Isarphilharmonie in Sendling.

$\leftarrow$

The Bavarian Junior Ballet performing at the Nationaltheater

DRINK

Gin City

A gem within Munich's Werksviertel, this bar offers over 400 gins, with bottles stacked from floor to ceiling. A vast selection of cocktails and perfectly curated gin tastings make this a firm city favourite.

⌂ Werksviertel, Speicherstraße 20
🌐 gincity.de

Paint the Town Red

Munich is becoming increasingly renowned for its DIY nightlife scene. The excellent Bahnwärter Thiel *(www.bahnwaerter thiel.de)*, a cultural hub made up of old tram and underground carriages, is a laid-back spot for a drink, as is the central Werksviertel, comprised of old shipping containers that have been transformed into ateliers, bars, restaurants and independent shops.

←
Bahnwärter Thiel's tram carriages, now home to bars and restaurants

Global Theatre

In Munich, inventive plays in German can be enjoyed by all, with the benefit of surtitles. The Residenztheater *(p82)*, next to the opera house, has a renowned ensemble cast of over 50 actors and a total staff of over 450; it's one of the largest theatres for drama in the German-speaking world. Then there's the Kammerspiele *(p95)* which puts on international, contemporary plays and traditional German staples, all noted for their striking stage design.

→
Actors performing on stage at the Kammerspiele

A YEAR IN
MUNICH AND THE BAVARIAN ALPS

JANUARY

△ **Four Hills ski-jumping tournament**
(Dec–Jan). A ski-jumping tournament held at
Oberstdorf and Garmisch-Partenkirchen.
Schäfflertanz *(2026)*. This Munich festival,
held every seven years, commemorates a
16th-century plague.

FEBRUARY

△ **Carnival** *(Shrove Tuesday)*. Known as
Fasching in Bavaria, Carnival is celebrated in
fancy dress at Munich's Viktualienmarkt.
Skifasching *(last Sunday of Carnival)*. A
renowned skiing show held during Carnival.

MAY

△ **Maibaumaufstellen** *(1 May)*. Virtually every
Bavarian community honours the custom of
Raising the Maypole.
Trachten- und Schützenumzug *(first Sunday
in May)*. In Passau, a large procession of folk
groups and bands from Bavaria and Austria
open this annual fair.

JUNE

△ **Munich Pride** *(mid-June)*. Known as
Christopher Street Day, over half a million
people gather in Munich to celebrate Pride.
Tollwood Sommerfestival *(mid-June to
mid-July)*. Held at the Olympic grounds,
Tollwood features food, music and stalls.

SEPTEMBER

△ **Oktoberfest** *(Days leading up to the first
Sunday in October)*. Munich's world-famous
folk and beer festival.
Viehscheid *(September–October)*. Held across
Bavaria, this celebration traditionally marked
the movement of cattle from higher pastures.

OCTOBER

△ **Lange Nacht der Museen** *(one night in
October, date varies)*. Some 90 museums in
Munich open late for tours and parties.
Medientage München *(second half of
October)*. Munich fair dedicated to media and
communications, with panels and debates.

APRIL

△ **Plärrer** (*early April*). The largest folk festival in Swabia, a small counterpart to Oktoberfest.

Flohmarkt (*mid-April*). Held annually, Munich's biggest flea market welcomes amateur sellers.

Frühlingsfest (*mid-April to early May*). A smaller version of Oktoberfest, Munich's spring festival takes place at Theresienwiese.

MARCH

△ **Starkbierfest** (*between Ash Wednesday and Good Friday*). Munich's Festival of Strong Beer commemorates the ale drunk by Pauline monks as they observed the Lenten fast.

Internationale Jazzwoche (*mid-March*). For one week in March, international jazz stars head to Burghausen with 11,000 spectators.

AUGUST

△ **Gäubodenvolksfest** (*mid-Aug*). This folk festival in Straubing features an agricultural and industrial fair.

Allgäuer Festwoche (*mid-August*) Held in Kempten, this exhibition recounts the Allgäu's economic and cultural achievements, and coincides with a popular folk festival.

JULY

Kocherlball (*early July*). This annual dance is held in the early morning at the Chinesischer Turm in Munich.

△ **Sommernachtstraum** (*early July*). A classical music concert rounded off with a fireworks display overlooking the lake at Munich's Olympic grounds.

Fischertag in Memmingen (*late July*). A medieval tradition centred around fishing trout in Memmingen's town centre stream.

DECEMBER

Winter-Tollwood (*end of November to New Year's Eve*). A major music and arts festival held at Theresienwiese.

△ **Christkindlmarkt** (*early December to Christmas Eve*). Across Bavaria, Christmas fairs inaugurate the festive season with the ritual raising of the tree in the main square.

NOVEMBER

Leonardifahrten und Leonardiritte (*first Sunday in November*). In many areas, such as Bad Tölz and Schliersee, processions on horseback take place in honour of St Leonard.

△ **Martinstag** (*11 November*). Processions are held across the state to honour St Martin.

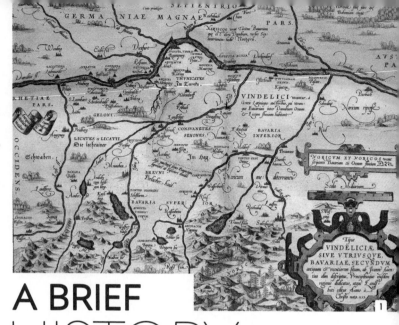

1

A BRIEF
HISTORY

Situated in southern Germany, Bavaria has long had a distinct cultural identity, from its early period as a Celtic settlement through centuries of Wittelsbach rule and on to the industrial flourishing of its capital, Munich, in the 20th century.

Early Settlement and the Celts

The first agricultural communities settled in southern Bavaria in the 4th millennium BCE. During the Hallstatt period of the late Bronze Age (750–450 BCE), these early farming communities were joined by a group who would go on to shape Bavaria's early period: the Celts. The origins of the Celts in this part of Central Europe remains a mystery, but these early arrivals left a compelling physical legacy throughout rural Bavaria in the form of burial mounds and flat grave cemeteries. Many later towns, like Straubing and Kempten, have Celtic roots.

1 One of the earliest known maps of Bavaria.

2 Wood engraving of rural life in the Allgäu.

3 Germanic peoples fight the Romans.

4 Charlemagne, Emperor of the Franks.

Timeline of events

4,000 BCE
The first agricultural settlers arrive in Bavaria.

750 BCE
The Celtic peoples arrive in the region.

15 BCE
The Roman army conquers the Celts.

400 CE
Germanic invasions topple Roman control.

The Roman Empire

Even flourishing societies can't last, however, and in 15 BCE the Roman army conquered the Celts and pushed forward to reach the Danube. Under Roman rule, southern Bavaria was divided into Raetia and Noricum. After two centuries of development, Raetia and Noricum were attacked by Germanic tribes; though the first attacks were suppressed by Emperor Marcus Aurelius, the province was destroyed shortly after. After 400 CE a new wave of Germanic invasions toppled Roman control.

A Tapestry of Bavarian Peoples

The fall of the Romans ushered in the age of the Bavarian peoples. It's widely believed that a group called the Baiovarii appeared south of the Danube in 450–550 CE, to be joined by groups of other Germanic and Celtic peoples. This social tapestry was unified under the Duchy of Bavaria in the mid-6th century, but the growing might of the dynasty alarmed the Frankish ruler Charlemagne, who put an end to the Bavarian tribes' first state. Bavaria lost its independence and became part of the East Frankish Empire (an embryo of Germany).

↑ Marble bust of Roman Emperor Marcus Aurelius, displayed in Munich

550 CE
The Duchy of Bavaria is founded.

843 CE
Bavaria becomes part of the East Frankish Empire.

590 CE
The Bavarian dynasty grows in strength under Gardibald I.

788 CE
Charlemagne deposes Bavarian duke Tassilo III.

The Wittelsbach Dynasty

The Saxons conquered the Bavarian throne in the 10th century, before the Welf dynasty took charge. The dynasty's Duke Henry the Lion founded Munich in 1158, when he allowed local monks to form a market in the square that would become Marienplatz. The city's population and wealth grew steadily, before Henry the Lion waged war against the Holy Roman Emperor Friedrich Barbarossa. Henry was defeated in 1180, and Barbarossa conferred the title of Duke of Bavaria on Otto I Wittelsbach, whose family would rule Bavaria until 1918.

Shifting Fortunes

Under Ludwig IV of Bavaria, the duchy was at the height of its powers. In 1314 Ludwig became king of Germany, and 14 years later he was crowned Holy Roman Emperor. After his death, Bavaria was shaken by an endless succession of conflicts and local wars. Despite the division and rivalry, the ducal courts encouraged the development of culture: the town of Landshut underwent a period of social flourishing, and in 1475 it was the venue of the wedding of the daughter of Casimir Jagiellon *(p194)*.

1 Henry the Lion at the founding of Munich in 1158.

2 Early depiction of Oktoberfest.

3 King Ludwig III, Bavaria's final king.

Did You Know?

The German name for Munich is München, or "Home of the Monks", referring to a monastery at Tegernsee.

Timeline of events

1158
Munich is founded by Henry the Lion.

1180
The Wittelsbach reign begins, lasting 738 years.

1610
Maximilian I orders huge political reforms.

1799
The outbreak of the Napoleonic Wars sees Bavaria lose its territories.

1810
Crown Prince Ludwig I marries Therese of Saxe-Hildburghausen; the celebrations inspire Oktoberfest.

3

Maximilian I (1573–1651) reorganized the administration of the state and the military, streamlined the fiscal system and took charge of the Catholic camp in the conflict that would lead to the Thirty Years' War. Conditions for ordinary Bavarians improved markedly during the 16th century as Bavaria consolidated its powers. With the outbreak of the Napoleonic Wars (1799–1815), Bavaria tried to remain neutral but was unable to protect its possessions from French occupation.

The Birth of Modern Bavaria

The modern state of Bavaria was established at the beginning of the 19th century and it has survived intact to this day. In the latter half of the 19th century, Bavaria made significant cultural advances: Munich saw new parks, gardens and buildings, while the wedding of Ludwig I led to celebrations that became today's Oktoberfest. Ludwig II acceded to the throne in 1864, aged just 18, but he died suspiciously (p243), to be succeeded by Otto, who was followed by Bavaria's last king, Ludwig III. After Germany's defeat in World War I, the monarchy was overthrown and the Free State of Bavaria was proclaimed.

THE LURID LIFE OF LUDWIG II

Ludwig II had a vivid imagination; he fell in love with Wagner's operatic worlds and began to create a vibrant fantasy. He had extravagant palaces built, modelled on Versailles, and spent time as a recluse in his grand mountain abodes while leaving the business of politics to a select group of anonymous officials.

1825
A suite of cultural advances in Munich sees new gardens and buildings.

1868
Ludwig orders the building of Schloss Neuschwanstein.

1918
The monarchy is overthrown, led by the revolutionary Kurt Eisner.

1864
Infamous Ludwig II takes to the throne.

1913
Bavaria's last king, Ludwig III, begins his reign.

The Rise of the Nazis

In 1923, the NSDAP, led by Adolf Hitler, attempted a coup d'état, known as the Beer Hall Putsch, by marching on Munich's Feldherrnhalle. Hitler was accused of treason and was sentenced to prison in Landsberg, where he wrote *Mein Kampf*. In 1931, the Nazis opened their headquarters at the Brown House, a mansion later destroyed by Allied bombing. Munich became a Nazi stronghold, and after the Nazis came to power in 1933, Munich's Neo-Classical Königsplatz was transformed into a space for rallies.

Darkness Descends

With the Nazis in power, a dark chapter in Bavaria's history began. The first concentration camp was built just outside of Munich, in Dachau. During World War II, Munich was a key target for Allied bombings because of its Nazi ties and its industrial prowess. The city suffered damage by air raids from 1940 onwards, with acute air bombardment starting in 1942, reducing large parts of the city to rubble; there were 74 air raids on the city alone. As the war came to an end, fierce

↑ The austere gate of the Dachau Camp

Timeline of events

1923
Launch of the coup d'état known as the Beer Hall Putsch.

1931
The Nazis open their headquarters at the Brown House.

1933
The doors of the Dachau Concentration Camp open.

1940
Allied bombardment of Munich begins.

debate began to rage throughout Germany about how to put the nation's shattered infrastructure back together.

Post-war Industry

Bavaria was occupied by the Americans after the war until 1949. Slowly, the state began to rebuild its industry, and corporations such as Siemens moved headquarters from Berlin to Munich, catalysing rapid economic growth. This was the era of the *Wirtschaftswunder*, or "The Economic Miracle", and both Munich and wider Bavaria enjoyed great prosperity – all the more remarkable given the region's decimated post-war state.

Modern Bavaria

Today, Munich is the third-biggest city in Germany and Bavarians enjoy a high standard of living. Politically conservative, the Bavarian CSU (Christian Social Union, the sister party to the Christian Democratic Union, which operates in other states) has enjoyed a largely unbroken rule since 1946. Bavarians continue to cultivate their customs, and the state's landscapes and cultural festivals attract hundreds of thousands of visitors.

1 A Nazi Party rally in Munich.

2 Munich after Allied air attacks.

3 The BMW Museum and headquarters in the heart of the industrial city.

1945
The end of WWII sees the start of US occupation.

1949
American occupation of Bavaria ends.

1972
Munich hosts the Summer Olympics.

2024
The opening game of the UEFA Euros brings thousands to Munich.

EXPERIENCE
MUNICH

Munich's bustling centre, Marienplatz

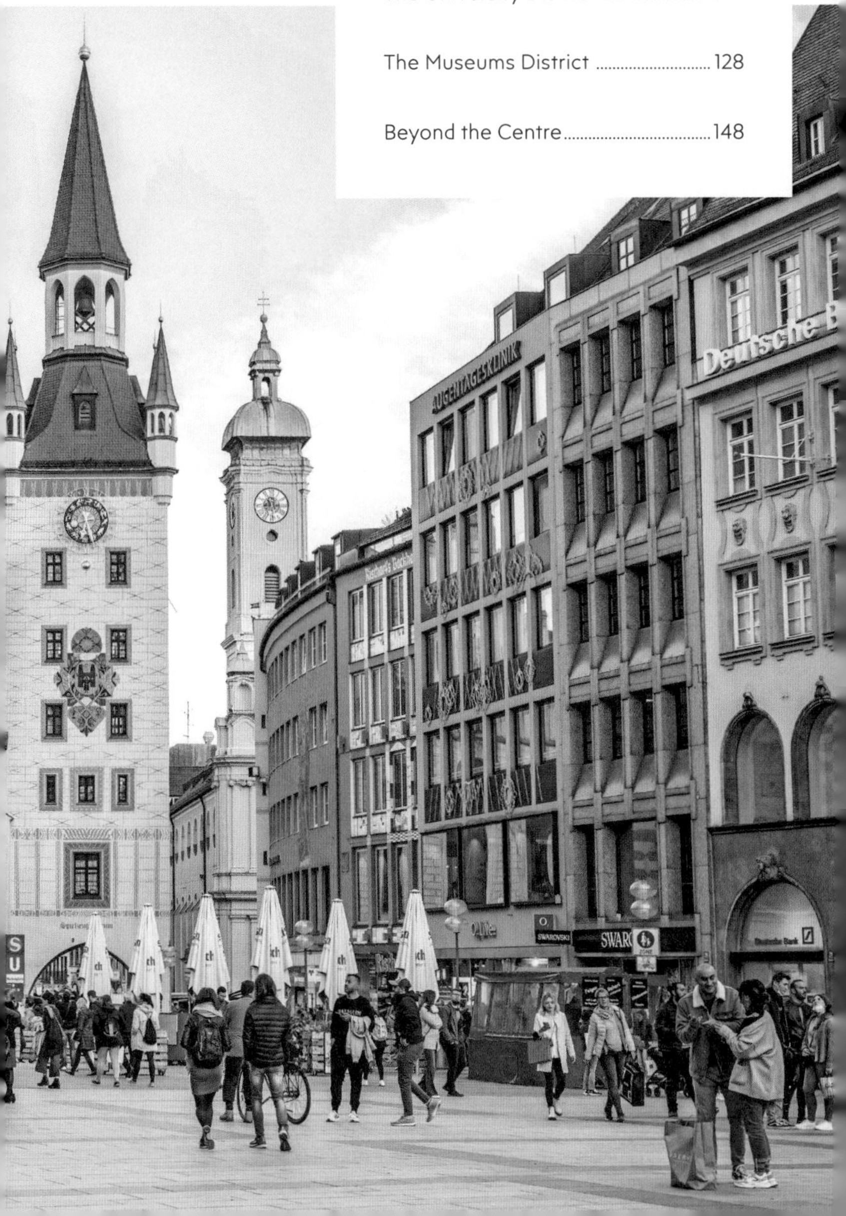

EXPLORE
MUNICH

This guide divides Munich into six colour-coded
sightseeing areas: the five on this map and one
for sights beyond the city centre *(p148)*. Find out
more about each area on the following pages.

Neue
Pinakothek

Löwenbräu-
keller

STIGLMAIER-
PLATZ

Alte
Pinakothek

Glyptothek

Pinakothek
der Moderne

KÖNIGS-
PLATZ

KAROLINEN-
PLATZ

**THE MUSEUMS
DISTRICT**
p128

WITTELS-
BACHER-
PLATZ

Alter
Botanischer
Garten

MAXIMILIANS-
PLATZ

LENBACH-
PLATZ

**OLD TOWN
(NORTH)**
p78

KARLS-
PLATZ

Frauenkirche

Neues
Rathaus

ALTSTADT

**OLD TOWN
(SOUTH)**
p56

Sendlinger
Tor

ST-JAKOBS-
PLATZ

GÄRTNER-
PLATZ

LOCATOR MAP

CZECH
REPUBLIC

GERMANY

BAVARIAN ALPS

★ **MUNICH**

AUSTRIA

Jugendstil-Haus

HABSBURGER-PLATZ

Leopold-Park

SCHWABING

Pacelli-Palais

Akademie der Bildenden Künste

Siegestor

PROF.-HUBER-PLATZ

Ludwig-Maximilians-Universität

THE UNIVERSITY DISTRICT
p112

Bayerische Staatsbibliothek

KISSKALT-PLATZ

Chinesischer Turm

Monopteros

Englischer Garten

Haus der Kunst

Bayerisches Nationalmuseum

Hofgarten

Staats-kanzlei

LEHEL

Klosterkirche St Anna

Friedensengel

EUROPA-PLATZ

Museum Villa Stuck

Residenz

AROUND THE ISAR
p98

Isar

Alter Hof

Museum Fünf Kontinente

ISARTOR-PLATZ

Alpines Museum

Maximilianeum

BAADER-PLATZ

Nikolaikirche

Gasteig

Deutsches Museum

0 metres 500
0 yards 500

N

GETTING TO KNOW
MUNICH

The largest city in southern Germany, Munich lies just 30 miles (50 km) north of the Bavarian Alps on the banks of the Isar river. To help you get your bearings in this large but conveniently walkable city, we've broken Munich down into six handy districts.

OLD TOWN (SOUTH)

PAGE 56

The south of Munich's Old Town is a gathering place for locals and tourists alike, with many of the city's finest historic buildings. The geographical centre of Munich is marked by the Mariensäule (Column of the Virgin), which stands proudly at the heart of Marienplatz, long the city's architectural and commercial hub. The towering domes of the Frauenkirche provide an unmistakeable symbol of the city, while the Asamkirche is a masterpiece of Bavarian Baroque. This part of town is also home to fine museums including the Bier- und Oktoberfestmuseum and the Jewish Museum.

Best for
Grand religious buildings

Home to
Frauenkirche, Asamkirche

Experience
The bustling Neuhauser Straße, lined with many of Munich's best shops

OLD TOWN (NORTH)

PAGE 78

Head north in Munich's Old Town to find a melange of architectural styles. Around the Alter Hof (Old Court), the first seat of the Wittelsbach family, there is a maze of medieval streets and buildings, among which is the Hofbräuhaus, Munich's most renowned brewery. A short walk away, the streets leading to the Altstadtring are home to some of the city's busiest shopping areas. But the crown jewel of this area is undoubtedly the Residenz, a former royal property set in the most elegant part of Munich, an area characterized by numerous Baroque palaces and royal houses.

Best for
Exploring Munich's royal history

Home to
The Residenz

Experience
The extravagance and grandeur of the Residenz

AROUND THE ISAR

PAGE 98

The banks of the Isar are home to some of Munich's most popular areas, flanked by wooded stretches that feel like you've left the city entirely. On the steep right bank spreads the Maximiliansanlagen, green areas densely planted with trees which are favourite places for locals to walk and cycle. The Praterinsel and Museumsinsel, two islands linked to the city by several foot-bridges, also contribute to the area's charm. The grand Maximilianstraße runs from the Old Town to the river.

Best for
Relaxing river walks

Home to
The Deutches Museum

Experience
A calming cycle along the river

PAGE 112

THE UNIVERSITY DISTRICT

This district differs starkly to the historic grandeur of Munich's Old Town. There's an endearing buzz about the place, caused in large part by the local student population popping in and out of independent bookshops, or relaxing in pubs and cafés. The busy area surrounding Ludwigstraße, known as Schwabing, abounds in trendy boutiques, independent shops and pubs. To the east of Schwabing is the verdant oasis of the Englischer Garten, Munich's largest park.

Best for
Bar hopping

Home to
Bayerisches Nationalmuseum, Englischer Garten

Experience
A resftul afternoon in the Englischer Garten

PAGE 128

THE MUSEUMS DISTRICT

Since the 19th century, the Museums District has been home to some of the city's greatest cultural institutions and galleries. Foremost among these are the Alte Pinakothek and the Pinakothek der Moderne, each home to countless masterpieces of European painting from the 14th century onward. For a sobering account of Bavaria's 20th century history, visit the remarkable NS-Dokumentationszentrum, before venturing further back in time with a foray into natural history at Munich's illustrious Palaeontology Museum.

Best for
Admiring European art

Home to
Alte Pinakothek, Pinakothek der Moderne

Experience
Art and artifacts from centuries past

BEYOND THE CENTRE

Munich's wonders aren't confined to the city centre. As the city expanded over the past two centuries, its outer districts became increasingly populous and diverse, with an array of sights and attractions. To the west lies the Nymphenburg district, with its palace, park and botanical gardens. Southwest of the Old Town is Theresienwiese, famous as the home of Oktoberfest. Head south for the Hellabrunn Zoo, in Thalkirchen, and the Bavaria Film Museum, in Geiselgasteig. With Munich's excellent public transport system, there's no reason not to head out and explore.

Best for
Superb palaces

Home to
Schloss Nymphenburg

Experience
Learning more about the history of BMW cars at the BMW museum

→

OLD TOWN (SOUTH)

In 1158, Henry the Lion, the Duke of Saxony and Bavaria, granted monks permission to establish a market in what is now Marienplatz; it would become the heart of Munich's Altstadt (Old Town). Marienplatz was quickly established as a focal point for a new settlement, with monks and traders arriving in the region by the late 12th century. Peterskirche, the city's oldest parish church, was founded on the square shortly after. As the city's population grew, the southern section of the Altstadt was fortified with three medieval gates, which still mark the area today: the Karlstor, Sendlinger Tor and Isartor.

As the city continued to expand throughout the 14th and 15th centuries, the population spread south of Marienplatz into the area that became Angerviertel, which was safer from the frequent flooding of the Isar river. Until the end of the 18th century, the city was confined to the Altstadt, and Marienplatz remained the focal point of social life in the city. In the early 19th century, the Viktualienmarkt was established in the district of Angerviertel, and the market has been held daily for over 200 years.

Today, the south of the Old Town remains the beating heart of Munich. Marienplatz was fully pedestrianized for the 1972 Olympics, and has since been a gathering point for both locals and tourists. The square also serves as the gateway to one of Munich's primary shopping avenues, the bustling Kaufingerstraße.

Hauptbahnhof

Karlsplatz

4 Karlsplatz

Karlstor **3** **5**

5

Michaelskirche **6**

Bürgersaalkirche

Augustinerbräu

Damenstift **23**
St Anna

ALTSTADT

4

LUDWIGS-
VORSTADT

25 Allerheiligenkirche
am Kreuz

2 Asamkir

Asamhaus **22**

3

Sendlinger Tor **21**

SENDLINGER-
TOR-PLATZ

Sendlinger
Tor

St-Matthäus-
Kirche **24**

Münchner
Marionettentheater

OLD TOWN (SOUTH)

Must Sees
1 Frauenkirche
2 Asamkirche

Experience More
3 Karlstor
4 Karlsplatz
5 Bürgersaalkirch
6 Michaelskirche
7 Deutsches Jagd- und
Fischerei museum
8 Peterskirche
9 Neues Rathaus
10 Marienplatz
11 Altes Rathaus
12 Ehemalige Stadtschreiberei
13 Heilig-Geist-Kirche
14 Isartor
15 Gärtnerplatz
16 Viktualienmarkt
17 Ignaz-Günther-Haus

18 Bier- und Oktoberfestmuseum
19 Jüdisches Zentrum
20 Münchner Stadtmuseum
21 Sendlinger Tor
22 Asamhaus
23 Damenstift St Anna
24 St Matthäuskirche
25 Allerheiligenkirche am Kreuz

Drink
① Cole and Porter Bar
② The Royal Dolores

Stay
③ Hotel MIO by AMANO
④ KOOS Hotel and Apartments

Shop
⑤ Oberpollinger
⑥ Hofstatt
⑦ Breuninger

N

P

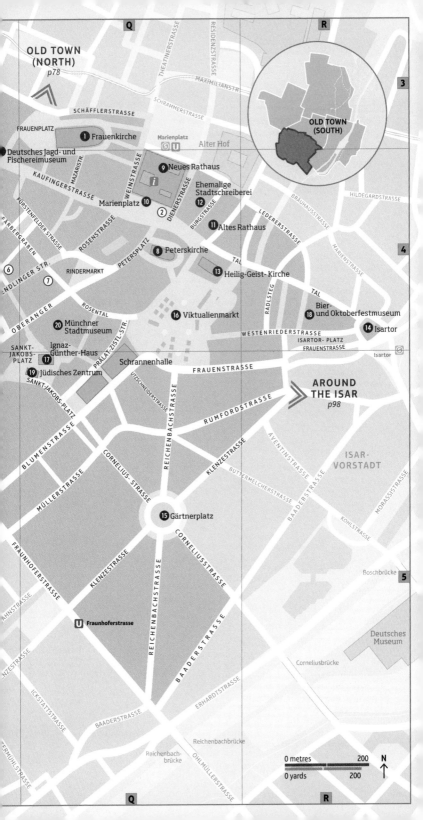

FRAUENKIRCHE

**◉ Q3 ⌂ Frauenplatz 1 ⑤Ⓤ Marienplatz 🚋 19 🚌 52
🕐 8am–8pm daily; South Tower: 10am–5pm daily
(from 11:30am Sun) Ⓦ muenchner-dom.de**

With two striking onion-shaped domes stretching high into the air, the Frauenkirche is an iconic landmark in Munich, visible around the city. It's the city's largest church, and the largest Gothic building in southern Germany.

The Frauenkirche, built in 20 years from 1468 to 1488, stands on the site of an earlier Romanesque parish church. The imposing triple-naved brick building was begun by architect Jörg von Halspach, and was continued after his death by Lucas Rottaler. The church's façade has a rather severe aspect – the towers have blind windows at their angles and are pierced by arched doors that echo the shape of the central portal. The distinctive onion domes crowning the high towers are typical of the Renaissance; the style is believed to have been inspired by the Dome of the Rock in Jerusalem. Since 1821, the church has been the seat of the archbishopric of Munich and Freising. Today, the building's distinctive silhouette is perhaps Munich's oldest and best-known symbol, and no buildings which block a view of the church are permitted, by law.

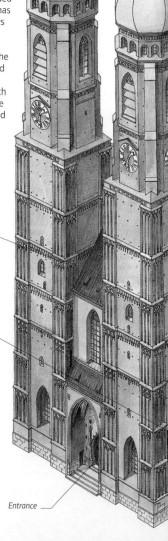

The onion domes crowning the towers are typical of the Renaissance style.

The church's towers have blind windows at their angles and are pierced by arched doors.

A Mannerist canopy of black marble covers the tomb of Emperor Ludwig IV of Bavaria. The sarcophagus is surrounded by the figures of four kneeling knights and putti.

Entrance

THE DEVIL'S FOOTPRINT

According to legend, the dip in the floor at the church's entrance was formed by the Devil's footprint. Some say he was angered that yet another building had been built in God's name, while others tell of a broken wager between the Devil and the cathedral's builder. Tall tales to entice tourists? Maybe. But there is no confirmed story about how the strange footprint was formed in the church's floor.

Columned nave of Frauenkirche, and *(inset)* its domed west towers

The main chapel features a painting by Jan Polack, Chorhauptkapelle (c 1510), which shows the Virgin protecting members of the patrician Sänftl family.

Legend says that the cathedral's builder wagered with the Devil that no window could be seen from within, so pillars were constructed to obscure the windows.

The Memminger Altar was built in 1500, incorporating reliefs by Ignaz Günther and a Rococo Madonna.

The stalls are decorated with various figures. One of them features the bust of St James, which was made by Erasmus Grasser.

↑ Illustration of the Gothic-style Frauenkirche

2

ASAMKIRCHE

◉P4 ⓐSendlinger Str. 62 ⓤSendlinger Tor 🚊16, 17, 18, 27 🚌52 🕐9am–7pm daily

Officially known as St Johann Nepomuk, the German Baroque Asamkirche is a highlight of Bavarian architecture. Its pièce de résistance is a ceiling fresco depicting the life of St Nepomuk, a Bohemian monk. With exquisite stucco and gold leaf decorations, the church is an ode to the Italian Baroque.

The Asamkirche was funded, designed and executed between 1733 and 1746 by the Asam brothers, the most famous builders and decorators of the time. Drawing on the full effects of Baroque artistry, the brothers created a mysterious, theatrical illusion of another world. The façade, set upon a plinth that imitates natural stone, gives no hint of the splendour within. The nave, with its low-key lighting, is full of small but striking architectural details, rich stuccowork and colourful frescoes that are some of most celebrated of their kind.

← The beautiful west façade of the Asamkirche

A statue of St John Nepomuk, surrounded by cherubs and two angels, graces the arch over the doorway.

The nave is a relatively small space, measuring up to just 28 m (92 ft) long and 9 m (29 ft) wide.

A fine carving on the doors of the west façade depicts St John Nepomuk being thrown into prison.

Entrance

A fine Rococo epitaph was sculpted by Ignaz Günther in 1758.

Did You Know?

St John Nepomuk is widely considered a protector against floods and natural disasters.

Illustration of the
↓ 18th-century
Asamkirche

The ceiling features trompe
l'oeil paintings depicting
scenes from the life and
martyrdom of St John Nepomuk.

THE ASAM BROTHERS

The fresco painter Cosmas Damian Asam and the sculptor and stuccoist Egid Quirin Asam were taught by their father, the painter Hans Georg Asam, and studied briefly at the Accademia di San Luca in Rome. From 1714 onwards, they built masterpieces of late Baroque art in Rohr, Weltenburg, Munich and Osterhofen. By combining architectural, sculptural and painterly effects, they created what was called *theatrum sacrum*, a means of portraying salvation through the contrast of light and shadow.

An undulating gallery
divides the walls of the
nave and the high altar
into two distinct parts.

A glass sarcophagus in the
high altar contains a robed wax
figure of a prelate representing
St John Nepomuk.

The pulpit is surrounded by a
relief with scenes from the life
of St John the Baptist and
symbols of the Evangelists.

→
Stunning bas-reliefs,
paintings and gold
leaf decorations inside
the church

EXPERIENCE MORE

③

Karlstor

♥ P3 **🏠 Karlsplatz 5** **🚋 16, 17, 18, 19, 20, 21, 22, 27, 28**

A vestige of the medieval town's fortifications, this gate stands at the western entrance to the Old Town. Originally known as the Neuhauser Tor, the gate received its present name in 1791 in honour of Karl Theodor, who recommended the demolition of the old walls to enable the city to expand. Initially, the Karlstor had three

Did You Know?

In 1970, a medieval escape tunnel used by soldiers in battle was discovered through the Karlstor.

towers. The tallest of them, the central tower, was destroyed in 1857 when the gunpowder that was stored there exploded. The gate was rebuilt to a Neo-Gothic design by Arnold Zenetti.

In 1899–1902 the architect Gabriel von Seidl added two wings, known as the Rondel-bauten, to the Karlstor. These Neo-Baroque buildings, with two tower-shaped projections, have shops in their ground-floor arcades.

④

Karlsplatz

♥ P3 **🏠 Karlsplatz (Stachus)** **🚋 16, 17, 18, 19, 20, 21, 22, 27, 28**

After the city's fortifications were blown up in 1791 on the orders of Elector Karl Theodor, a vast square was laid out on the western side of the Old

Town. Like the Karlstor, it was named Karlsplatz in honour of the ruler. The square also had a popular name – Stachus – which is still used today. It refers to the most popular inn in Munich, which since 1759 has stood on the southwest side of the square.

⑤

Bürgersaalkirche

♥ P3 **🏠 Neuhauser Str. 14** **🚋 16, 17, 18, 19, 20, 21, 22, 27, 28** **⏰ Lower church hall: 9am-7pm daily; upper church hall: daily, only during mass**

The name of this church reflects its original purpose as the headquarters of the Marian congregation. It was designed by Giovanni Antonio Viscardi and consecrated in 1778. The rather austere façade fronts a two-storey interior. The lower

↑ Strolling through the Neo-Gothic Karlstor to Neuhauser Straße

Intricately carved ceilings on display in the Michaelskirche ↑

SHOP

Oberpollinger

Originally opened in 1905, this luxury department store, one of the largest in Germany, is home to many of the best designer brands.

📍P3 🏛Neuhauser Stra. 18
🌐oberpollinger.de

Hofstatt

A sleek retail space in a historic building designed by architect Max Littmann. Expect high-end stores, as well as an array of good restaurants.

📍P3 🏛Sendlinger Stra. 10
🌐hoftstatt.info

Breuninger

Breuninger's flagship store is a vast repository of contemporary fashion's biggest brands. It also stocks staples of high-quality traditional Bavarian dress.

📍P3
🏛Diener Str. 12
🌐breuninger.com

church contains the tomb of the beatified Rupert Mayer, a staunch fighter against the Nazis. The upper church, which was the main meeting place of the Marians, glitters with Rococo stuccowork by Joseph Georg Bader and paintings by Anton von Gumpp. The interior of the church was damaged during World War II. Surviving original features include the bas-relief on the high altar by Andreas Faistenberger, dating from 1710, the famous Guardian Angel of 1763 and the group of figures crowning the pulpit by Ignaz Günther.

6
Michaelskirche

📍P3 🏛Neuhauser Str 6 🚋
16, 17, 18, 19, 20, 21, 22, 27
🕙10am–5pm Mon–Sat

The founder of this church, built for the Jesuit order, which was prominent in this area from 1559 onwards, was Duke Wilhelm V. The complicated construction process began in 1585, but when the tower collapsed in 1590, it was decided to enlarge the transept and to add a choir to designs by Italian-Dutch painter Friedrich Sustris. The Michaelskirche, which aimed to bolster the Counter-Reformation and reinforce the Jesuits' presence, is the largest late-Renaissance religious building north of the Alps. It is reminiscent of the church of Il Gesú in Rome.

The three-tier façade, with its double doorway, is an out-standing example of Mannerist architecture. Between the pilasters, there are windows and rows of niches containing the figures of Bavarian and imperial rulers engaged in the expansion and defence of Christendom. The ground floor is dominated by a bronze figure of St Michael slaying the Dragon, with a figure of Christ the Saviour on his shield, made by Hubert Gerhard in 1585. The two portals, designed by Sustris, lead into a strikingly spacious interior. The complex barrel vaulting over the nave spans the second-largest space after St Peter's Basilica in Rome. The elongated choir ends with the massive high altar, where a large painting by Christoph Schwarz depicts the dramatic fall from heaven of the rebellious angels. In the crypt beneath the choir area lie members of the Wittelsbach family, including Maximilian I and Ludwig II, along with the church's founder. Beside the church is a monastery and a college. The latter was built in 1585–97, also by Sustris. It is known as the Alte Akademie.

 Boar sculpture at Deutsches Jagd- und Fischereimuseum

7 Deutsches Jagd- und Fischereimuseum

📍P4 🏛Neuhauser Str. 2
🚊16, 17, 18, 19, 20, 21, 22, 27, 28 🕐9:30am–5pm daily 🌐jagd-fischerei-museum.de

The German Hunting and Fishing Museum holds one of the largest collections of field sports equipment in the world. First formed in the early 20th century, when hunting was particularly fashionable among the European elite, the collection includes hunting weapons, bags and sleighs, and some 1,000 stuffed animals and birds in lively re-creations of their natural surroundings. There are also trophies and pictures of hunting scenes from across the continent. The large angling section illustrates the development of fishing tackle, and shows numerous specimens of fish, from local catches to rare, prized species.

The museum is housed somewhat incongruously in an Augustinian basilica, which was first erected in the late 13th century. It was rebuilt several times, and became the first building in Munich to be decorated in the Baroque style. In 1911 it was converted into a concert hall, and in 1966 the hunting and fishing collection was moved here from Bavaria's Schloss Nymphenburg.

8 Peterskirche

📍Q4 🏛Rindermarkt 1
🕐9am–7:30pm daily (Nov–Mar: to 6:30pm)
🌐alterpeter.de

St Peter's Church, standing on the highest point of the Old Town, is Munich's earliest public building. Built in the 12th century, the basilica formed part of the monastery from which the city received its name (*Mönchen* meaning "monks"). In 1278–94 it was replaced by a new church in the Gothic style. In the 14th century the twin towers were replaced with a single tower. In the 17th century the church was redecorated in Baroque style, and in the 18th century it was remodelled in the Rococo style. The church's famous tower, known as Alter

 GREAT VIEW
Tower Views

The Peterskirche is famous for panoramic views from its high tower. Climb the tower's 500 stairs and look out from the 56-m (180-ft) observation deck. Here you can snap a grand panorama looking out over Marienplatz.

Peter (Old Peter), has eight clocks, seven bells and a viewing gallery that offers a splendid view over the Old Town. The high altar is crowned with a statue of St Peter by Erasmus Grasser, surrounded by the Church Fathers by Egid Quirin Asam. The choir contains five figures by Jan Polack with scenes from the life of St Peter.

9 Neues Rathaus

📍Q4 🏛Marienplatz 8
🕐Viewing tower: May–Oct: 10am–7pm daily; Nov–Apr: 10am–5pm Mon–Fri; Clock chimes: Nov–end Feb: 11am & noon

In the second half of the 19th century, the civic authorities decided to build new headquarters for themselves, choosing the north side of Marienplatz for their new town hall. To accommodate the building, 24 large houses were demolished, leaving enough space for the grand construction. The building that emerged, with its six courtyards, is a prime example of German pseudo-historical architecture, in this case mock-Netherlands

→ Alfresco dining at the Marienplatz in front of the towering Neues Rathaus

Gothic. The decoration of the façade abounds in sculptures alluding to Bavaria's many legends and history. The steeple is topped by a bronze figure of the Münchner Kindl (Munich Child), the symbol of the Bavarian capital.

The clock in the tower is the fourth-largest chiming clock in Europe. Every day a concert is played on its 43 bells, with coloured copper figures dancing to four different melodies. The figures dance two tradtional Bavarian scenes: a knightly tournament in honour of the grand wedding of Duke Wilhelm V and Renata of Lotharingia, and the Schäfflertanz, or Dance of the Coopers (p40), which is performed every seven years in the streets of Munich to this day, to commemorate the passing of an epidemic of the plague in 1515–17.

In the evening, in the bays of the tower's seventh storey, appear the figures of a night-watchman blowing on his horn and the Angel of Peace blessing the Münchner Kindl. The viewing tower commands a fine view.

⑩ Marienplatz

📍 Q4

Ever since the city was planned by Henry the Lion, Marienplatz has been Munich's focal point. Until 1807 it was a marketplace. It acquired its present name in 1854, when Munich's citizens asked the Virgin Mary to protect them from a cholera epidemic. For centuries the square was the place where major public events, proclamations, tournaments and executions took place. Today it is the venue for the famous Christkindlmarkt (Christmas Fair), which is held in the days leading up to Christmas.

The square is dominated by the Neues Rathaus (New Town Hall). Crowds of tourists and local people gather in the square every day to watch the mechanical figures on the central clock tower perform their concert.

The Mariensäule (Column of the Virgin) in the square was erected in 1638 in gratitude for the end of the Swedish invasion. The golden statue of the Virgin (1593) is by Hubert Gerhard and the four putti around the plinth (1639) are by Ferdinand Murmann. The putti are shown overcoming

hunger, war, heresy and pestilence. Another attraction of the square is the 19th-century Fischbrunnen (Fish Fountain), which was rebuilt after being destroyed in World War II.

⑪ Altes Rathaus

📍 Q4 🏠 Marienplatz 15
🚫 To the public

The original Old Town Hall was built by Jörg von Halspach, who also built the Frauenkirche (p60). The building lost its official role in 1874, when it was replaced by the Neues Rathaus (New Town Hall). The old building was rebuilt on many occasions, most recently in 1861–4, when it acquired its present Neo-Gothic character. In 1877 and then in 1934 two gateways were cut through in order to accommodate the increasing flow of traffic.

The oldest part of the building is the tower of 1180–1200, part of the original city fortifications. Since 1983 it has housed the **Spielzeugmuseum** (Toy Museum), which as well as antique doll's houses, tin cars and copper soldiers contains a display tracing the history of the Barbie doll.

The Gothic interior of the Altes Rathaus survives. The ceremonial hall occupying the ground floor has wide wooden barrel vaulting, and a wall with a frieze of 96 coats of arms dating from 1478. This hall is used to exhibit the Moriscos (Moriskentänzer) that sculptor Erasmus Grasser carved in 1480. The figures currently on display here are copies of the originals.

Spielzeugmuseum
♿ 📷 🏠 Marienplatz 15
🕐 10am–5:30pm daily
🌐 spielzeugmuseum muenchen.de

⑫ Ehemalige Stadtschreiberei

📍 Q4 🏠 Burgstr. 5

A visit to Munich's oldest surviving townhouse is the perfect excuse to enjoy a beer and some food; even better when it's served in a late Gothic cloistered courtyard. In 1510 the town council bought this pair of houses between Burgstraße and Dienerstraße. The house on Burgstraße, rebuilt in 1551–2, housed the offices of the city writers' guild (Stadtschreiberhaus) from 1552 to 1612. The house has an interesting façade with a large window in the centre. The perfectly preserved large main doorway conceals the entrance passage. To the right of the façade is a small late Gothic side entrance framed by a donkey-back arch. The façade, which had been under restoration, was unveiled in 1964, revealing most of the restored Renaissance decoration executed by Hans Mielich in 1552. An attractive addition to the courtyard is a late Gothic tower with a spiral stair-case. The townhouse is now also home to German-Japanese chef Tohru Nakamura's popular fusion restaurant, Tohru (schreiberei-muc.de/en/tohru).

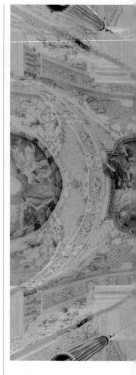

⑬ Heilig-Geist-Kirche

📍 Q4 🏠 Prälat-Miller-Weg 3
🕐 8:30am–7pm daily

The Church of the Holy Spirit is one of Munich's oldest buildings, ranking in importance along-side the Frauenkirche and the Peterskirche. It stands on a site of historic importance: it was once home to a chapel, a hospital and a pilgrims' hostel. In the mid-13th century a hospital church was built here, which was replaced by a new, larger church in the 14th century. In 1724, the church was decorated in the Baroque style, with fine vaulting and stuccowork by the Asam brothers. In 1729 a tower was added. Its Neo-Baroque façade dates from 1895, when the hospital next to the church was demolished.

The interior is a fine example of the combination

↑ The Alte Rathaus at the eastern end of Marienplatz

↑ Vaulted ceiling covered in intricate stuccowork at Heilig-Geist-Kirche, and *(inset)* the church itself

of Gothic and late Baroque elements for which Bavaria is renowned. The ceiling frescoes depict scenes from the hospital's history. The high altar was made by sculptors Nikolaus Stuber and Antonio Matteo in 1728–30 and rebuilt after World War II. Original elements of the altar include the painting of the Pentecost (1644) by Ulrich Loth and the flanking angels by Johann Georg Greiff. The bronze figures in the vestibule (1608) by Hans Krumpper originally formed part of the ornate tomb of Ferdinand of Bavaria.

14

Isartor

🅿 R4

Entry into the city from the southeast is through the Isartor. This gate is the only vestige of the city's original fortifications. The central tower was built in 1337, and in 1429–33 two eight-sided towers, connected by walls, were added. In the 19th century arcades were made in the towers. They were decorated with friezes representing the triumphal procession of Ludwig IV of Bavaria after his victory at the Battle of Ampfing (1322).

The southern tower houses the **Valentin-Karlstadt-Musäum**, a museum dedicated to the actor and comedian Karl Valentin (1882–1948), a master of the absurd who wrote theatre sketches and short films.

Valentin-Karlstadt-Musäum

🔗 🅰 Tal 50 🕐 11am–6pm Mon–Tue & Thu–Sat, 10am–6pm Sun 🆆 valentin-karlstadt-musaeum.de

---

🔍 HIDDEN GEM
The Cauldron

Visit the Isartor in December, and you might just notice an invitingly fragrant aroma. The gate is home to a huge winter cauldron serving steaming mugs of *Feuerzangenbowle*, a festive mulled drink.

15

Gärtnerplatz

🅰 Q5 🚋 16, 17, 18
🚌 132 🌐 gaertnerplatz
theater.de

The hexagonal square lying at the intersection of Reichenbachstraße, Corneliusstraße and Klenzestraße is named after the prominent 19th-century architect Friedrich von Gärtner. It is the focal point of the district known as the Gärtnerplatzviertel, built in the second half of the 19th century. It was the first large district of purpose-built apartment blocks in Munich to be designed in a unified style.

In 1864–5 a theatre was built on the south side of Gärtnerplatz. It was designed by Franz Michael Reiffenstuel and was known as the Gärtnerplatztheater. It was a slightly less upmarket response to the courtly Nationaltheater. Its decorative façade stands out among the somewhat monotonous architecture that surrounds it and it is considered by many to be the most beautiful theatre in Munich.

The Gärtnerplatztheater stages minor operas, operettas and musicals. Rare works are often staged, including operas that have never been performed in Munich before.

16

Viktualienmarkt

🟥 Q4 🅰 Between
Petersplatz and Frauenstr.
🚌 52

This is Munich's oldest and most picturesque market. Since the beginning of the 19th century, food of all kinds has been sold here – fruit and vegetables, milk, meat, the finest French wines and cheeses, fish and shellfish and delicacies from all corners of the world, albeit at fairly high prices. The market still attracts locals who come for their regular shop, as well as many tourists; it's common for visitors to sample *Weißwürste* (white sausage) or to sip hot soup and drink beer in the market's beer garden. The market is also home to several fountains topped with statues, each dedicated to German singers and entertainers. The fountains are celebrated with a fountain festival in August, during which market vendors decorate the many statues.

EAT

Café Frischhut
It's a tradition for workers to start their day with a visit to Café Frischhut. This spot serves Schmalznudel and Bavarian-style doughnuts close to Viktualienmarkt.

🟥 Q4 🅰 Prälat-Zistl-
Str. 8
📞 (+49 089) 26023156

💲💲💲

⑰ Ignaz-Günther-Haus

Q5 🅰 St-Jakobs-Platz 15
🔒 To the public

Ignaz Günther (1725–75) was one of Europe's finest Rococo sculptors. He worked throughout southern Germany, but primarily in Munich. His work can be seen in the Peterskirche, Bürgersaal, Frauenkirche, the grounds of Schloss Nymphenburg and Schleißheim Palace, as well as the churches and abbeys of Upper and Lower Bavaria. He moved into this house on St-Jakob's-Platz in 1761.

The Ignaz-Günther-Haus is a very fine example of late Gothic residential architecture. The reception room on the first floor has an early 16th-century wooden ceiling. The façade on the side of the Oberanger contains a statue of the Virgin carved by Günther and known as the Hausmadonna. This is a copy of the original, which is housed in the Bayerisches Nationalmuseum in Munich.

↑ Traditional beer mugs at the Bier- und Oktoberfestmuseum

⑱
Bier- und Oktoberfestmuseum

R4 🅰 Sterneckerstr.
🚋 16, 18 🕐 1–6pm Tue–Sat
🌐 bier-und-oktoberfest museum.de

This fine museum covers both the history of beer as well as the story of the Oktoberfest, telling how the festival became such an important part of Munich's tradition and global reputation. Visitors can learn how beer was first made in ancient Egypt, as well as how the beer-making process developed in Munich itself.

Up until 1870, beer was only brewed in the city during the winter months, with ice from the lakes necessary for the cooling process. After the invention of refrigerators, beer was brewed all year round, with a rapid expansion in the number of breweries in Munich. At one time there were as many as 70 breweries in the city; today just six major breweries remain in Munich.

There is also a collection of artifacts from Oktoberfests over the years, including a collection of tankards. The museum has a restaurant serving beer and typical Bavarian snacks. The building housing the museum was constructed under an ambitious city expansion scheme, spear-headed by Ludwig IV after the great fire of 1327.

←
Browsing the varied food stalls at the Viktualienmarkt

Jüdisches Zentrum

Q5 **St-Jakobs-Platz 16** **w** juedischeszen
trumjakobsplatz.de

The Jewish Centre is the focal point of Munich's Jewish community, which was almost obliterated during World War II. Located on St-Jakobs-platz, the complex comprises the Ohel Jakob Synagogue, the Jewish Community Centre of Munich and Upper Bavaria, and the Jewish Museum.

The **Jewish Museum** is housed in a cube-shaped, free standing building intended to resemble the Wailing Wall in Jerusalem. The transparent ground floor lobby, glazed on all sides, emphasizes the museum's role as a place for open discussion. Three floors of exhibitions, plus a library and a learning centre, all offer extensive information on Jewish culture and history and highlight important aspects of contemporary Jewish life.

The synagogue, also cube-shaped, is crowned by a light-flooded roof. The community centre contains the administrative department, the rabbinate, conference rooms, a kinder-garten, a public full-time school, a youth and

arts centre, and a kosher restaurant. There is also a sobering memory wall inscribed with the names of Jewish Munich residents who were killed during the Nazi regime. The synagogue can be viewed on a guided tour.

Jewish Museum

 St-Jakobs-Platz 16
10am–6pm Tue–Sun
w juedisches-museum-muenchen.de

Münchner Stadtmuseum

Q4 **St-Jakobs-Platz 1**
For renovation until 2027
w muenchner-stadtmuseum.de

The Munich City Museum is housed across six adjoining buildings. Two of them, the Marstall and the Zeughaus, were built in the 15th century as granaries but later became the city's stables and arsenal. The museum is home to a vast collection of art and photo-graphy and a film museum. The exhibitions are closed for renovations for the fore-seeable future, but the museum's café and cinema remain open. The spacious café is a comfortable haven on rainy days and the cinema is popular among film buffs.

↑ Cube-shaped Ohel Jakob Synagogue, part of the Jüdisches Zentrum

Sendlinger Tor

P4 **Sendlinger-Tor-Platz** **16, 17, 18, 27, 28,
N16, N27, N40, N41** **62**

The southern end of the bustling thoroughfare

STAY

Hotel MIO by AMANO
Conveniently located on Sendlinger Straße, this hotel has a modern, designer vibe.

P4 **Sendlinger Str. 46** **w** amanogroup.com

KOOS Hotel and Apartments
This family-run aparthotel is located in the centre of Munich and has friendly staff.

N4 **Sonnenstr. 18b**
w kooshotel.de

known as Sendlinger Straße passes through the Sendlinger Tor, a large Gothic gate overgrown with vines.

The gate was first mentioned in 1318 and, with the Karlstor and Isartor *(p69)*, this gate is all that remains of the secondary city fortifications that were built in 1285–1347 during the reigns of Ludwig II and Ludwig IV of Bavaria. An important trade route to Italy via Innsbruck once passed along here.

The tall gatehouse that formerly stood in the centre of the Sendlinger Tor was demolished in 1808. The octagonal tower which then functioned as a gatehouse dates from the end of the 14th century. In 1906, because of the increasing volume of traffic, the three arches were converted into a single large arch, with pedestrian arches made through the side towers.

Beyond the gate is Sendlinger-Tor-Platz, a square named after the gate. It is one of Munich's crossroads, with pedestrian subways leading to the metro station. The Sonnenstraße, which continues from here, was the first 19th-century thoroughfare to be built along the course of the old city walls. Its name, meaning "sun street", reflects its bright, open design compared with the narrow, shady passages of the Old Town. Sendlinger-Tor-Platz has a park on the west side with St Matthew's Church rising over it.

___

㉒
Asamhaus

🚇 P4 🏠 Sendlinger Str. 34
🚊 16, 17, 18, 27, 28, N16, N27 🚌 62
🚫 To the public

One of the most important artist's residences in Munich, the Asamhaus affords special insights into the life and work of two of the city's most esteemed creatives, the Asam brothers *(p63)*. When the fresco painter Cosmas Damian Asam decided to settle in the suburban Maria Einsiedel Palace, which he renovated, his brother Egid Quirin Asam purchased four adjoining properties on Sendlinger Straße in 1729–33. He converted them into his own residence, adding a church and presbytery. Asam designed each building in the same lavish style, adding an interior window looking from the house towards the church's altar.

Rather than decorating his home with the fresco paintings that were customary at the time, Egid Quirin Asam showed off his mastery of stucco and added intricate stucco decorations, depicting Christian and Classical motifs, to the medieval façades. Personifications of the fine arts, poetry and music are watched over by St Joseph, patron saint of craftsmen, who is surrounded by symbols of Faith, Hope and Mercy. Visitors can also admire a large relief designed to represent Perfection, with a range of religious imagery symbolizing the Christian concept of heaven.

This remarkable decorative work covers the exterior of the house. An additional design on the left of the property constructs a vision inspired by Classical Antiquity, whose ideals were adopted by Baroque artists. The figure of Pallas Athenae leads a childlike figure into the world of art and science under the aegis of Pegasus, with Apollo watching over them all. These visions are complemented by the world of sensations, which are represented by Cupid, satyrs and fauns.

↑ The lavishly decorated façade of the Asamhaus

Beautifully decorated interior of the Damenstift St Anna church

23 Damenstift St Anna

Q P4 **A** Damenstiftstr. 1
◷ 8am–8pm daily

Princess Henrietta of Savoy, founder of Munich's Catholic Theatine Church, brought the Salesian order of sisters to Munich in 1667. During the 18th century the order acquired its own church, this one. In time the convent passed into the hands of an order of aristocratic ladies, hence the name "Damenstift" (an institution for ladies of rank). This single-nave church, with side chapels behind mighty arches and a presbytery at one end, is a typically Baroque attempt to combine the centrally planned church with the elongated model, a style seen across Bavaria.

Today the building houses a high school for girls. The façade is in the late Baroque style, as is the opulent decoration of the interior, which was executed by the Asam brothers. After suffering total destruction during World War II, the paintings inside the church were restored in sepia, as black-and-white photographs were the only existing record of the original decorative scheme. The paintings depict the oath of angels, the Glory of St Mary and St Anne, and the concert of angels (above the gallery). The realistic group of the *Last Supper* to the right of the high altar is unusually lifelike. The life-sized statues sitting at the table, which seem to be conversing and gesticulating, were probably copied directly from their Spanish originals.

24 St Matthäuskirche

Q N5 **A** Nußbaumstr. 1
🚋 16, 17, 18, 27, 28 **🚌** 62
◷ 9am–4pm Tue–Fri
W stmatthaeus.de

The original St Matthäuskirche was built in 1827–33 at the junction of Stachus and Sonnenstraße, and was the earliest Protestant church in Munich. Known as "Stachuskirche" due to its original location, the church was demolished in 1938 by command of the National Socialists, who

St Matthäuskirche was demolished in 1938 by command of the National Socialists, who planned an expansion of the area on a scale of that found in Berlin.

In addition to being the ministry of the regional bishop, St Matthäuskirche offers a wide range of activities, including a healthcare chaplaincy, exhibitions of Munich's religious history, the "You Dare" children's circus, art installations and performances of church music by the Münchner Motettenchor.

Allerheiligenkirche am Kreuz

P4 Kreuzstr. 10
8am–8pm daily

All Hallows' Church was built in 1478 by German architect Jörg von Halspach, and was the first cemetery church in the parish of St Peter. In centuries past, four streets converged outside the church, hence the name "am Kreuz" ("at the crossing").

The church's bare brick walls, Gothic vaults and tall steeple make it a prominent and distinctive religious landmark in Kreuzstraße. The interior was refurbished during the Baroque era, so that the only vestiges of its Gothic appearance are the web vaulting over the nave, fragments of a fresco of Christ in a mandorla (circle of light) and a crucifix made in 1520 by esteemed sculptor Hans Leinberger, whose works can be found throughout the state.

Fine examples of the transitional style of art that developed between the Mannerist period and led into the Baroque can be seen in the tombs designed by sculptor Hans Krumpper, and in the depiction of the Virgin appearing before St Augustine on the high altar, which was created by German painter Hans Rottenhammer in 1614. Today Allerheiligenkirche is designated a Uniate (Greek Catholic) church.

> ### PROTESTANT AND CATHOLIC CHURCHES
>
> Most churches in Munich are Catholic, but there are a few striking examples of Protestant churches in the city, among them St Matthäus, St Lukas and the Erlöserkirche. Historically, Munich has been a predominantly Catholic city, but this is changing as the population becomes increasingly secular – now, around a quarter of residents belong to the Catholic Church.

planned an expansion of the area on a scale of that found in Berlin. The replacement church was built in 1953–5 to a design by Gustav Gsaenger at the southern end of the Sendlinger-Tor-Platz, between Nußbaumstraße and Lindwurmstraße. The modern, red-brick building is one of two Lutheran episcopal churches of the Protestant Church in Bavaria (the other is the Lorenzkirche in Nuremberg). The church's free standing 51-m- (167-ft-) high tower has six bells, two of which hang at the level of the clock, while the other four sit a floor above.

St Matthäuskirche is graced by a large organ designed by Steinmeyer, one of the leading European organ manufacturers in the late 19th century. Since 2014, the grand organ has gradually been restored and extended by leading organ specialists.

↑ The striking Allerheiligenkirche am Kreuz towering over the city

A SHORT WALK
AROUND MARIENPLATZ

Distance 600 m (0.4 miles) **Time** 10 minutes
Nearest U-Bahn station Karlsplatz

Ever since Munich was founded, Marienplatz has been the city's architectural and commercial hub. The geographical centre of the city is marked by the Mariensäule (Column of the Virgin), from which all distances in Munich are measured. The square and the streets around it, which have been pedestrianized since the Munich Olympics in 1972, are always lively. This area is Munich's busiest, bustling with shoppers, visitors taking walking tours and office workers going about their business.

*Known as the **Karlstor** (Karl's Gate), the west entrance to the Old Town was part of the medieval fortifications. It was given its present name in 1791, in honour of Elector Karl Theodore.*

KARLS PLATZ

START

HERZOG-MAX-STR.

NEUHAUSER STRASSE

KAPELLE

HERZOG-WILHELM STR.

HERZOGSPITALSTR.

EISENMANNSTR.

Bürgersaal (p64) was built in 1710 for a Marian congregation (followers of the Virgin Mary) as a place of meeting and worship. It includes an upper and lower church.

*Founded by monks in 1328, **Augustiner-Bräu** is the oldest and most celebrated brewery in Munich. It occupies two 19th-century houses with picturesque façades.*

Neuhauser Straße *is Munich's largest shopping street. It is filled with typical 19th-century buildings and with cafés and shops that are busy from morning till night.*

 The ornate interior of Bürgersaal's Upper Church

↑ Visitors gathering to see the mechanical dolls dance on the Neues Rathaus's clock tower

Around Marienplatz

OLD TOWN (SOUTH)

Locator Map

The interior of **Michaelskirche** (p65) is surprisingly large. The massive barrel vaulting over the nave is the second largest after St Peter's Basilica in Rome.

Housed in the Augustinerkirche, a deconsecrated church with a Rococo interior, the **Deutsches Jagd-und Fischereimuseum** (p66) has a huge collection of hunting and fishing exhibits.

Despite heavy damage during World War II, the iconic dome-topped towers of the **Frauenkirche** (p60) still stand tall.

The figures in the **Neues Rathaus's** (p66) chiming clock enact a joust and perform a dance.

The high altar of **Peterskirche** (p66) is decorated with a figure of the saint surrounded by the four Church Fathers.

The **Altes Rathaus** (p68) was remodelled several times, and restored after damage in World War II. It now houses a small toy museum.

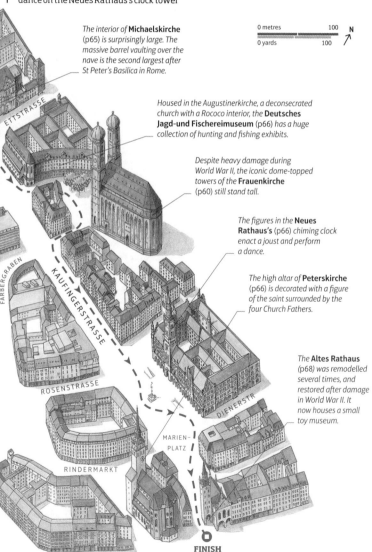

0 metres 100
0 yards 100

N

ETTSTRASSE

FÄRBERGRABEN

KAUFINGERSTRASSE

ROSENSTRASSE

RINDERMARKT

DIENERSTR

MARIEN-PLATZ

FINISH

OLD TOWN (NORTH)

The section of the Altstadt (Old Town) to the
north of Marienplatz can be traced back to the
city's medieval expansion. It was only when the
Wittelsbach dynasty came to power in Bavaria
in the late 12th century that the area became a
centre of royal life, with the construction of the
huge Alter Hof, the first fortified residence of the
Wittelsbachs. The Residenz was built shortly after;
it was to be the home of the Wittelsbachs for
centuries. Heavy royal investment meant the area
became increasingly elegant throughout the 14th
and 15th centuries, with the development of lavish
residences, numerous Baroque palaces and the
fine Theatinerkirche and opera house. In 1589,
Wilhelm V opened an inn as part of the Royal
Brewery, which was to become the Hofbräuhaus,
Munich's most famous drinking house.

The north of the Old Town soon became
renowned for its modern shopping streets and
bustling promenades; the principal thoroughfares
traversing the Old Town are Theatinerstraße and
Residenzstraße. West of Theatinerstraße is the old
Kreuzviertel district, formerly known as the centre
of the city's clergy. Today the north of the Old
Town is enclosed by the Altstadtring (ring road).

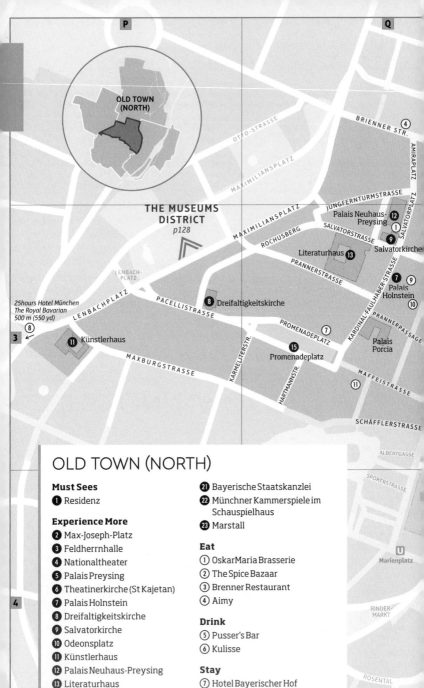

OLD TOWN (NORTH)

Must Sees
1. Residenz

Experience More
2. Max-Joseph-Platz
3. Feldherrnhalle
4. Nationaltheater
5. Palais Preysing
6. Theatinerkirche (St Kajetan)
7. Palais Holnstein
8. Dreifaltigkeitskirche
9. Salvatorkirche
10. Odeonsplatz
11. Künstlerhaus
12. Palais Neuhaus-Preysing
13. Literaturhaus
14. Alter Hof
15. Promenadeplatz
16. Palais Toerring-Jettenbach
17. Hofbräuhaus
18. Alte Münze
19. Maximilianstraße
20. Hofgarten
21. Bayerische Staatskanzlei
22. Münchner Kammerspiele im Schauspielhaus
23. Marstall

Eat
① OskarMaria Brasserie
② The Spice Bazaar
③ Brenner Restaurant
④ Aimy

Drink
⑤ Pusser's Bar
⑥ Kulisse

Stay
⑦ Hotel Bayerischer Hof
⑧ 25hours Hotel München The Royal Bavarian

Shop
⑨ Fünf Höfe
⑩ Hugendubel
① LODENFREY

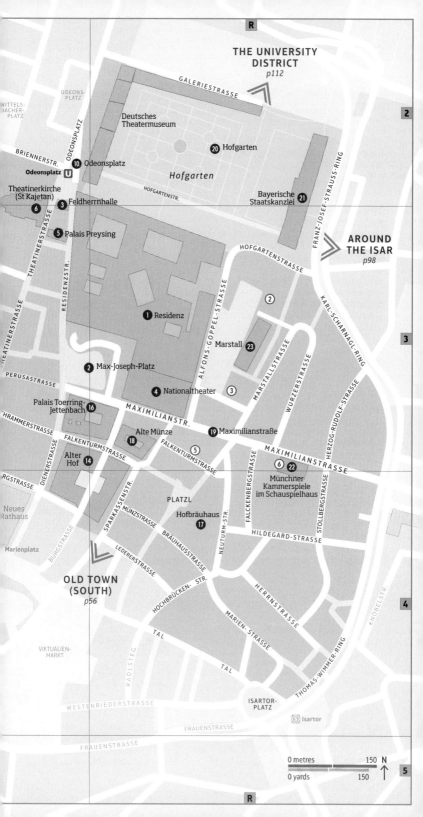

RESIDENZ

❑R3 ▣Max-Joseph-Platz 3 ⓤOdeonsplatz 🚊19 🚌100 🕐Apr-mid-Oct: 9am-6pm daily; mid-Oct-Mar: 10am-5pm daily �🌐residenz-muenchen.de

The former royal palace of Bavaria's Wittelsbach monarchs, the Residenz is one of the most eminent palace museums in Europe. Here, one can explore the lavish Renaissance Hall of Antiquities, marvel at the Rococo decorations in the Ancestral Gallery and take in the striking Neo-Classical flourishes of the Charlotte rooms.

Germany's largest city palace, the Residenz has ten courtyards, 130 rooms, a treasury, church, theatre, stables and a huge park, the Hofgarten. The buildings date back to 1385, when the Neuveste (castle) was built in the part of Munich enclosed by city walls. In the 16th century the Antiquarium and another wing were added, creating the Grottenhof courtyard. The Kaiserhof was added in the 17th century. After rebuilding in the Baroque and Rococo periods, the ensemble was enclosed by new buildings, the Königsbau and Festsaalbau, in the 19th century.

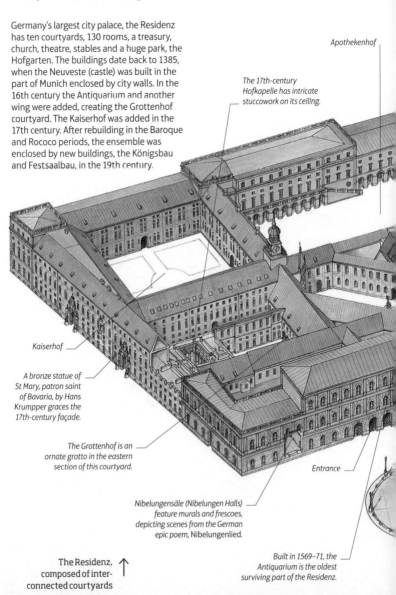

Apothekenhof

The 17th-century Hofkapelle has intricate stuccowork on its ceiling.

Kaiserhof

A bronze statue of St Mary, patron saint of Bavaria, by Hans Krumpper graces the 17th-century façade.

The Grottenhof is an ornate grotto in the eastern section of this courtyard.

Entrance

Nibelungensäle (Nibelungen Halls) feature murals and frescoes, depicting scenes from the German epic poem, Nibelungenlied.

The Residenz, composed of inter-connected courtyards ↑

Built in 1569-71, the Antiquarium is the oldest surviving part of the Residenz.

↑ Lamplit archways on the outer wall of the Residenz

Cuvilliés-Theater, opened in 1753, is considered to be Europe's finest surviving Rococo theatre.

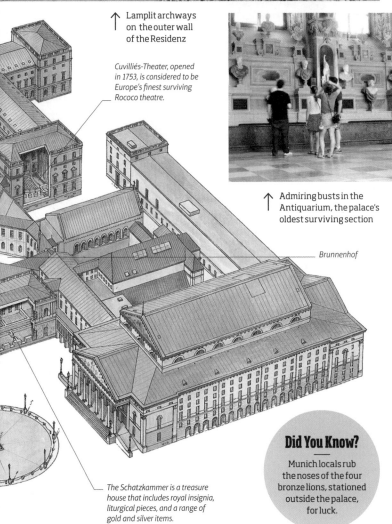

↑ Admiring busts in the Antiquarium, the palace's oldest surviving section

Brunnenhof

The Schatzkammer is a treasure house that includes royal insignia, liturgical pieces, and a range of gold and silver items.

Did You Know?

Munich locals rub the noses of the four bronze lions, stationed outside the palace, for luck.

EXPLORING THE RESIDENZ

A thorough exploration of this unusual palace would take a few days. The first parts to see are the three monumental façades and the many courtyards that are open to the public. Much of the palace's interior is home to the Residenzmuseum, where you can explore the vast halls and admire many wonders of European painting. Away from the museum, there is separate admission to the Schatzkammer, where royal treasures are housed, and the striking Rococo Cuvilliés-Theater.

↑ Wittelsbach Fountain decorated with bronze sculptures at the Brunnenhof

The Courtyards

The palace is home to several large courtyards. The one that lies on the side of the Residenzstraße features two Mannerist doorways with figures representing the four cardinal virtues: Justice, Prudence, Fortitude and Temperance. The south doorway leads into the Kapellenhof (Chapel Yard). It's enclosed by the Residenz's tower, built in 1615. The Grottenhof (Grotto Court) is visible through the gates to the right. This Mannerist courtyard, designed by Friedrich Sustris, encloses the Perseus Fountain.

The north doorway leads to the Kaiserhof, the centre of a section of the Residenz that was built in Maximilian style in the early 17th century. This leads in turn to the monumental Apothekenhof, which is closed on its northern side by the Festsaalbau (Ceremonial Hall Wing) of 1835–42. Parallel to the Antiquarium is the elongated octagonal Brunnenhof, with the famous Wittelsbach Fountain by Hans Krumpper and Hubert Gerhard (1611–23). It depicts Otto I surrounded by personifications of the rivers of Bavaria.

Schatzkammer

In 1565, Albrecht V ordered that the jewels of the Wittelsbachs were not to be sold after his death. This led to the creation of a treasure house, or "Schatzkammer". To it Elector Karl Theodor added the contents of the Palatinate treasury from Heidelberg, Düsseldorf and Mannheim. Later, religious works of art confiscated after the secularization of the knightly orders, and the insignia of the new kingdom of Bavaria were added.

Highlights include the royal insignia, the *cyborium* (covered cup) of Arnulf of Carinthia (c 890), the Rappoltsteiner Cup (1540), a statue of St George (1597), a 17th-century ornamental cup made of rhinoceros horn, and the royal insignia (crown and orb) made by Martin Guillaume Biennais in 1806.

Museums and Rooms

The Residenzmuseum, opened to the public in 1920, showcases the many wonders of the palace's interior. Enter the museum from Max-Joseph-Platz and through Königsbau, built by Leo von Klenze in 1826–35. Visits start from the vestibule and the two garden halls leading to the Ahnengalerie (Ancestral Gallery) with its lavish stuccowork and 121 portraits of the Wittelsbachs. After passing François Cuvilliés' porcelain cabinet, visitors reach the Grottenhof and the Antiquarium, the oldest part of the Residenz, which was built in 1568–71 for Prince Albrecht V. The final room on this floor is the Schwarzer Saal (Black Hall) of 1590, with

→ Equestrian figure of St George, inlaid with precious stones

The opulent Cuvilliés-
Theater, with elaborate
carvings on its tiers ↑

trompe l'oeil paintings on the ceiling. It in turn leads to the Gelbe Treppe (Yellow Stairs), where there is a statue of Venus Italica by Antonio Canova, and rooms in which European and Oriental porcelain and Persian divans are displayed.

Beyond the bedrooms of Maximilian III Joseph and his wife, designed by Cuvilliés in 1763, is the Allerheiligengang (All Saints Passage). It is decorated with 18 paintings by Carl Rottmann, which were moved here from the Hofgarten arcades in 1966. The Charlottentrakt that leads away from here is named after Princess Karoline Charlotte Auguste von Bayern, daughter of Maximilian I Joseph, who once lived in the Residenz.

Next is the 17th-century Trierzimmer (Trier Room). The ceiling was painted by Peter Candid and others and the walls are hung with tapestries dating from 1604–15. The St Georgs-Rittersaal (Knights' Hall) leads to the Reiches Zimmer (Rich Room), built in the 1730s to a design by Cuvilliés, with early Rococo decoration.

East Asian Collection

The collection of East Asian art comprises over 500 porcelain objects and some lacquer items. Most of the pieces on display were acquired around 1700 by Elector Maximilian Emanuel.

The earliest porcelain wares in the collection are the blue-and-white bowls and plates made in China around 1600, during the period of the Ming dynasty. The collection also contains items of Japanese and Chinese Imari porcelain.

Cuvilliés-Theater (Altes Residenztheater)

Europe's finest surviving Rococo theatre was built in 1751–53 by Maximilian Joseph III, who designed the spot to be his new opera house. The theatre was originally reserved exclusively for members of the royal court.

1781
—
The year the world premiere of Mozart's *Indomenio* was staged at the Cuvilliés-Theater.

The predominantly gold and red woodcarvings on the balconies, royal loggia and proscenia still survive. Largely destroyed in World War II, the theatre was rebuilt soon after, reusing many of the original carvings.

Coin collection

The Residenz contains the largest coin collection in the world. Its nucleus originated in a collection formed by Albrecht V and Ludwig I. It contains coins and medals dating from all periods and originating from all over the world. Seals, weights and banknotes also form part of the display.

EXPERIENCE MORE

2

Max-Joseph-Platz

Q3 19

During the 1820s, Karl von Fischer and Leo von Klenze laid out a grand square outside the Residenz, flanking it with the monumental façades of Neo-Classical buildings: Königsbau to the north, the National Theatre to the east, and the arcaded Toerring-Jettenbach Palace (p92) to the south. The latter is now an exclusive residence and also houses high-end stores.

In the square is a statue of Maximilian I Joseph, the first king of Bavaria, who drew up the Bavarian constitution, the first in Germany, in 1818. The statue was created by Leo von Klenze and Christian Daniel Rauch.

The building of the National Theatre doubles as the National Opera.

The interior also obeys Classical canons. The large circular auditorium is decorated predominantly in purple, gold, ivory and sky blue. It is surrounded by five-tiered galleries, with the royal box in the centre. The National Theatre became famous for its performances of Wagnerian operas. It was here that *Tristan und Isolde*, *Die Walküre* and *Rheingold* were first performed. Today it is the venue for opera festivals. Next door is the Residenztheater.

3

Feldherrnhalle

Q2 Odeonsplatz 100

On the site of the Schwabinger Tor, a medieval watchtower, the architect Friedrich von Gärtner raised a building that blends perfectly with the old and new towns between which it stands. The aim had been to create a focal point that would close off Ludwigstraße and give the irregular Odeonsplatz a more ordered appearance. At the request of Ludwig I, a loggia in honour of the heroes of Bavaria was built, modelled on the famous Loggia dei Lanzi in Florence. The Feldherrnhalle was completed in 1844. It consists of an open hall 20 m (65 ft) high with a triple arcade

---

HITLER AND THE FELDHERRNHALLE

On 8 November 1923, Adolf Hitler announced the start of the "people's revolution" in the Bürgerbräukeller and ordered the takeover of the central districts of Munich. The following day, people acting on his orders were stopped by a police cordon outside the Feldherrnhalle. Four policemen and 16 of Hitler's supporters were shot. When Hitler finally came to power in 1933, he turned what became known as the Beer Hall Putsch into a central element of the Nazi cult.

→

Statue of Maximilian I on Max-Joseph-Platz in front of the Nationaltheater

approached by a stairway in the central span. The statues of lions flanking the stairway were added in 1906. The niches in the arcade contain statues of Count Tilly, a renowned military leader in the Thirty Years' War, and of Count von Wrede, a marshal of the Bavarian Napoleonic era. There is also an allegorical memorial to the Bavarian army of Ferdinand von Miller the Younger, built in 1892.

Nationaltheater

◎R3 ⌂Max-Joseph-Platz 2 ◷10am–7pm Mon-Sat ⓦstaatsoper.de

Modelled on a Greek temple, the National Theatre is Munich's historic opera house. It has seen the premieres of many significant operas over the years: Wagner's *Tristan und Isolde* and *Die Walküre* premiered here, as did Strauss's *Friedenstag* and *Capriccio*. Original building work was thwarted by fires and financial trouble, and after it opened in 1918, it burned to

the ground in 1923. The second opera house was opened in 1925 but was destroyed in an air raid in 1943. The present building was finalized in 1963, with a Neo-Classical edifice featuring imposing Corinthian columns. Guided tours, bookable online, offer a behind-the-scenes glimpse of the theatre.

Palais Preysing

◎Q3 ⌂Residenzstr. 27

On an irregular plot of land between Theatinerstraße and Residenzstraße, which leads to Odeonsplatz, Count Emanuel Graf von Preysing built the first Rococo palace in Munich. It was designed by the court architect Joseph Effner and built in 1723–8. Novel designs were used for the three sides of the palace (the fourth adjoins Feldherrnhalle). For the first time exuberant mouldings covered the entire façade, partially obscuring the architectural divisions of the building.

The finest example of rich Baroque design at the palace is the grand staircase, in

the centre of the north wing. It is reached today via an internal passage that was once a hall and is now lined with elegant shops. The staircase has decorative balustrades and is supported by giant caryatids, and the walls are covered with lavish stuccowork. Few Baroque palaces built after Palais Preysing display such a wealth of interior decoration and lavish attention to detail.

6

Theatinerkirche (St Kajetan)

☐ Q2 ☐ Theatinerstr. 22 ☐ 19 ☐ 6:30am–8pm daily

To celebrate the birth of their long-awaited son in 1662, the Elector Ferdinand Maria and his wife Henriette Adelheid von Savoyen ordered the construction of a church and monastery for the Theatine order. It was designed by Agostino Barelli of Bologna.

Work began in 1663. The church was also designed for use as a court chapel. It was based on Sant' Andrea della Valle in Rome. Thus a building of pure Roman Baroque form rose in Munich. It is a barrel-vaulted cruciform basilica with an apse, a dome over the crossing and arcades opening onto side chapels. From 1675 work was supervised by Enrico Zucalli, who completed the dome, designed the interior and added twin towers which had not formed part of Barelli's original design. Almost 100 years later, the completion of the façade was entrusted to Cuvilliés and his son, who finished the work in 1765.

The distinctive form of the church brought considerable variety to Munich's cityscape. The huge domes of the towers are 70 m (230 ft) high. The volutes on the towers are inspired by those of Santa Maria della Salute in Venice.

The Cuvilliés' late Baroque façade is brought forward and broken up by pilasters and scrolled cornices. It also has niches with the figures of Ferdinand and Adelaide, Maximilian and Kajetan, the patron saint of the church. The portico contains a cartouche with coats of arms, including those of Bavaria and Saxony.

The crypt contains the tombs of the dukes and kings of Bavaria, among them the founders of the church and their son Maximilian Emanuel and his wife Therese Kunigunde Sobieska.

7

Palais Holnstein

☐ Q3 ☐ Kardinal-Faulhaber-Str. 7 ☐ 19 ☐ To the public

This palace, which consists of four wings enclosing a court-yard, was commissioned by the Elector Karl Albrecht and built by François Cuvilliés in 1733–7. It became the seat of the archbishops of Munich and Freising in 1821. It is the only surviving urban palace built by Cuvilliés.

The building is fronted by finely moulded pilasters. The tympanum contains the crest of Count von Holnstein, Karl Albrecht's illegitimate son, the division across the coat of arms indicating his illegitimate status. A bas-relief over the doorway depicts the Virgin surrounded by cherubs.

The interiors of the palace were completed in about 1735 by Johann Baptist Zimmermann to a design by Cuvilliés. They are among the finest examples of late Baroque decoration in Munich.

8

Dreifaltigkeitskirche

☐ P3 ☐ Pacellistr. 6 ☐ 19 ☐ 7am–7pm daily

In the war of the Spanish Succession (1700–14) the townswoman Anna Maria Lindmayr had a vision in which the city was consumed by the flames of war. To ward

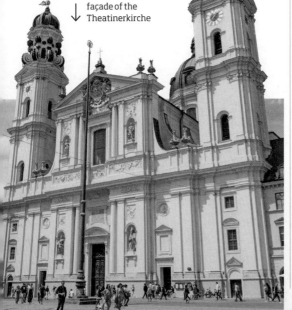

Magnificent Baroque-style façade of the Theatinerkirche

off such disaster, the burghers pledged to build a church.

Work began in 1711, and the result is an unusually interesting piece of architecture. The design, inspired by the Roman architecture of Francesco Morrominiego, is by Giovanni Antonio Viscardi, and construction was supervised by Enrico Zucalli and Johann Georg Ettenhofer. It was completed in 1718.

The broken façade is set with a multitude of columns, pilasters and cornices, and windows of different shapes are set in surprising places. A niche in the upper storey contains a statue of St Michael by Joseph Fichtl. The plan combines elongated and centralized schemes.

The interior is profusely decorated with stuccowork and with paintings by Cosmas Damian Asam. The high altar (1717) has a painting of the Holy Trinity, to whom the church is dedicated, by Andreas Wolff and Johann Degler. The Rococo tabernacle of 1760 is by Johann Baptist Straub.

9
Salvatorkirche

🚩Q3 🏠Salvatorplatz 17
🚌19 🚊100
🕙10am–8pm daily

In the late 15th century, the population of Munich increased greatly, and the existing cemeteries at

↑ Intricate rib vaulting inside the Greek Orthodox Salvatorkirche

Frauenkirche and Peterskirche were no longer sufficient. A new cemetery was created near the city walls, and cemetery chapels were built – the Allerheiligenkirche am Kreuz for the parish of St Peter and the Frauenkirche for that of St Mary.

Salvatorkirche was completed in a single year (1493–4). It was built by Lukas Rottaler, who brought the Gothic style to Munich. The combination of brick, stone and terracotta, the intricate fan vaulting and the delicate division of the walls give the church a distinctive elegance. It is complemented by a slender tower ending in a steeple. Vestiges of late Gothic frescoes can be seen over the north door.

In 1829 Ludwig I donated the church to the Orthodox community. The iconostasis (screen) at the end of the nave is in Romanesque style, and the combination of Gothic architecture with Greek Orthodox furniture creates a unique effect. A plaque on the outer wall

commemorates those who lie in the cemetery. They include the painter Hans Mielich, the composer Orlando di Lasso, and the architects François Cuvilliés and Johann Baptist Gunetzrhainer.

10
Odeonsplatz

🚩Q2 🚊100

In the early 19th century, when the Schwabinger Tor was demolished, a decision was made to impose order on the haphazard arrangement of buildings to the north of the Residenz and the Theatinerkirche. In 1817 Maximilian I Joseph approved Leo von Klenze's plan for the Odeonsplatz, unaware that its originator was in fact his son, Ludwig I. The heir to the throne wished to create a magnificent square marking the start of the main thoroughfare to the northern districts and also acting as a triumphal entry point into Munich.

The Odeonsplatz takes its name from the Odeon, a concert hall built by Leo von Klenze in 1826–8 as a counterpart to the Leuchtenbergpalais of 1816–21. Set back from the square, both buildings serve to elongate it.

The equestrian statue of Ludwig I flanked by personifications of Religion, Art, Poetry and Industry in the centre of the square was created by Max Widmann in 1862. It faces the side of the square containing the Market Hall of 1825–6 and the arch leading to the palace court. On the side of the Old Town, the square is bounded by the Feldherrnhalle (p86), intended as a monument to the heroes of Bavaria.

> **In the early 19th century, a decision was made to impose order on the haphazard arrangement of buildings to the north of the Residenz.**

EAT

OskarMaria Brasserie

This lovely brasserie in the Literaturhaus does great Bavarian dishes, as well as reasonably priced, delicious pasta. Popular jazz brunches are held on Sundays from 11am.

 Q3 Salvator-platz 1 oskar maria.com

€€€

The Spice Bazaar

This sophisticated restaurant offers innovative Middle Eastern mezze; there are many excellent vegetarian options.

R3 Marstallplatz 3 thespicebazaar.de

€€€

Brenner Restaurant

Fine, traditional Italian dishes served in a lavish interior modelled on restaurants in Rome, with a large open-plan kitchen.

R3 Maximilianstr. 15 brennergrill.de

€€€

Aimy

Inventive South East Asian food served in a casual setting. The dumplings and tamarind glazed meats are particularly worth sampling.

R3 Brienner Str 10 aimy-restaurant.de

€€€

---

 11 🍽

Künstlerhaus

P3 Lenbachplatz 8
19, 20 N40, N41
kuenstlerhaus-muc.de

The Künstlerhaus, on the southern side of Lenbachplatz, was designed by Gabriel von Seidl and built in 1892–1900. This attractive building, with wings set around an inner courtyard, is in mock northern German Renaissance style, which is characterized by stepped gables and bronze decoration.

The Munich painter Franz von Lenbach made a great contribution to its completion. Having collected sufficient funds, he set to work on the interior. The rooms are decorated in Italian Renaissance and Art Nouveau styles.

Despite wartime destruction, the vestibule and the Venetian Room – which today houses a restaurant – have been preserved. The Künstlerhaus

---

→

Enjoying a book at the Literaturhaus, with a view of Theatinerkirche

is now the headquarters of an art foundation with the same name. It hosts regular literary festivals, as well as dance, cabaret and theatre performances. Small exhibitions, workshops and concerts are also held here.

12

Palais Neuhaus-Preysing

Q3 Prannerstr. 2
19 To the public

This palace – not to be confused with the nearby Palais Preysing (*p87*) – was built in 1737, probably by German architect Karl Albrecht von Lespilliez.

A small attic was added to the palace during the Neo-Classical period. The interior was completely

destroyed during World War II, although the original façade somehow survived. The palace was restored and renovated in 1956–8.

A little farther along the same street are two fine late Baroque palaces, also probably designed by Lespilliez in a similar style: the Palais Seinsheim at No. 7, built in 1764, and the Palais Gise at No. 9, built in 1765.

Patrons enjoying alfresco dining at L'Osteria, Künstlerhaus

13

Literaturhaus

Q3 **Salvatorplatz 1**
For exhibitions: hours vary, check website
literaturhaus-muenchen.de

Munich's great literary traditions and its influential position in the European publishing market were marked by the opening of the Literaturhaus in 1997.

This monumental building, which blends with the closely aligned façades of town-houses and the outline of the Salvatorkirche, dominates Salvatorplatz. Until the beginning of the 20th century this was the site of the city market. In 1887 a large school building designed by Friedrich Löbel was built here, its open ground floor fulfilling the function of a market hall up until 1906.

In 1993 the building, which had been partially destroyed during World War II, was extensively renovation and would open a few years later as the Literaturhaus.

The present building skilfully combines the period style of the lower storeys with a light steel and glass structure for the two upper storeys. These provide a breathtaking view on to the dome of the Theatinerkirche *(p88)* and the city's rooftops.

The Literaturhaus is the home of literary institutions and foundations that organize literary conferences and seminars as well as readings. Part of the ground floor hall is occupied by a display area where temporary exhibitions are held. There is a library on the first floor.

One of the institution's great attractions is the literary café. Its decor includes an installation by the American artist Jenny Holzer devoted to the Bavarian poet and novelist Oskar Maria Graf.

LITERARY MUNICH

In the latter part of the 19th century, Munich's Maxvorstadt and Schwabing districts became hubs for the arts and literature. It is said that the Norwegian playwright Henrik Ibsen would have breakfast daily at the Café Maximilian and study his journals during the meal. Nobel Prize winner Thomas Mann, originally a north German, wrote all his major works while living in Munich; poet Rainer Maria Rilke and feminist Fanny zu Reventlow also lived in the area. They each frequented cafés also visited by the likes of playwright Bertolt Brecht and even Lenin, the Russian revolutionary.

⑭ Alter Hof

Q3 **Burgstr. 8**
19

The first fortified residence built for the Wittelsbachs within the walls of Munich was constructed in 1253–5. The purpose was to protect them not only from outside invaders, but also from rebellious citizens. In 1328–47 the Alter Hof was the residence of Emperor Ludwig IV of Bavaria. In the second half of the 14th century construction began on a larger residence, and gradually the seat of power was moved there.

The west wing ends with a gatehouse decorated with the crests of the Wittelsbachs, and it retains its original Gothic character. Another original feature is the distinctive bay window known as the Monkey Tower. According to legend, when Ludwig IV was a baby he was carried off by a monkey from the royal menagerie. The monkey climbed to the top of the tower, and it took a long time for it to be coaxed into returning the child.

⑮ Promenadeplatz

Q3 **19**

This elongated rectangular square, whose origins date back to the Middle Ages, was once the site of the salt market, and storehouses for salt and the customs house stood here. At the end of the 18th century, the buildings were demolished and the square was planted with linden trees. Fine palaces and townhouses also rose up all round the square.

On the northern side is the Bayerischer Hof, a high-class hotel, where many famous people have stayed. In addition to the main building, in the Maximilian style, the adjoining Palais Montgelas also forms part of the hotel. It was designed for the king's ministers and important advisers by prominent architect Emanuel Joseph von Herigoyen.

The decoration is by Jean-Baptiste Métivier. The grand interior has been preserved, including the Royal Hall, Montgelas Hall and Library, all in Empire style. It was beside the building on Kardinal-Faulhaber-Straße that Kurt Eisner, first president of the Bavarian Republic, was shot in 1919.

Situated on the other side of the square, at No. 15, is the house belonging to the architect Johann Baptist Gunetzrhainer.

⑯ Palais Toerring-Jettenbach

Q3 **Residenzstr. 2**
19

The Baroque palace that originally stood on this site

Famous Monkey Tower in the medieval Alter Hof

Fünf Höfe
The Fünf Höfe shopping complex is home to a gallery, several stores, cafés and restaurants.

Q3 **Theatinerstr. 15** **funfhoefe.de**

Hugendubel
The city's most popular bookstore offers a range of bestsellers as well as some English-language titles.

Q3 **Theatinerstr. 15** **hugendubel.de**

LODENFREY
This luxury department store has been open since 1850, with designer goods spread over six floors.

Q3 **Maffeistraße 7** **lodenfrey.com**

was at odds with ideas of town planning that had inspired the creation of Max-Joseph-Platz, particularly after the Neo-Classical wing of Königsbau and the Opera House were built.

In 1835–8 Ludwig I commissioned Leo von Klenze to rebuild the original palace, extending it and creating a façade based on that of the Ospedale degli Innocenti in Florence. The Baroque doorway was moved inside, as were two of the nine sculptures by Johann Baptist Straub (the remaining statues are today housed in the Bayeriches Nationalmuseum). The new arcade-style loggia was painted in ochre, contrasting with the red walls behind. This aristocratic palace, once home to a post office, is now an exclusive residence and also houses high-end stores.

⓱ ⬚
Hofbräuhaus

📍R4 🏠Platzl 9
☎29 01 36 100 🚊19
🕐11am-midnight daily

Munich's greatest tourist attraction, and the epitome of the Bavarian lifestyle, is the Hofbräuhaus. An inn, it formed part of the Royal Brewery that was founded by Wilhelm V in 1589. The opening ceremony of the inn in 1830 was attended by Ludwig I. Extended on numerous occasions, the building was given its present Neo-Renaissance exterior in 1896.

The ground floor contains the Schwemme, a large hall that can hold 1,000 people seated at long tables. On the first floor is the vaulted

Enjoying a meal at the ↑ immensely popular Hofbräuhaus, and (inset) its Neo-Renaissance façade

Festsaal, a ceremonial hall seating 1,300, and many smaller side-rooms. Every day 10,000 litres (17,600 pints) of beer are consumed here.

⓲
Alte Münze

📍R3 🏠Hofgraben 4 🚊19
🕐Courtyard: 8:30am-4pm Mon-Thu, 8:30am-2pm Fri

The Alte Münze (Old Mint Yard) is a Renaissance building which originally served as the ducal stables before housing the art collections of Albrecht V, Duke of Bavaria. Designed by the architect Bernhard Zwitzel of Augsburg, the building was constructed by court architect Wilhelm Egkl in 1563. Despite the involvement of these prominent Bavarian architects, the building revealed Albrecht's style.

The courtyard was surrounded by a three-storey loggia housing the stables and coach houses. The loggia also contained Albrecht V's book collection and some of the earliest collections of fine art in Europe.

When the building was rebuilt in the 19th century as the state mint, it was given a Neo-Classical east façade. The north façade, meanwhile, is in the Maximilian style.

MUNICH'S "BIG SIX" BREWERIES

Munich has six major breweries (these are the only ones legally permitted to serve beer at Oktoberfest): Hofbräu, Augustiner, Paulaner, Spaten, Löwenbräu and Hacker-Pschorr. These six are also the only breweries that produce what is collectively known as "Münchner Bier" (Munich beer), and there are strict requirements for every batch of beer produced. The Augustiner is the oldest of the bunch, founded in 1328, and Spaten is the largest. The beers are available in bars around the city and throughout wider Bavaria.

19 Maximilianstraße

R3 19

When he came to power, Maxmilian I Joseph continued the fierce passion for building that had gripped his father Ludwig I. His wish to make his own architectural mark on Munich manifested itself in Maximilianstraße. Built in 1852–5, this was a reaction to the outmoded Neo-Classicism of Ludwigstraße.

Maximilianstraße was built to connect the Residenz and the Old Town with the green areas along the banks of the River Isar. It is divided into two separate parts, the showpiece square closed off by the Maximilianeum, and the commercial part located within the Old Town.

Friedrich Bürklein, who designed the thoroughfare, created a novel architectural and decorative scheme that combined English Gothic with Italianesque arcades and depended on new skeleton construction methods. The arcades of the imposing Neo-Gothic buildings are home to Munich's luxury shops.

The famous Kempinski Vier Jahreszeiten hotel and the Museum Fünf Kontinente are the only buildings not designed by Bürklein.

The opera house, the theatre, the numerous art galleries, where private views are a social event, and the clientele of the bustling cafés combine to create a thriving urban atmosphere in the area.

Did You Know?

Ludwig I disliked his son Maximilian's architectural choices so he often avoided Maximilianstraße.

20 Hofgarten

R2 **North side of the Residenz**

The Hofgarten is one of the largest Mannerist gardens north of the Alps. It was laid out in front of the north wing of the Residenz in 1613–17. The geometrically designed gardens are divided by two straight main paths that intersect at right angles. At the intersection is the polygonal Hofgartentempel, or Temple of Diana, built by Heinrich Schön in 1615. The figure of Diana crowning the cupola was completed by Hubert Gerhard in 1594 (the present one is a copy). In 1623 Hans Krumpper remodelled the figure, transforming it into a symbol of Bavaria and adding putti bearing the ducal insignia.

The garden is bounded to the west and north by a gallery built in the reigns of Albrecht V and Maximilian I. The engaging art gallery, built in the garden in 1781, was the precursor of the present Alte Pinakothek (*p132*) and Neue Pinakothek. Next to it is the famed German Theatre Museum, the oldest of its kind in Europe. Its exhibitions – showcasing stage sets, props, costumes and photographs – illustrate the history of drama in all parts of the world.

The triumphal arch at the entrance gate is Leo von Klenze's first work in Munich. The carvings are by Ludwig Schwanthaler and the frescoes, by Peter von Cornelius, depict the history of the Wittelsbachs and Bavaria. The northern arcades feature landscapes by Richard Seewald of 1962. South of the gardens rises the imposing Festsaalbau, with von Klenze's huge doorway of 1835–42.

 The Bayerische Staatskanzlei, as seen through an archway

21
Bayerische Staatskanzlei

R2 **100**

After a dispute between the city council and the government that went on for almost 30 years, the Bavarian State Chancellery was finally completed in 1992. A design proposed in the 1980s – by which the ruins of the former army museum at the end of the Hofgarten would be linked to a modern architectural complex – seemed too invasive

 The impressive Maximilianstraße, lined with trees

to most of Munich's residents. It interfered with green areas, and the wings of the new building would result in the demolition of the 16th-century garden wall. After large-scale protests and litigation, the government altered the original plans.

22
Münchner Kammerspiele im Schauspielhaus

R3 **Maximilianstr. 28** **muenchnerkammerspiele.de** **Box office: 10am–6pm Mon–Fri, 10am–1pm Sat**

One of the few surviving Art Nouveau theatres in Germany, the stunning Schauspielhaus (meaning "playhouse") was built in 1900–01. It adjoins the backs of two buildings in Maximilian style.

The interior is also in Art Nouveau style. The walls of the auditorium are bright red with ornamental outlines. The green ceiling has six stucco beams and imaginative floral strands lit by spotlights in the shape of flower buds. The typical Art Nouveau device of softening lines with floral motifs can be seen everywhere – around the stage and the balconies and on door handles. The decorative stage curtain was made in 1971. Equally imaginative and colourful are the foyers on the two floors and the ticket office.

The theatre was long renowned for the controversial works that were performed there, such as Frank Wedekind's *The Awakening of Spring*. The theatre's avant-garde traditions were instrumental to the development of Naturalism in Munich.

 DRINK

Pusser's Bar
A classy cocktail bar, Pusser's has been an institution in Munich since 1974. It has long welcomed famous patrons, including Andy Warhol.

R3 **Falkenturmstr. 9** **pussersbar.de**

Kulisse
Located in the Kammerspiele theatre, this charming café has outdoor tables and is a great spot for a drink. On Saturdays, DJ sets contribute to a laid-back atmosphere.

R3 **Maximilianstr. 26** **muenchner-kammerspiele.de**

23
Marstall

R3 **Marstallplatz 4** **21 85 19 40** **19**

Leo von Klenze's first major work on the Residenz was the royal stables, on which he worked from 1817 to 1822. The large hall-like building is based on Renaissance and Baroque palace architecture.

The row of semicircular windows is topped by medallions depicting horses' heads. Busts of Castor and Pollux, the sons of Zeus who were excellent horsemen, crown the columns at the entrance. The reliefs on the gates depicting the epic battle between the Lapiths and the Centaurs were made by Johann Martin von Wagnerin in 1821.

Today the Marstall houses the Marstalltheater, which is known for its experimental performances combining theatre with dance and music.

A SHORT WALK
AROUND THE RESIDENZ

Distance 1 km (0.5 miles) **Time** 15 minutes
Nearest U-Bahn station Odeonsplatz

The Residenz is set in the most elegant part of Munich, an area characterized mainly by the Wittelsbach residences, numerous Baroque palaces and the fine silhouettes of the Theatinerkirche and the opera house. The streets leading to the nearby Altstadtring (ring road) are lined with cafés and shops selling luxury goods. This area is also the centre of Munich's cultural life, with several theatres as well as concert and banqueting halls within the residences themselves.

*Until the end of the 18th century **Salvatorkirche** stood in the middle of the city cemetery. It is now a Uniate church.*

START

KARD.-FAULHABE...

SALVATORSTR.

*The façade of the **Erzbischöfliches Palais** (Archbishop's Palace) was decorated by the great stuccoist Johann Baptist Zimmermann.*

*The arcades of **Eilleshof**, an enchanting late Gothic courtyard, hidden behind the Residenzstraße, are an oasis of peace.*

PERUSASTR.

← The Theatinerstraße shopping district in winter

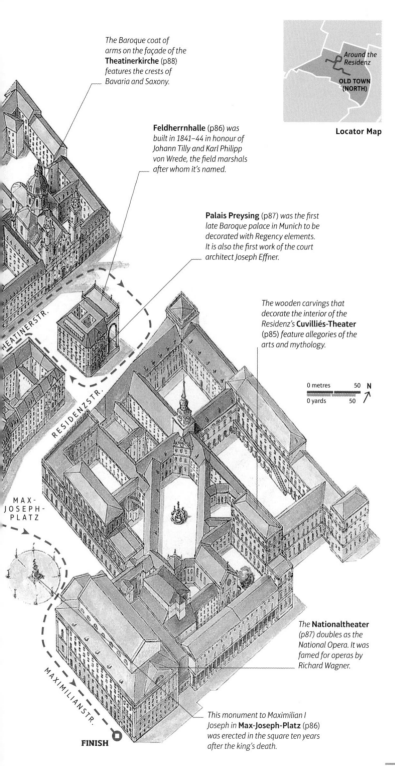

The Baroque coat of arms on the façade of the **Theatinerkirche** (p88) features the crests of Bavaria and Saxony.

Feldherrnhalle (p86) was built in 1841–44 in honour of Johann Tilly and Karl Philipp von Wrede, the field marshals after whom it's named.

Palais Preysing (p87) was the first late Baroque palace in Munich to be decorated with Regency elements. It is also the first work of the court architect Joseph Effner.

The wooden carvings that decorate the interior of the Residenz's **Cuvilliés-Theater** (p85) feature allegories of the arts and mythology.

Around the Residenz

OLD TOWN (NORTH)

Locator Map

THEATINERSTR.

RESIDENZSTR.

MAX-JOSEPH-PLATZ

MAXIMILIANSTR.

0 metres 50 N
0 yards 50

The **Nationaltheater** (p87) doubles as the National Opera. It was famed for operas by Richard Wagner.

This monument to Maximilian I Joseph in **Max-Joseph-Platz** (p86) was erected in the square ten years after the king's death.

FINISH

AROUND THE ISAR

The Isar river has played a vital role throughout Munich's history, shaping both its landscape and its culture. Over millennia, the Isar's rapid flow carved out the city's riverside topography, with gravel forming small islands between its banks (today's Museuminsel and Praterinsel). Shortly after the market was established in what is now Marienplatz in the 12th century, a new bridge was built over the river, allowing the city's growing population to settle on both banks. The city's first districts were constructed on the higher banks of the river where flooding was less likely, and residents used water wheels to provide energy. Since these first districts were established, the banks of the river have become increasingly populous, while an assortment of canals, weirs and embankments have channelled the river's flow.

Today, the main attractions that draw visitors to this part of Munich are centred around the area of the Luitpoldbrücke, Maximiliansbrücke and Ludwigsbrücke. On the steep right bank of the Isar are the Maximiliansanlagen, green areas densely planted with trees, which have become favourite places for walking and cycling. The Maximilianstraße leads to the Maximilianeum, the great parliament building, and the road is flanked by one of Munich's prettiest districts, Lehel, home to the city's fashion quarter.

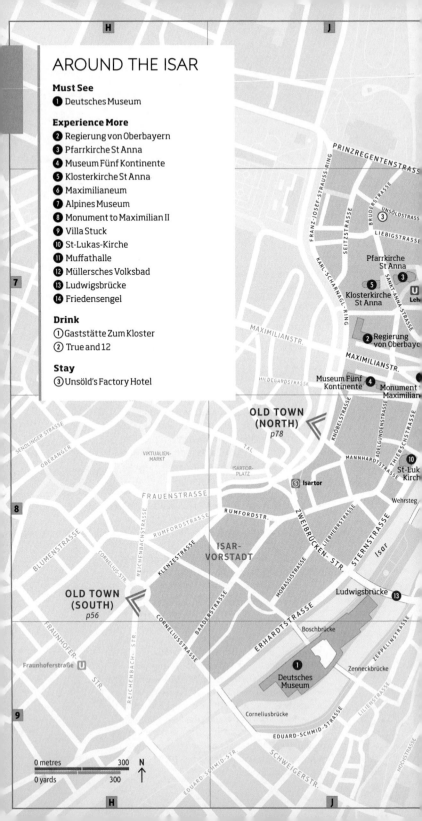

AROUND THE ISAR

Must See
1. Deutsches Museum

Experience More
2. Regierung von Oberbayern
3. Pfarrkirche St Anna
4. Museum Fünf Kontinente
5. Klosterkirche St Anna
6. Maximilianeum
7. Alpines Museum
8. Monument to Maximilian II
9. Villa Stuck
10. St-Lukas-Kirche
11. Muffathalle
12. Müllersches Volksbad
13. Ludwigsbrücke
14. Friedensengel

Drink
1. Gaststätte Zum Kloster
2. True and 12

Stay
3. Unsöld's Factory Hotel

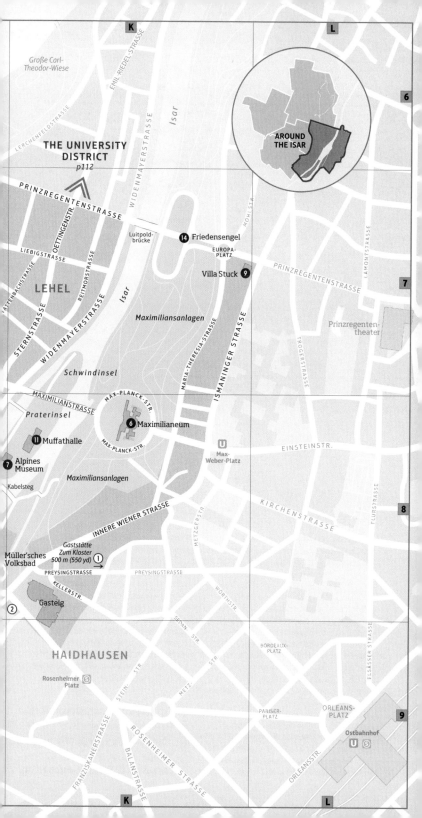

① ⚒ ♫ 🍴 🖥 🛍

DEUTSCHES MUSEUM

📍 J9 🏛 Museumsinsel Ⓢ Isartor Ⓤ Fraunhoferstr. 🚊 17, 18 🚌 132
🕐 9am–5pm daily 🌐 deutsches-museum.de

The Deutsches Museum is one of the world's oldest and largest museums of technology and engineering, with an array of permanent exhibits covering everything from innovative hydraulic devices to musical instruments.

The Deutsches Museum, which turns 100 in 2025, has been undergoing renovations that will make it one of the world's most modern science and technology museums. Some sections were reopened in 2022, while others are likely to reopen by 2028. The museum is designed to take visitors on a journey of scientific discovery, with permanent exhibitions touching on topics such as aviation, chemistry, robotics and health, and a host of special exhibitions shedding light on cutting-edge developments including quantum mechanics. There are also live experiments and interactive exhibits which bring science to life.

To view every exhibit would take a whole month, since the entire route through the permanent and temporary exhibition spaces is around 17 km (10.5 miles) long. With more than 20 sections currently open, it's best to concentrate on just a few areas. The museum has other branches in Munich – the Verkehrs-zentrum dedicated to transport and the Flugwerft Schleißheim, which is dedicated to the history of aviation.

> **To view every exhibit would take a whole month, since the entire route through the permanent and temporary exhibition spaces is around 17 km (10.5 miles) long.**

↑ The 65-m- (213-ft-) high tower of the museum and *(above)* engines on display

Design and Technology

The museum contains displays of such classic aspects of engineering as machine building, mining, metallurgy, and hydraulic and civil engineering. The display of machines and turbines features many prototypes and the first diesel engine.

Physics, Chemistry and Pharmaceuticals

▷ In the physics and chemistry section, there are fascinating reconstructions of the laboratories of great scientists and also a collection of the original instruments used in some of the greatest scientific discoveries, as well as many pieces of prototype apparatus.

Musical Instruments

Here, exhibits are displayed in chronological order, with over 1,800 instruments on display. The centrepiece of the keyboard instruments section is the earliest harpsichord, which was made in 1561. You can also hear a live demonstration of the workings of a large organ that was built for the museum, before being taught about the acoustics and mechanics of the instrument.

A Tour of the Body

This interactive journey through the human body starts with a huge walk-in head, with themed exhibits inside featuring the eyes, ears and teeth. The tour of our biology continues past a large heart on stilts, where visitors can learn about the cardiovascular system, before continuing down the body to the legs and other joints.

Kids' Kingdom

▷ Kids' Kingdom is a play area where children between the ages of three and eight can learn about science and technology. There are many exciting exhibits, including a giant guitar, a fire engine and an electric light cinema.

MUSEUM RENOVATIONS

Note that until the renovation work in the second part of the building is completed, visitors enter the museum via an entrance on Corneliusbrücke. Modernization work has seen numerous new exhibits opening, including chemistry laboratories with scientists offering live demonstrations. There is also a huge sculpture made entirely from scrap electronics.

↑ Neo-Gothic building of the Regierung von Oberbayern

EXPERIENCE MORE

2
Regierung von Oberbayern

 J7 Maximilianstr. 39
 18, 19

This monumental building, the seat of the government of Upper Bavaria, is one of the finest examples of the Maximilian style.

The eponymous king, Maximilian II, endeavoured to create a new architectural style, distancing himself from the severe Classicism of his father, Ludwig I. The result was an eclectic mixture of elements drawn from such diverse styles as English Gothic and Moorish architecture.

Solid and imposing, the Regierung von Oberbayern was built in 1856–64 to a design by Friedrich Bürklein. The façade, 170 m (558 ft) long, was conceived as part of the grand new city plan. It is vertically divided into 17 bays of arched windows, which are arranged above an imposing arcade. Its strong horizontal lines and fine ornamentation are highly reminiscent of those of English Gothic cathedrals.

Indeed, the building's pseudo-ecclesiastical appearance was specifically designed to underline its civic importance and dignity. This symbolism is further reinforced by the large statue of Justice,

created by German sculptor Johann Halbig, that crowns the roof of the building.

3
Pfarrkirche St Anna

 J7 St-Anna-Platz 5 18, 19
 8am–6pm daily

A competition for the design of a parish church for the Lehel district was held in 1885. The winner was Gabriel von Seidl. Work began in 1887, continuing until 1892. The design of the church is based on that of the Romanesque imperial cathedrals of the Rhineland, in the great German nationalist style that was prevalent after 1871.

The monumental triple-nave basilica has a square plan, the transept and apse ending in a chapel and the west front having a large tower and an impressive Neo-Romanesque doorway. The interior is decorated with late 18th- to early 19th-century wall paintings. An interesting feature is the hybrid iconography in the

---

BAVARIAN RULE

Lower Bavaria is typically considered the most conservative region in Germany. The Christian Social Union (CSU) is a political party that only operates in Bavaria, and is typically further to the right than its national counterpart, the Christian Democratic Union. There are also district governments: the Regierung von Oberbayern (Government of Upper Bavaria) is one of seven in Bavaria. It coordinates the Bavarian state ministries and supports private and public projects in the state, with half a billion euros in funds annually.

figure of Christ on the west front, dating from 1910, in which he is depicted on horseback holding a bow and an olive branch.

Museum Fünf Kontinente

📍 J7 🏛 Maximilianstr. 42
🚋 18, 19 🕐 9:30am–5:30pm Tue–Sun 🌐 museum-fuenf-kontinente.de

The Five Continents Museum features non-European artworks and artifacts. It was built in 1859–65 to a design by architect Eduard Riedel in the Maximilian style. Its iconic façade is set with eight figures personifying the virtues of the Bavarian people: Piety, Patriotism, Diligence, Loyalty, Magnanimity, Justice, Courage and Wisdom.

The building was originally intended to house the collections of the Bavarian National Museum. From 1900 to 1923 it served as the first main building of the Deutsches Museum. From 1926 to 2014, it was the home of the State Ethnographic Museum (Staatliches Museum für Völkerkunde), then the second largest such museum in Germany after that in Berlin. The museum changed its name as part of a broader rebranding in 2014.

The collection dates from as early as 1782, when curiosities from the collections of Bavarian rulers were displayed in the galleries of the Residenz. The museum's extensive collection now consists of more than 150,000 pieces relating to the life and culture of non-European peoples. The Far East (China and Japan), South America (Peru) and East and Central Africa are well represented. Because of the size of the collection, many exhibits are displayed on a rotating basis.

---

❺ Klosterkirche St Anna

📍 J7 🏛 St-Anna-Platz 21
🚋 18, 19 🕐 6am–7pm daily

In 1725 Lehel, then still a suburb, was settled by an order of Hieronymite monks. A monastery church was built here in 1727–33. Designed by Johann Michael Fischer, it was a real architectural jewel for the city: Munich's first Rococo religious building. It is also said to have shaped the development of religious architecture in Bavaria.

The oval interior is lined with scalloped niches that are separated by arches supported on pilasters. The interior decoration was executed by the Asam brothers *(p63)*. The ceiling paintings, which glorify St Anne, were executed by Cosmas Damian Asam and completed in 1730. In 1737 the Asam brothers completed the high altar and most of the side altars, their stuccowork and paintings harmonizing with the fluid forms of the interior. The pulpit and tabernacle, by German sculptor Johann Baptist Straub, date from around 1756.

An air raid during World War II completely destroyed the monastery church,

The "Blue Rider Post", on display at the Museum Fünf Kontinente

↑ Lavish interior of the Rococo Klosterkirche St Anna

down to the outer walls. Extensive post-war reconstruction on the church began in 1946, with the interior restored using a record of colour photographs. Today, the church remains a stunning example of Munich's early Rococo style.

 6

Maximilianeum

K8 | **Max-Planck-Str. 1**
15, 16, 19, 25 | **190, 191**

The largest building on Maximilianstraße is, not surprisingly, the monumental Maximilianeum. It was built as a commission from Maximilian II by Friedrich Bürklein in 1857–74 and stands on an elevation on the right bank of the Isar.

The building is the headquarters of a royal fund that gave school students the opportunity to study at university without paying fees. Since 1949 it has also been the seat of the Bavarian parliament (and until 1999 the Bavarian senate).

It took almost 17 years to complete the Maximilianeum, progress being hampered by the sloping terrain of the river bank. The focal point of the slightly concave façade is the tall, triple-arched projecting entrance, topped by the figure of an angel. Wings, arcaded in their lower storey, extend on either side. The terracotta façade is decorated with busts and statues, while coloured mosaics on a gold background fill the semicircular blind windows over the upper storey. The interior is decorated with historical and allegorical paintings by Wilhelm and Friedrich von Kaulbach.

 7

Alpines Museum

K8 | **Praterinsel 5**
18 | **10am–6pm Tue–Sun** | **alpenverein.de/museum**

This unique museum stands in scenic parkland in the southern part of Praterinsel, one of the islands in the Isar in central Munich. The building that it occupies, dating from the late 19th century, was presented to the German-Austrian Mountaineering Association in 1938.

The museum's exhibits illustrate both the scientific and the aesthetic aspects of the Alps. There's an informative geological section on the exploration and study of Alpine rocks and minerals,

THE PRATERINSEL

The Praterinsel *(praterinsel.de)*, a small island on the Isar river on which the Alpines Museum is located, has become a popular event location in the city. The Stroke modern art fair *(stroke-artfair.com)* is hosted here, usually in May, with some of the best local artists and crafters exhibiting their work. The exciting Anotherday electronic music festival also takes place on the island in June, and Christmas markets take over at the end of the year.

Maximilianeum towering over Maximilianstraße, and *(inset)* the building's conference room

a statue of Maximilian II, patron of the arts and industry, and inspirer of the new architectural style to which he gave his name. Maximilian II conceived the urban planning of this part of the city. The monument was erected by the citizens of Munich in homage to their ruler and in honour of the monarchy.

The impressive bronze statue, designed by Kaspar Zumbusch and cast in 1875, stands on a red marble plinth surrounded by personifications of the four royal virtues. Four putti hold the coat of arms of the four tribes of Bavaria: the Franconians, Bavarians, Swabians and Palatines.

9

Villa Stuck

📍K7 🏠Prinzregent-enstr. 60 🚋16, N16 🚌100 🕐Noon-8pm Tue-Sun 🌐villa stuck.de

Franz von Stuck (1863–1928), the talented son of a miller from Lower Bavaria, made a giddy career for himself in Munich. He not only achieved great success as a painter, sculptor and graphic artist, but also became a professor at the Academy of Fine Arts, was given an aristocratic title and earned himself the nick-name "prince of art".

In 1897–8 Stuck built himself a magnificent home, to which a large studio was added in 1913–14. This villa on Prinzregentenstraße is now one of the most important artist's residences in Europe. Both the architectural con-ception and the interior

featuring a vast number of paintings and drawings of Alpine scenery. Temporary exhibitions and workshops led by researchers are also organized regularly.

The museum also houses the world's largest library of books on Alpine subjects, and has a mountaineering archive. An information centre serves the needs of mountaineers intending to set out on expeditions into the Alps.

8

Monument to Maximilian II

📍J7 🏠Rondo Maximilianstr. 🚋18, 19

As you saunter along Maximilianstraße you pass a circus that has at its centre

decoration of the house were his own work. In it, he combined Neo-Classical, Art Nouveau and Symbolist elements, thus underlining his tenet that art and life were connected.

The house contains finely decorated reception rooms which, after the artist's death, were used for meetings by Munich's high society. The walls of the drawing rooms and studios are covered with mosaics and paintings in a Pompeiian style. As well as ostentatious furniture, there are examples of Stuck's own sculpture. The museum also has an Art Nouveau display and hosts visiting exhibitions.

10

St-Lukas-Kirche

📍 J8 🚊 Mariannenplatz
🚋 18 Ⓤ Isartor Ⓢ Lehel
🕐 9am–5pm daily
🌐 sanktlukas.de

St-Lukas-Kirche is located on the banks of the Isar, between Steinsdorfstraße and Mariannenplatz and near the Isartor (p69). Its 64-m- (210-ft-) high dome dominates the cityscape near the central stretch of the Isar. The church was built between 1893 and 1896 in historicist style, to a design by Albert Schmidt, with a layout based on the shape of a Greek cross.

There is a Steinmeyer organ and in the northeast tower there are four bells. Music has long been an important part of St-Lukas-Kirche. In addition to traditional Protestant church music, there are concerts, as well as gospel, dance and contemporary music performances, and the church has been awarded a cultural prize by the Evangelical Churches of Germany.

From late 2024, renovation will be undertaken inside the church building, though it is expected that the church will remain open throughout.

11

Muffathalle

📍 K8 🚊 Zellstr. 4
Ⓢ Isartor 🕐 Hours vary, check website
🌐 muffathalle.de

This laid-back, alternative concert venue is housed in a former hydropower station, originally built by Franz Karl Muffat in 1837. The power station's turbine hall is now home to the Muffatcafe, an intimate bar area that opens an hour before gig entrance times. The Muffathalle hosts popular international bands on tour, regular poetry slams and free concerts featuring local musicians.

12

Müllersches Volksbad

📍 J8 🚊 Rosenheimer Str. 1 Ⓢ Isartor 🚋 16, 18
🚌 132 🕐 7:30am–11pm daily (to 5pm Mon); sauna: 9am–11pm daily 🌐 swm. de/baeder/mueller sches-volksbad

This vast bathing complex has been offering the people of

> ### Did You Know?
>
> The Volksbad were the first public baths to open in Munich.

Munich prime relaxation for over a century. Built from 1897 to 1901 by renowned German engineer Karl Müller to an architectural design by Carl Hocheder, these baths were considered to be the finest in Germany at that time, and they still retain their sophisticated allure today.

In addition to the many relaxation rooms, showers and baths, there is also a barrel-vaulted men's swimming pool, a domed ladies' swimming pool, a Roman bath and an excellent Art Nouveau café that should not be missed.

The whole building reflects the new concepts of hygiene that were coming into vogue in the late 19th century, together with an interest in Roman bathing

traditions. From an architectural point of view, the building is notable for the Neo-Baroque, Art Nouveau and Moorish elements that it incorporates.

---

⑬ Ludwigsbrücke

❷ J8 **🏠** Zweibrückenstr./
Rosenheimer Str. **Ⓢ** Isartor
Ⓤ Rosenheimer Platz,
Isartor 🚋 16, 18

The history of Munich began at Ludwigsbrücke in 1158, when Henry the Lion destroyed the toll bridge over the Isar belonging to the Bishop of Freising. Duke Heinrich wished the Salzstraße, the salt route that had existed since Roman times, to cross the Isar near the place where Benedictine monks had established a settlement. He therefore built a new toll bridge, and the settlement became a centre of trade, having trading rights and issuing its own coinage.

The present bridge dates from 1935. It is decorated with figures personifying Industry and River Navigation (these were made in 1892

for the previous bridge) and Art (made in 1979).

Beside the bridge, on Museumsinsel, is the Fountain of Father Rhine, built in 1897–1902 by the sculptor Adolf von Hildebrand. The bronze statue of Father Rhine originally formed part of the fountain that stood outside the theatre in Strasbourg. When it was brought to Munich, it was placed in the centre of a fountain and was surrounded by putti standing on plinths.

---

⑭ Friedensengel

❷ K7 **🏠** Prinzregentenstr. 🚋 16 🚌 100

High on the right bank of the Isar stands the Angel of Peace, a monument raised to mark 25 years of peace after the Franco-Prussian War of 1870–71, in which Germany was victorious.

Commissioned by the city council, this monument has become something of an icon in Munich, featured on countless postcards and

↑ The Friedensengel, or Angel of Peace, depicting Nike

guidebooks. It was designed by the architect Jacob Möhl in 1891 and built in 1896–9 by Heinrich Düll, Georg Pezold and Max Heilmeier. It stands on the Maximilian Terraces, which are supported by a wall pierced by three niches. The central niche is in the form of a grotto that acts as a backdrop to the fountain. The monument is also flanked by a stairway with a decorative balustrade. The plinth, on a tall podium, is in the form of an open hall with Classical caryatids and columns. It contains portraits of the rulers, chancellors and generals of the Franco-Prussian War.

The monument was modelled on the Erechtheum on the Acropolis in Athens. Inside the hall, gold mosaics depicting the allegories of Peace, War, Victory and Culture cover a pedestal from which rises a Corinthian column 38 m (125 ft) high. The golden figure of the angel, 6 m (19 ft) high and crowning the column, imitates the Greek statue of Nike Paioniosa on Mount Olympus. In the evenings in summer, the monument is a popular place to gather to watch the sunset over the city, with the ornate fountain in the foreground.

↑ Distinctive domes of the St-Lukas-Kirche, as seen from the banks of the Isar river

A SHORT WALK
ALONG
MAXIMILIANSTRASSE

Distance 2 km (1.25 miles) **Time** 30 minutes
Nearest U-Bahn Lehel

Maximilian II, with the aid of his court architect Friedrich Bürklein, translated his lofty vision of urban planning into reality in the Maximilianstraße. Designed in what became known as the Maximilian style, it opens out from the Old Town into a kind of forum flanked by monumental buildings. It is completed by a circus with a statue of the king contemplating his creation. This short walk is one of the city's most iconic, offering a great insight into Maximilian's ambitious style.

START

BÜRKLEINSTR.

ST-ANNA-STR.

ST-ANNA-STR.

MAXIMILIANSTR.

The niche in the finial of **Klosterkirche St Anna** (p104) *holds a statue of its patron saint.*

These Neo-Gothic buildings house the **Regierung von Oberbayern** (p105), *the government of Upper Bavaria.*

The rich collection of the **Museum Fünf Kontinente** (p105) *illustrates the culture and everyday life of people from around the world.*

The **Monument to Maximilian II** *was designed in 1875. The king, whose great ambition was to be a professor rather than a monarch, is surrounded by figures symbolizing Peace, Liberty, Justice and Strength.*

The **Isar**, *although flanked by embankments, retains its woodland charm.*

← Entrance to the Museum Fünf Kontinente (Museum of Five Continents)

↑ The Alpines Museum on Prater Island, seen from the across the Isar

Did You Know?

With its abundance of designer outlets, Maximilianstraße is known as Munich's "luxury mile".

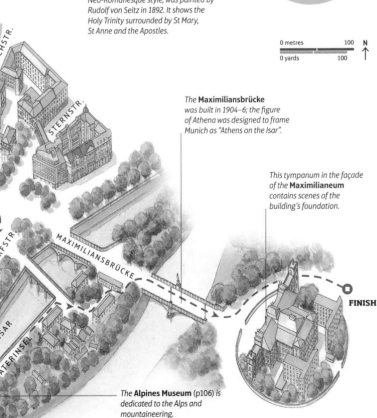

The monumental apse of **Pfarrkirche St Anna** (p104), *built in Neo-Romanesque style, was painted by Rudolf von Seitz in 1892. It shows the Holy Trinity surrounded by St Mary, St Anne and the Apostles.*

0 metres	100	N
0 yards	100	↑

The **Maximiliansbrücke** *was built in 1904–6; the figure of Athena was designed to frame Munich as "Athens on the Isar".*

This tympanum in the façade of the **Maximilianeum** *contains scenes of the building's foundation.*

THIERSCHSTR.

STERNSTR.

NSDORFSTR.

MAXIMILIANSBRÜCKE

ISAR

PRATERINSEL

FINISH

The **Alpines Museum** (p106) *is dedicated to the Alps and mountaineering.*

THE UNIVERSITY DISTRICT

The area to the north of the Old Town has long been defined by the Bavarian State Library, the sprawling university and an array of administrative buildings. The district arose during the planned extension of Munich in the 19th century, when the city required new infrastructure to facilitate its burgeoning role as an administrative and cultural centre. King Maximilian I Joseph levelled old buildings to create space for a distinctly modern district arranged on a grid system (differing starkly from the winding streets of the Old Town). The district was intersected by Ludwigstraße, lined exclusively with elegant Neo-Classical buildings.

Today, the west and north of Ludwigstraße are home to the lively Schwabing district, full of trendy shops and student pubs. To the east of Schwabing is the Englischer Garten, one of Europe's largest city parks.

THE UNIVERSITY DISTRICT

Must Sees
1. Bayerisches Nationalmuseum
2. Englischer Garten

Experience More
3. Wittelsbacherplatz
4. Ludwigstraße
5. Bayerische Staatsbibliothek
6. Ludwigskirche
7. Ludwig-Maximilians-Universität
8. Siegestor
9. Jugendstilhaus in der Ainmillerstraße
10. Pacelli-Palais
11. Akademie der Bildenden Künste
12. Archäologische Staatssammlung
13. Sammlung Schack
14. Haus der Kunst

Eat
1. Salzkruste
2. Julius Brantner

Drink
3. SEEHAUS
4. Chinesischer Turm
5. Goldene Bar in Haus der Kunst

Stay
6. Hotel Biederstein am Englischen Garten

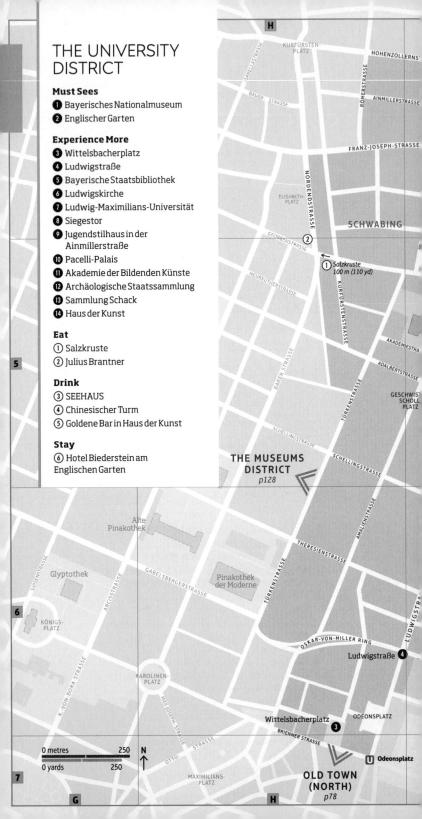

H
KURFÜRSTEN-PLATZ
HOHENZOLLERNS
SABELLISTRASSE
BAUER STRASSE
RÖMERSTRASSE
AINMILLERSTRASSE
FRANZ-JOSEPH-STRASSE
NORDENDSTRASSE
ELISABETH-PLATZ
SCHWABING
GEORGENSTRASSE
②
① Salzkruste 100 m (110 yd)
NEUREUTHERSTRASSE
KURFÜRSTENSTRASSE
AKADEMIESTRA
BARER STRASSE
TÜRKENSTRASSE
ADALBERTSTRASSE
GESCHWIST SCHOLL PLATZ
SCHELLINGSTRASSE
SCHELLINGSTRASSE

THE MUSEUMS DISTRICT p128

Alte Pinakothek
LUISENSTRASSE
Glyptothek
GABELSBERGERSTRASSE
Pinakothek der Moderne
ARCISSTRASSE
AMALIENSTRASSE
THERESIENSTRASSE
TÜRKENSTRASSE
LUDWIGSTR

KÖNIGS-PLATZ
K.-VON-BORA STRASSE
KAROLINEN-PLATZ
OSKAR-VON-MILLER RING
Ludwigstraße ④

Wittelsbacherplatz ③
ODEONSPLATZ
BRIENNER STRASSE
U Odeonsplatz

0 metres 250
0 yards 250
N ↑

MAXIMILIANS-STRASSE
OTTO STRASSE
MAXIMILIANS-PLATZ

OLD TOWN (NORTH) p78

G   H

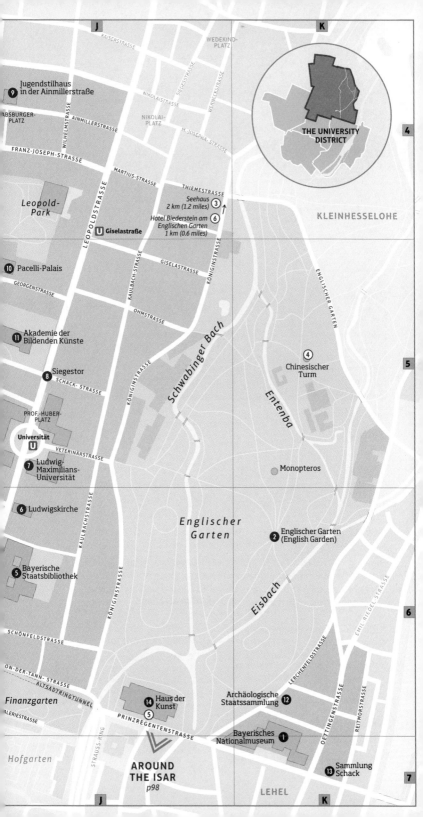

Seehaus
2 km (1.2 miles)

Hotel Biederstein am
Englischen Garten
1 km (0.6 miles)

J

K

KAISERSTRASSE

WEDEKIND-
PLATZ

NIKOLAISTRASSE

SIEGESSTRASSE

WERNECKSTRASSE

4

⑨ Jugendstilhaus
in der Ainmillerstraße

ABSBURGER-
PLATZ

NIKOLAI-
PLATZ

M.-JOSEPHA-STRASSE

THE UNIVERSITY
DISTRICT

WILHELMSTRASSE

AINMILLERSTRASSE

NIKOLAISTRASSE

KLEINHESSELOHE

FRANZ-JOSEPH-STRASSE

MARTIUS-STRASSE

THIEMESTRASSE

Leopold-
Park

LEOPOLDSTRASSE

③

⑥

U Giselastraße

ENGLISCHER GARTEN

⑩ Pacelli-Palais

KAULBACHSTRASSE

GISELASTRASSE

KÖNIGINSTRASSE

GEORGENSTRASSE

OHMSTRASSE

5

⑪ Akademie der
Bildenden Künste

④
Chinesischer
Turm

⑧ Siegestor

SCHACK-STRASSE

KÖNIGINSTRASSE

Schwabinger Bach

Entenba

PROF.-HUBER-
PLATZ

Universität U

VETERINÄRSTRASSE

⑦ Ludwig-
Maximilians-
Universität

Monopteros

⑥ Ludwigskirche

KAULBACHSTRASSE

Englischer
Garten

❷ Englischer Garten
(English Garden)

❺ Bayerische
Staatsbibliothek

KÖNIGINSTRASSE

Eisbach

6

SCHÖNFELDSTRASSE

LERCHENFELDSTRASSE

EMIL-RIEDEL-STRASSE

ON-DER-TANN-STRASSE

ALTSTADTRINGTUNNEL

Finanzgarten

⑭ Haus der
Kunst

❺

Archäologische
Staatssammlung ⑫

OETTINGENSTRASSE

REITMORSTRASSE

ALERIESTRASSE

PRINZREGENTENSTRASSE

STRAUSS-RING

**AROUND
THE ISAR**
p98

Bayerisches
Nationalmuseum ❶

Hofgarten

⑬ Sammlung
Schack

7

LEHEL

J

K

BAYERISCHES NATIONALMUSEUM

⚑K6 ⌂Prinzregentenstr. 3 ▦17 🚌100 ⏱10am–5pm Tue–Wed & Fri–Sun, 10am–8pm Thu 🌐bayerischesnationalmuseum.de

Founded in 1855 by King Maximilian II, the Bayerisches Nationalmuseum is one of Europe's largest art history museums. The museum features a suite of fascinating exhibits ranging from 17th-century ivory safes to one of the world's oldest depictions of the Resurrection.

One of the most important museums of decorative arts in Europe, the Bavarian National Museum's collections span Classical antiquity to the 19th century. In architectural terms, the museum was intended to embody the idea of a 19th-century artistic shrine. It was built by Gabriel von Seidl in 1894–1900, and features a mixture of styles that expresses the richness and variety of the collections within. The nucleus of the collection is that of the Wittelsbachs, which Maximilian II donated to the country in 1855.

MUSEUM GUIDE

The collections are laid out in separate wings across three floors, connected by grand staircases. The basement contains a collection of Christmas cribs and a section devoted to folk art. Painting, sculpture and crafts up to the 18th century are exhibited on the ground floor. The upper floor contains collections of musical instruments, porcelain and Biedermeier art.

Did You Know?

The museum is big enough to house entire palace rooms from 18th-century royal residences.

TOP 3 MUSEUM HIGHLIGHTS

Judith with the Head of Holofernes
This alabaster figure was made by sculptor Conrad Meit in 1515, with the figure of Judith depicted nude.

Christmas Crib
This 18th-century Neapolitan crib forms part of the largest and most important collection of nativity scenes in the world, with many from Italy.

Model of Munich
Commissioned by Albrecht V, this wooden model of the city was made by Jakob Sandtner in 1570. It is one of many Munich models on show.

↑ Religious art and tombstones in the Gothic hall, Bayerisches Nationalmuseum

1 Suits of armour are displayed in the museum's arms and armour collection.

2 This delicate 18th-century Meissen vessel is decorated with flowers and small figurines.

3 The Neo-Classical edifice of the Bayerisches Nationalmuseum is fronted by a garden on Prinzregentenstraße.

② Ⓜ️ 🖵

ENGLISCHER GARTEN

📍K6 Ⓤ Giselastraße 🚌54

Stretching from the centre to the city's northern limits, the Englischer Garten is as vast as it is beautiful. The park is popular among locals and visitors alike, with a replica Greek temple, meandering paths, a large herd of sheep and the iconic Eisbach standing wave.

The Englischer Garten (English Garden) is so named because it is naturalistically laid out in the manner of English landscaped grounds. One of Europe's largest city parks, it came into existence thanks to the vision of Sir Benjamin Thompson, an American officer on whom the elector Karl Theodor bestowed the title Count Von Rumford. As Bavaria's Minister of War, he ordered the clearing of the swampy terrain around the Isar; it became a municipal park in 1789. Today the park is a valued green area for the people of Munich. The Eisbach wave at the park's entrance draws large crowds, as hardy surfers take to the standing crest generated as water flows over a stone.

DRINK

SEEHAUS
This lakeside beer garden is a perfect place to relax with a local beer or wine in summer; it offers an excellent seafood menu, too.

📍K4 🏠Kleinhesselohe 3
🅦kuffler.de/de/seehaus

Chinesischer Turm
Munich's second-largest beer garden seats 7,000 people and has food stalls serving hearty dishes near the Chinese Tower.

📍K5 🏠Englischer Garten 3 🅦chinaturm.de

Did You Know?

With 78 km (48 miles) of pathways, the park is even bigger than New York's Central Park.

↑ A surfer riding the wave on the River Eisbach

← Relaxing in the beer garden near the Chinese Tower

Must See

TOP 3 ATTRACTIONS IN THE GARDEN

Chinese Tower
The Chinese Tower was built in 1789-90 as a viewing tower and bandstand. One of the city's most famous beer gardens is laid out around it.

The Monopteros
The Monopteros is a Neo-Classical building designed by Leo von Klenze which offers panoramic views.

The Eisbach
The Eisbach, despite the chilly water, is an excellent place to practise surfing.

← Taking in the view from the Monopteros in the Englischer Garten

Equestrian statue of Maximilian I in the centre of Wittelsbacherplatz ↑

EXPERIENCE MORE

❸
Wittelsbacherplatz

 H6 🚇 Odeonsplatz 🚌 100

This square is situated on Briennerstraße, one of the city's most elegant streets, which leads off from Odeonsplatz. Wittelsbacherplatz was laid out in the 1820s and is one of Munich's finest squares. It is lined on three sides by Neo-Classical palaces, and the square itself is laid with paving slabs and stones arranged to form various patterns.

Leo von Klenze lived in the Ludwig-Ferdinand Palais on the north side of the square. From 1878 the palace belonged to Duke Ludwig Ferdinand, after whom it was named. It is now owned by the Siemens corporation.

On the west side of the square is Arco-Zinneberg Palace, also designed by Leo von Klenze, which today houses upmarket shops. To the east is the Odeon and the Palais Méjean, which was rebuilt after being destroyed in World War II.

In the centre of the square stands a monument to the Elector Maximilian I. It was designed by the prominent Danish Neo-Classical sculptor Bertel Thorvaldsen and was unveiled in 1839.

THEMED CHRISTMAS MARKETS

Munich has many Christmas markets, and the medieval Christmas market at Wittelsbacherplatz is one of the most popular. Here, you can drink mead from a medieval stone mug and listen to musicians play the lute. Other themed markets include Pink Christmas, an LGBTQ+-friendly market complete with drag acts, and another focused on arts and handmade pottery at Schloss Blutenburg.

❹
Ludwigstraße

 H6 🚇 Odeonsplatz, Universität 🚌 100, 154

One of the most splendid city streets in Europe is Ludwigstraße. It was built from 1815 to 1852, the gen-

royal collection of books – particularly of early editions – was made when the Jesuit order was disbanded in 1773 and again when the monasteries were dissolved in 1803.

Today the Bayerische Staatsbibliothek contains almost 10 million volumes, including 95,900 manuscripts, 29,000 maps and over 62,000 periodicals.

The library was the first architectural project undertaken by German architect Friedrich von Gärtner, who started work in 1832 and completed the building in 1843. The Classical design echoes the style of Italian Renaissance palaces. The great interior staircase is flanked by figures of Classical sages carved by Ludwig Schwanthaler and overlooked by ornate figures of the library's founders, Albrecht V and Ludwig I. Equally impressive is its grand external staircase, adorned with the seated figures of ancient thinkers and luminaries including Thucydides, Hippocrates, Homer and Aristotle.

> In building Ludwigstraße, Ludwig I departed from the city's planning rules to satisfy his aesthetic and political ideals.

eral plan and the first group of buildings being designed and completed by Leo von Klenze. The street begins at Odeonsplatz, whose Italian Renaissance-style palaces harmonize perfectly with the buildings at the beginning of Ludwigstraße. In 1827 the project was taken over by Friedrich von Gärtner, who was responsible for the buildings north of Theresienstraße, which he gave Romanesque and Byzantine elements. The principal buildings on this part of the street are the Bavarian State Library, Ludwigskirche and university buildings. In the mid-19th century, the Feldherrnhalle and Siegestor were added, at the south and north ends of the street respectively. In building this triumphal route, Ludwig I departed

from the city's planning rules to satisfy his aesthetic and political ideals.

---

⑤

Bayerische Staatsbibliothek

📍 J6 **🏛** Ludwigstr. 16
Ⓤ Odeonsplatz, Universität
🚌 100 **🕐** 8am–midnight daily **🌐** bsb-muenchen.de

The monumental Bayerische Staatsbibliothek, Germany's second-largest library after the German national library in Leipzig, has its origins in the collections of books that were amassed by Duke Albrecht V and Wilhelm V in the 16th century. It was enhanced from 1663, when the Elector Friedrich Maria ordered that one copy of every new book published in Bavaria or published by a Bavarian abroad should be kept in the library. An enormous addition to the

→

Statue of Ludwig I, king of Bavaria and founder of Bayerische Staatsbibliothek

⑥ Ludwigskirche

📍 J6 🏛 Ludwigstr. 20
Ⓤ Universität 🚌 154
🕐 8am-8pm daily
(except during services)

Its distinct façade set with
tall, pointed twin steeples,
St Ludwig's Church is in sharp
contrast to the neighbouring
Staatsbibliothek *(p121)*.
It was built in the Italian
Romanesque style by
Friedrich von Gärtner in
1829–43. The niches in
the façade contain figures
of Christ and the four
Evangelists. The wings
connect the church
to the presbytery

and to Friedrich von Gärtner's
former house. The interior is
decorated with Italian
Renaissance-style paintings
by Peter von Cornelius and his
pupils. The painting of the
Last Judgment is the second
largest in the world after
Michelangelo's in the
Sistine Chapel.

⑦ Ludwig-Maximilians-Universität

📍 J5 🏛 Geschwister-Scholl-
Platz/Professor-Huber-
Platz Ⓤ Universität
🚌 154 🕐 6:15am-10pm
Mon–Fri, 8am-6pm Sat
🌐 lmu.de

This institute of higher
education is named in honour

The interior and
vaulted ceiling
of Ludwigskirche,
and *(inset)* its Neo-
Romanesque façade

of its first sponsors. In 1472
Ludwig der Reiche (the Rich)
founded a Jesuit Studium
Generale in Ingolstadt. In
1771 it became a university.
Maximilian I Joseph moved
it to Landshut in 1800 and
in 1826 Ludwig I transferred
it to Munich.

Today there are some
52,000 students. The noisy
crowds of young people
ensure that the streets in
the vicinity are always full of
life. The university's assembly
hall and seminar rooms are
set round two quadrangles.
The latter are named after
Hans and Sophie Scholl and
Professor Kurt Huber, who
together founded the White
Rose movement that
opposed Hitler.

In 1943 members of the
group distributed anti-Nazi
leaflets at the university.
The group was arrested
and most of its members
were executed. The event,
and the movement, are
commemorated with a
free exhibition on the
ground floor.

⑧ Siegestor

📍 J5 🏛 Ludwigstr.
Ⓤ Universität 🚌 154

Following the early
19th-century fashion
for erecting triumphal
arches, Friedrich von Gärtner
designed the Siegestor for
Ludwig I. The monument was
built in 1843–50, and with its
three grand arches, it echoes

←

The monumental Siegestor, crowned by the statue of Bavaria

the architecture of the Feldherrnhalle *(p86)*. It stands on Ludwigstraße at the junction with Leopoldstraße.

The design of the Siegestor is based on the Arch of Constantine in Rome. It honours the Bavarian army and its role in the country's victory against Napoleon. The arch is covered in bas-reliefs depicting battle scenes, medallions, personifications of the Bavarian provinces, and figures of Victory at the top of the columns. The arch is crowned by the figure of Bavaria riding in a chariot drawn by four lions.

Passing through the Siegestor and entering Leopoldstraße, the architectural uniformity of Ludwigstraße is replaced by stylistic variety in houses of the late 19th and early 20th centuries. The cafés, restaurants, music shops, bookstores, cinemas and discos here make for a vibrant atmosphere.

9

Jugendstilhaus in der Ainmillerstraße

J4 Ainmillerstr. 22 Giselastr. 27, 28, N27 154, N40, N41
To the public

The house at Ainmillerstraße 22 was the first residential building in Munich to be given an Art Nouveau (Jugendstil) façade. It was designed by Ernst Haiger and Henry Helbig in 1899–1900. The intricate scheme features decorative floral and mock-antique motifs.

10

Pacelli-Palais

J5 Georgenstr. 8-10
Universität, Giselastr.
To the public

This grand city palace provides an opportunity to compare two distinct architectural styles that were prevalent in Munich around 1900. The right-hand half of the building is in a late historical style, with columns, tympanums, small towers, carved loggias and sculptures. The flat but colourful Neo-Classical decoration on the left-hand half is typical of the Munich Art Nouveau style. It is now a private residence.

11

Akademie der Bildenden Künste

J5 Akademiestr. 2-4
Universität 154
To the public

During the 19th century Munich was one of the most important centres of painting, although it was regarded as being rather conservative.

Munich's artistic community developed around the Academy of Graphic Arts, which was founded in 1808. Many painters who subsequently became famous studied here, including the Germans Wilhelm Leibl and Franz Marc, the German-Swiss Paul Klee, the Russian-born Wassily Kandinsky, and the Italian Giorgio de Chirico.

The imposing façade is pierced by a series of arched windows and the building is approached by a driveway leading to a grand staircase, with equestrian statues of Castor and Pollux.

EAT

Salzkruste

The colourful Mediterranean fare served at this popular restaurant is consistently excellent.

H4 Georgenstr. 45
salzkruste.de

€€€

Julius Brantner

One of the best bakeries in the city, this spot makes great traditional German loaves, pretzels and, if you come on the right day, croissants.

H5 Nordendstr. 23
julius-brantner.de

€€€

← Burial object from
Wittislingen at
Archäologische
Staatssammlung

Archäologische Staatssammlung

K6 🏛 **Lerchenfeldstr. 2**
🚋 **18** 🚌 **100** 🕐 **10am–7pm Tue–Sun (to 5pm Thu & Sun)** 🌐 **archaeologie.bayern**

The Archaeological Museum, at the southern end of the Englischer Garten, is a modern glass and steel construction consisting of six blocks arranged in chequerboard formation. Formerly known as the Museum of Prehistory, it is one of the largest regional museums of archaeology in Germany.

The collections date back to the foundation of the Bavarian Academy of Sciences in 1759. The exhibits, which span a period of time from as early as 100,000 BCE to 800 CE, are chronologically presented in three separate sections:

Prehistoric, Roman and Early Medieval. Implements and jewellery, coins and religious artifacts illustrate the history of human settlement in Bavaria. There is a rich collection of Roman exhibits, including bronze masks from Eining, the Straubing Treasure and many mosaics. A popular but grisly attraction is the mummified body of a 16th-century woman.

Sammlung Schack

K7 🏛 **Prinzregentenstr. 9** 🚌 **100** 🚋 **18**
🕐 **10am–6pm Wed–Sun** 🌐 **pinakothek.de/de/sammlung-schack**

The interesting collection of 19th-century paintings at Sammlung Schack was formed by Friedrich von Schack (1815–94), a wealthy baron from Mecklenburg. As well as an art collector, he was a man of letters, a translator and an avid traveller. In 1857 Schack bought a palace near the Propyläen, where he housed his art collection. Von Schack's main interest was in contemporary Munich painters, and he often sponsored young artists. Under the terms of his will, von Schack's art collection was bequeathed to Emperor

Wilhelm II, who then decided to give the collection a home in Munich, commissioning a building especially for it.

Designed by Max Littmann and completed in 1910, the Schack-Galerie has a Neo-Classical façade and is similar to the Berlin castle of the collection's founder, who is praised in an inscription on the façade.

In 1939, the Sammlung Schack was merged with the Bavarian State Art Collection. Spread over 17 halls, the museum showcases stunning German landscapes and portraits from the late Romantic period. Among the 270 paintings are works by Austrian artist Moritz von Schwind – including *Turnip-counter*, *Morgenstunde* and *King Olch* – and German Neo-Classical painter Anselm Feuerbach's famous *Portrait of a Roman Woman* and *Paolo and Francesca*. Also of interest are the paintings by Karl Spitzweg, Leo von Klenze and Franz von Lenbach.

> 🏔 **GREAT VIEW**
> ### A Terrace with a View
>
> In summer, the terrace of the Archäologische Staatssammlung offers excellent views over the lovely Englischer Garten. Sit back and relax with a drink in the evening at the lovely rooftop bar here.

→ Impressive façade of the Neo-Classical Haus der Kunst

Haus der Kunst

📍J6 🏛Prinzregenten-str.1 🚌100 🕐10am-8pm Mon, Wed, Fri-Sun, 10am-10pm Thu 🚫24 & 31 Dec 🌐haus derkunst.de

Built between 1933 and 1937, the Neo-Classical building that houses the Haus der Kunst was designed by architect Paul Ludwig Troost; Adolf Hitler laid the foundation stone. The building became the model for the nascent National Socialist architecture. The museum, known as the House of German Art under the Nazi regime, opened its doors in July 1937 with a display of propaganda art, proclaimed by the Nazis as "truly German". At the same time, "The Exhibition of Degenerate Art" opened in the Hofgarten Arcades, now the German Theatre Museum, with works confiscated from Munich's galleries. At the Haus der Kunst, the "Great German Art Exhibition" displayed only the work of officially approved artists, but public reaction was muted, and attendance was low – an inauspicious start for what the Nazis hoped would be the rebirth of German art.

In the decades following the war, the Haus der Kunst became a showcase of pioneering European works. In 2002, the National Collection of Modern and Contemporary Arts moved into the Pinakothek der Moderne, meaning the Haus der Kunst has no permanent collection. Instead, the museum shows temporary exhibitions of modern artists and photographers.

DRINK

Goldene Bar in Haus der Kunst

This chandelier- and fresco-adorned café and cocktail bar offers classic charm and sophisticated tipples.

📍J6 🏛Prinzregentenstr.1 🌐hausderkunst.de

STAY

Hotel Biederstein am Englischen Garten

This small hotel offers boutique rooms with balconies overlooking the nearby gardens.

📍J5 🏛Keferstr.18 🌐hotel-biederstein.de

€€€

A SHORT WALK
ALONG LUDWIGSTRASSE

Distance 1km (0.5 miles) **Time** 10 minutes
Nearest U-Bahn Odeonsplatz

The University District's monumental Neo-Classical architecture was designed to a unified urban plan. There are no shops or pubs; instead the Ludwigstraße is lined with palaces whose façades are reminiscent of Italian Romanesque or Renaissance architecture, and the long avenue is punctuated by large squares. While walking this grand royal route, it's hard to imagine that the bustling and culturally varied Schwabing district is just next door (but, thankfully, its plethora of bars and restaurants makes for a delightful break after this short stroll through Munich's royal history).

Did You Know?

Ludwig I's love of Italy is reflected along Ludwigstraße, with many grand Italianate designs.

↑ The Monument to Maximilian I on Wittelsbacherplatz

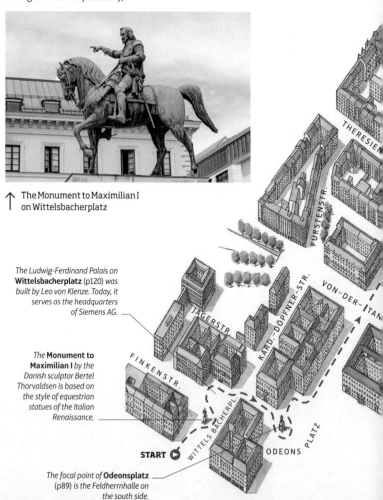

The Ludwig-Ferdinand Palais on **Wittelsbacherplatz** *(p120) was built by Leo von Klenze. Today, it serves as the headquarters of Siemens AG.*

The **Monument to Maximilian I** *by the Danish sculptor Bertel Thorvaldsen is based on the style of equestrian statues of the Italian Renaissance.*

THERESIEN

FÜRSTENSTR.

VON-DER-ITAN

TAGERSTR.

KARD.-DÖPFNER STR.

FINKENSTR.

WITTELS BACHERPL.

PLATZ

START 🔴

ODEONS

The focal point of **Odeonsplatz** *(p89) is the Feldherrnhalle on the south side.*

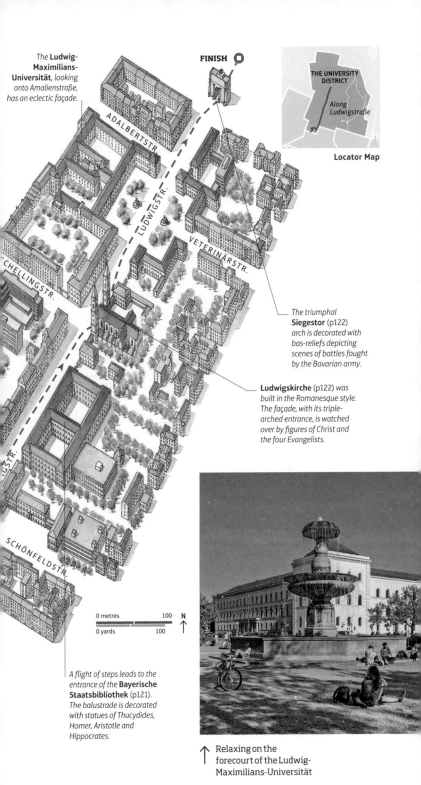

The **Ludwig-Maximilians-Universität**, *looking onto Amalienstraße, has an eclectic façade.*

FINISH

THE UNIVERSITY DISTRICT

Along Ludwigstraße

Locator Map

ADALBERTSTR.

LUDWIGSTR.

VETERINÄRSTR.

SCHELLINGSTR.

SCHÖNFELDSTR.

The triumphal **Siegestor** *(p122) arch is decorated with bas-reliefs depicting scenes of battles fought by the Bavarian army.*

Ludwigskirche *(p122) was built in the Romanesque style. The façade, with its triple-arched entrance, is watched over by figures of Christ and the four Evangelists.*

0 metres 100
0 yards 100

N ↑

A flight of steps leads to the entrance of the **Bayerische Staatsbibliothek** *(p121). The balustrade is decorated with statues of Thucydides, Homer, Aristotle and Hippocrates.*

↑ Relaxing on the forecourt of the Ludwig-Maximilians-Universität

THE MUSEUMS DISTRICT

This district is rooted in the cultural ambitions of Maximilian I Joseph and Ludwig I, who dreamed of turning Munich into a city of the arts in the early 19th century. As such, they commissioned the flagship institutions of what was to become the Museums District: the Alte Pinakothek and Neue Pinakothek, as well as the grand buildings on Königsplatz. To enhance the grand infrastructure of this section of the city, a popular architectural competition was launched in 1807; whoever devised the best proposal to embellish the royal route between the Residenz and Schloss Nymphenburg won. The winning design was one jointly produced by architects Friedrich Ludwig von Sckell and Karl von Fischer, although it was later modified by Leo von Klenze, and the district's layout has remained largely the same ever since.

The omnipresence of art is now underscored by the district's many private galleries, antique shops and bookstores. A cultural tour around the district leads past the main venues of the Bayerische Staatsgemäldesammlungen (Bavarian State Painting Collection), comprised of the Alte Pinakothek, Neue Pinakothek, Pinakothek der Moderne and Museum Brandhorst.

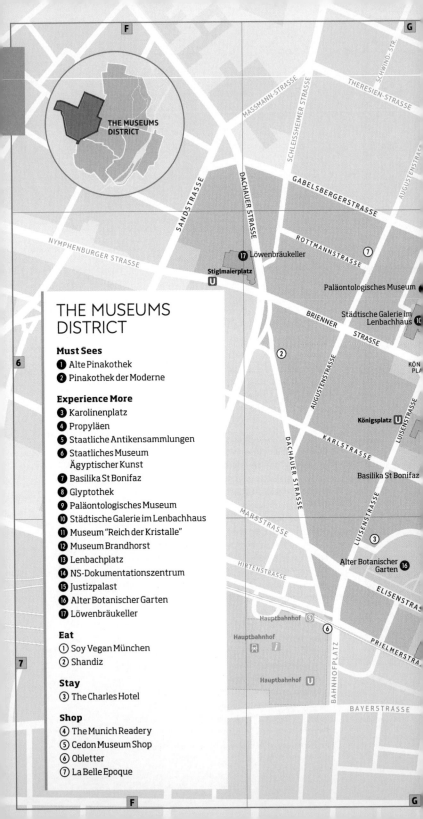

THE MUSEUMS DISTRICT

Must Sees
1 Alte Pinakothek
2 Pinakothek der Moderne

Experience More
3 Karolinenplatz
4 Propyläen
5 Staatliche Antikensammlungen
6 Staatliches Museum Ägyptischer Kunst
7 Basilika St Bonifaz
8 Glyptothek
9 Paläontologisches Museum
10 Städtische Galerie im Lenbachhaus
11 Museum "Reich der Kristalle"
12 Museum Brandhorst
13 Lenbachplatz
14 NS-Dokumentationszentrum
15 Justizpalast
16 Alter Botanischer Garten
17 Löwenbräukeller

Eat
① Soy Vegan München
② Shandiz

Stay
③ The Charles Hotel

Shop
④ The Munich Readery
⑤ Cedon Museum Shop
⑥ Obletter
⑦ La Belle Epoque

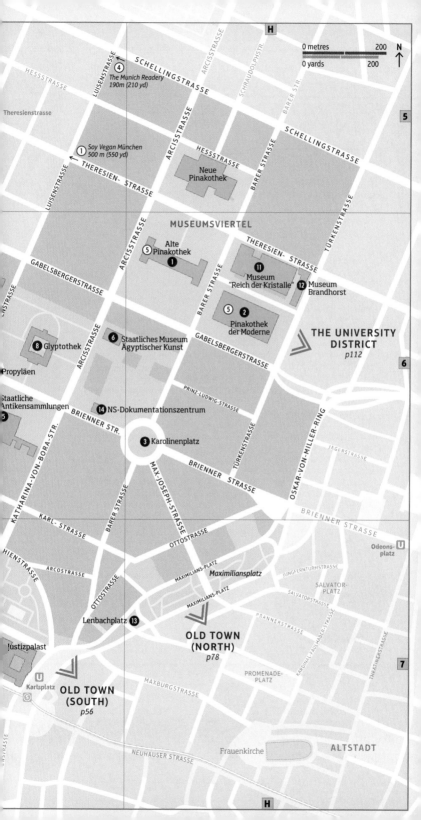

① ⊘ Ⓜ 🖼 🏛

ALTE PINAKOTHEK

📍 H6 🏛 Barer Str. 27 🕙 10am–6pm Tue–Sun (to 8pm Tue & Wed) 🌐 pinakothek.de

The Alte Pinakothek is a treasure trove showcasing the golden ages of European painting. It has an extensive collection that includes more than 700 beautiful artworks from the 14th to 18th centuries.

Opened in 1836, the Alte Pinakothek was designed in the Italian Renaissance style by Leo von Klenze. The history of its collections goes back to the Renaissance, when Wilhelm IV the Steadfast (ruled 1508–50) decided to decorate his residence with historic paintings. His successors were equally keen art collectors and, by the 18th century, an outstanding collection of paintings had been amassed. King Ludwig I ordered the construction of a gallery to showcase the collection, which covers European art styles from the Middle Ages to the late Rococo period.

The collections are laid out over two floors, with Flemish paintings and works from the Neue Pinakothek (closed until 2029) on the ground floor. On the first floor are works by German painters as well as Dutch, Flemish, French, Italian and Spanish paintings. Taken together, the museum houses many jewels of the Bayerische Staatsgemäldesammlungen (Bavarian State Painting Collection).

LEO VON KLENZE (1784-1864)

Leo von Klenze is one of the most prominent representatives of Neo-Classicism in Germany. In the reign of Ludwig I, von Klenze evolved the new face of Munich, fashioning the city as the new Athens. He designed important buildings including the Alte Pinakothek and the Residenz, and also built the Befreiungshalle in Kelheim and the New Hermitage in Russia's St Petersburg.

Gallery Highlights

Pietà (c 1490)

▽ The rich, contrasting colours, strong effects of light and shadow and homogeneous composition are typical of Botticelli's later works.

Peasants Playing Cards (c 1625–49)

This is an expressive, semi-satirical scene from Flemish peasant life painted by Adriaen Brouwer.

The Battle of Issus (1529)

△ This famous painting by Albrecht Altdorfer depicts the decisive moment in Alexander the Great's victory over the Persians.

Portrait of Karl V (1548)

▷ This portrait of the emperor, once attributed to Titian, was in fact painted by Lambert Sustris, who worked in his studio.

↑ Photographing works in the museum's galleries and *(inset)* the museum's façade

The Deposition (c 1633)

△ Here, Rembrandt challenges Rubens' idealised version of Christ's sacrifice by focusing on the pained expressions of the other figures in the composition.

Portrait of the Marquise de Pompadour (1756)

▷ This is one of the finest French Rococo paintings by François Boucher.

Adoration of the Magi (c 1502)

▷ This scene by Hans Holbein the Elder forms part of an altarpiece from Kaisheim.

EXPLORING THE ALTE PINAKOTHEK

After World War II, the Alte Pinakothek was rebuilt by Hans Döllgast. The entrance hall, ticket office, bookshop and café are on the ground floor, as are the sections on German Gothic painting, the Breughel Room and the temporary exhibitions gallery. The collections on the first floor are grouped according to the great national schools. The larger paintings are exhibited in the main rooms, and smaller ones in the side galleries. While Munich's Neue Pinakothek undergoes renovation until 2029, a selection of the museum's 19th-century paintings are shown on the ground floor of the Alte Pinakothek.

German Painting

The Alte Pinakothek is renowned for its collection of German late Gothic and Renaissance art. The section opens with a set of paintings by the Cologne School, from the Master of St Veronica (c 1420) to the fine altar of St Bartholomew (1500–10). Late 15th-century art is depicted in Michael Pacher's *Altar of the Church Fathers*, with a bold handling of perspective. The paintings by Albrecht Dürer document the development of his work over time, while two paintings by Matthias Grünewald show a strong Renaissance influence, as does the *Crucifixion* (1503) by Lucas Cranach the Elder. Albrecht Altdorfer of Regensburg, a painter of the Danube School, is represented by his *Battle of Issus*, with its inventive use of landscape. Mannerism is exemplified by the allegories of Hans Baldung Grien and Hans von Aachen.

Painting of the 17th century includes works by Adam Elsheimer and Johann Liss.

Dutch Painting

This school, which split into the Flemish and Dutch schools in the 16th century, is introduced by the fine works of Rogier van der Weyden, particularly his Cologne Altarpiece with the famous *Adoration of the Magi*. Hans Memling's *Seven Joys of the Virgin* depicts scenes from the life of Christ in an extensive symbolic landscape. A glimpse of the grotesque world of

Did You Know?

After World War II, the museum was rebuilt using a new shade of brick to highlight the extensive damage.

Hieronymus Bosch is given by his *Last Judgment*, while a completely different climate bathes Pieter Breughel's *Land of Cockaigne* (1567). An outstanding example of the assimilation of Italian Renaissance style is *Danae* by Jan Grossaert.

Flemish Painting

The largest collection of works by the great 17th-century painter Peter Paul Rubens can be seen here. They range from the intimate *Rubens and Isabella Brandt in the Honeysuckle Bower* (1609) to *The Battle of the Amazons* in the High Baroque style. Here also are the large-scale *Last Judgment* and *Women of the Apocalypse*, as well as sketches for the scenes from the life of Marie de Medici. This section also includes paintings by Rubens' pupils Anthony van Dyck and Jacob Jordaens, as well as the peasant scenes of Adriaen Brouwer.

Dutch Painting

The gallery's rich collection of 17th-century Dutch art includes an outstanding series of Baroque Passion scenes by Rembrandt executed in the 1630s. Notable among the wealth of portraits is a self-portrait by Carel Fabritius and the *Portrait of Willem van Heythuysen* by Frans Hals. Landscape painting is represented by the work of Jacob van Ruisdael and Jan van Goyen. Among the genre painters, Jan Steen, Gabriel Metsu and Gerard Terborch are particularly noteworthy.

Italian Painting

Most of the early Italian works came to the gallery thanks to Ludwig I's infatuation with the art of this particular period. Paintings of the 14th century include Giotto's *Last Supper*.

Central panel of the altarpiece at the church of St Colomba, Cologne

Admiring the works
of Jacopo Bassano and
other Old Masters ↑

Florentine art, which flowered a century later, is represented by the religious paintings of Dominico Ghirlandaio and Fra Filippo Lippi. Other highlights include Leonardo da Vinci's *Madonna and Child* (c 1473), Perugino's *Vision of St Bernard* and works by Raphael. The Venetian School is depicted in Titian's *Crown of Thorns* and Tintoretto's series of battle scenes glorifying the Gonzaga family. Great works of the 18th century include the religious canvases of Tiepolo and the fascinating Venetian townscapes of both Canaletto and Francesco Guardi.

Spanish Painting

Although smaller than the other sections, the collection of Spanish painting is no less interesting. The dramatic *Disrobing of Christ* by El Greco is one of three versions of this famous work. There are also paintings by Diego Velázquez, as well as the Mannerist scenes from the *Legend of St Catherine* by Francisco de Zurbarán, one of his finest works. Also of interest are Murillo's paintings,

in particular his genre scenes depicting street urchins in Seville. Other notable works include studio paintings by the lesser-known Claudio José Antonílez of about 1670.

French Painting

Despite their political connections with France, the Wittelsbachs did not collect French art on a large scale. The museum has three small paintings by Nicolas Poussin that, as early works, are not representative of his mature style. The work of Claude Lorrain is better documented, including his melancholic *Banishment of Hagar.*

By contrast, 18th-century French painting is well represented, most of the works having been acquired with the help of various banks. Noteworthy among them are paintings by Jean-Baptiste Pater and Nicolas Lancret, followers of artistocratic painter Antoine Watteau, and Jean-Marc Nattier's *Portrait of the Marquis of Baglion.* The work of François Boucher is generously represented, from the

exquisite *Portrait of the Marquise de Pompadour* to his intimate study of the young Louise O'Murphy, mistress of Louis XV. The eroticism of the Rococo age is illustrated by sketches by Jean-Honoré Fragonard, while Jean-Baptiste Greuze's moralistic *Grievance of Time* heralds the sentimentality of Neo-Classicism.

② ⌖ ⌖ 🍴 🖵 🛍

PINAKOTHEK DER MODERNE

📍 H6 🚇 Barer Str. 40 🚌 100, 58 🚊 27 🕐 10am–6pm Tue–Sun (to 8pm Thu) 🌐 pinakothek.de

Opened in 2002, the Pinakothek der Moderne is a celebrated repository of modern art. It includes several museums and has outstanding collections dedicated to art, works on paper, architecture and design from the 20th and 21st centuries.

The Pinakothek der Moderne is located on the site of a former army barracks, which was largely destroyed during World War II. The famous German Circus Roncalli moved there after the war, until, in 1990, the Bavarian government decided to create a Kunstareal – an art district – right in the heart of Munich. German architect Stefan Braunfels designed the Pinakothek der Moderne as a vast concrete and glass building with a light and airy interior.

The museum complements the nearby Alte Pinakothek (p132) and Neue Pinakothek, bringing together the worlds of art, design, graphics, jewellery and architecture under one roof. It houses outstanding works of art, including Cubist masterworks, works from the German Neue Sachlichkeit (New Objectivity) movement and paintings by Giorgio De Chirico and Max Beckmann. It also features central works of Pop Art, Photo-realism and the Junge Wilde movement of the 1980s. The gallery is also home to Die Neue Sammlung – the International Design Museum – which holds more than 120,000 items on industrial design, graphic design, technology, mobility, and arts and crafts.

GALLERY GUIDE

The collections are laid out over three floors. The basement level is home to the International Design Museum, from here stairs lead down to the Danner Rotunda. The ground floor contains exhibition rooms for architecture and works on paper. A leading collection of painting, sculpture and new media is located on the first floor.

TOP 3 GALLERY HIGHLIGHTS

Still Life with Geraniums (1910)
This painting by Henri Matisse shows his bold use of colour and lack of detail.

The Falling Man (1915)
This bronze cast of a naked youth by Wilhelm Lehmbruck mirrors the artist's feelings about World War I.

Proust's Armchair (1978)
Designed by Alessandro Mendini, this is one of 60,000 objects that illustrate the history of design.

↑ Modern concrete and glass façade of the Pinakothek der Moderne

→ *Tänzerin (Die Geste)* by Oskar Schlemmer at the Pinakothek der Moderne

↑ Exhibits at the
Design Museum in the
Pinakothek der Moderne

EXPERIENCE MORE

❸ Karolinenplatz

⊙ H6 🚊 27, 28, N27

Maximilian I Joseph, who continued the development of Munich that was begun by his predecessor Karl Theodor, focused his attention on the area around Briennerstraße. The Royal Route connecting the Residenz with Schloss Nymphenburg was opened up, and it became the focal point of the development of this suburb, which was named Maxvorstadt in the king's honour.

In 1809–12 a square was built at the junction of Briennerstraße and Barer Straße. This square was Karolinenplatz, the first star junction in Munich. Designed by Karl von Fischer, it was modelled on the Place de l'Étoile in Paris. In the centre of the square stands a bronze obelisk 29 m (95 ft) high, designed by Leo von Klenze and cast from Turkish guns captured at the Battle of Navarino in 1827.

On the south side of the Karolinenplatz is the Staatssammlung für Anthropologie und Paläoanatomie, the only anthropological collection of its kind in Germany, with a curious assortment of skulls.

❹ Propyläen

⊙ G6 Ⓤ Königsplatz 🚊 27, 28, N27 🚌 100

From 1815, Ludwig I and Leo von Klenze planned the layout of the Royal Square, or Königsplatz, west of Karolinenplatz. Königsplatz was laid out as an almost perfect square, with the Glyptothek and what the Antikensammlungen facing one another. To the west of the square was a Greek-inspired gate, also built by Leo von Klenze, in 1854–62, named the Propyläen.

According to the designs of the king and the architect, the buildings on three sides of the square would each represent one of the orders of architecture. The Propyläen would represent the Doric order, the Glyptothek the Ionic, and the exhibition hall the Corinthian.

The Propyläen was based on the Propylaeum in Athens, which consists of a central entrance way crowned by a grand tympanum and flanked by towers. Munich's Propyläen was intended to function as the western gate into the city, the Neo-Classical equivalent of the medieval Isar Gate.

When, however, the city's development rendered it superfluous, Ludwig I and von Klenze emphasized the Hellenistic character of the Propyläen, turning it into a kind of monument to the Greek War of Liberation against Turkey (1821–9).

MUNICH'S NAZI PAST

In 1933, students burned books deemed to be "un-German" at Königsplatz, which was also used for rallies during the Third Reich. In an effort to move beyond this dark legacy, the renovated square is now used for a host of functions, including open-air concerts and outdoor cinema screenings in summer.

❺ Staatliche Antikensammlungen

⊙ G6 🏛 Königsplatz 1 Ⓤ Königsplatz 🚊 27, 28, N27 🚌 100 ⏰ 10am–5pm Tue–Sun (to 8pm Wed) 🌐 antike-am-koenigsplatz.mwn.de

In 1838 Ludwig I, temporarily at loggerheads with the court architect Leo von Klenze, commissioned Georg Friedrich Ziebland to design the southern side of the Königsplatz. The king wished for an exhibition hall that would adjoin the Benedictine monastery and Basilica of St Boniface at the rear. The building, completed in 1848, was modelled on the design of a late Classical Greek temple, its proportions differing from those of the Glyptothek on the opposite side of the square. Over the large colonnaded portico is a tympanum containing a figure of Bavaria as patroness of art

↑ Propyläen, Leo von Klenze's grand city gate in the Neo-Classical style

Egyptian sarcophaguses at the Staatliches Museum Ägyptischer Kunst

and industry. From 1898 to 1916 the hall housed the gallery of the Munich Secession (Art Nouveau movement), after which it was taken over by the Neue Staatsgalerie. Since 1967 it has housed the National Collection of Antiquities. This impressive collection includes an important assemblage of Greek and Etruscan vases, plus fine pottery and glass, bronze and terracotta figures and jewellery.

Staatliches Museum Ägyptischer Kunst

📍 G6 🏛 Gabelsbergerstr. 35 Ⓤ Königsplatz 🚋 27 🕙 10am–6pm Tue–Sun (Tue until 8pm) 🌐 smaek.de

The State Museum of Egyptian Art is located below

Dionysus Cup on display in the Staatliche Antikensammlungen

the building of the University of Television and Film Munich. Visitors enter the exhibition rooms down a ramp and through a monumental walled portal sunk into the ground like a pharaoh's tomb.

The exhibits are thousands of years old so the highest levels of conservatorial protection are essential. Items are displayed in three large halls and smaller, darker catacombs, organized into themes such as The Pharoah, Realm of the Dead and Egypt in Rome.

7

Basilika St Bonifaz

📍 G6 🏛 Karlstr. 34 🕙 7am–7pm daily 🚋 27, 28, N27 🌐 smaek.de

The Basilica of St Boniface functioned as the parish church of the Maxvorstadt but was later dedicated to the Benedictine monks who moved to Munich. The church, modelled on an early Christian basilica, was first built in 1835–48 by Georg Friedrich Ziebland.

Did You Know?

The subterranean entrance to the Staatliches Museum resembles the entrance to a pharaoh's tomb.

Behind the portico, which is supported by Ionic columns, are three arched doorways. The central one is flanked by statues of St Peter and St Boniface, and the arch is crowned by a portrait of the architect himself – a rare occurrence – in medieval dress. The location of the church and monastery at the rear of the Kunstausstellungsgebäude (now the Antikensammlung) illustrates contemporary ideas about architecture, in which religion was to be linked with art and science, as represented by the Benedictine order.

Today's basilica, which was rebuilt after the destruction brought by World War II, carries no resemblance to the original double-aisled church, which had colourful paintings and an open-beam roof on 66 monolithic columns. Of its furnishings, the white marble tomb of Ludwig I survives, with the tombstone of his wife Therese behind it.

↑ Gallery with Greek and Roman sculptures at the Glyptothek

Glyptothek

📍G6 🏛Königsplatz 3
🚇Königsplatz 🚋27, 28, N27
🚌100 ⏰10am–5pm Tue–Sun (to 8pm Thu) 🌐antike-am-koenigsplatz.mwn.de

The idea of building a museum to house Greek and Roman sculpture originated in 1805, when Ludwig I, the future king, was on his first tour of Italy. In 1816, Leo von Klenze was given the task of designing a museum for his collection. It was named the Glyptothek, from the Greek word *glypte*, meaning "carved stone". It is regarded as von Klenze's finest Neo-Classical work.

The Glyptothek's hall contains the world's finest collection of antique sculpture, including archaic figures from the Temple of Aphaia on Aegina of 500 BCE,

---

INSIDER TIP
Thursday Tours

The Glyptothek offers early evening guided tours on a Thursday, when the museum is open later. Tour groups typically meet around Königsplatz, and tickets should be booked online in advance.

---

the famous Barberini Faun of 220 BCE and the Rondanini Alexander of 338 BCE.

Paläontologisches Museum

📍G6 🏛Richard-Wagner-Str. 10 🚇Königsplatz
🚌100 ⏰8am–4pm Mon–Thu, 8am–2pm Fri, 10am–4pm first Sun of the month
🌐bspg.snsb.de

Since 1950, the Bavarian palaeontological collection has occupied an eclectic building dating from 1899–1902. Built by Leonhard Romeis as a school for crafts, there are several decorative motifs in the main entranceway. The main hall is a beautiful arcade with a glass roof, where skeletons of large animals are exhibited.

The displays are divided into various thematic groups. Skeletons found in Bavaria include a mastodon, woolly rhinoceros and giant tortoise. There are also exhibits on fossilized palm trees that show the existence of a tropical climate here in prehistoric times.

> **The Glyptothek's hall contains the world's finest collection of antique sculpture, including archaic figures from the Temple of Aphaia on Aegina of 500 BCE.**

Städtische Galerie im Lenbachhaus

📍G6 🏛Luisenstr. 33
🚇Königsplatz 🚌100
⏰Hours vary, check website 🔒24 Dec
🌐lenbachhaus.de

The portraitist Franz von Lenbach (1836–1904) commissioned Gabriel von Seidl to build him a grand residence behind Königsplatz. Completed in 1891, the house and its garden are in the style of an Italian suburban villa, with Renaissance and Baroque elements.

The exhibition area contains galleries of Munich painting from the Gothic to

the Art Nouveau periods, the 19th and early 20th centuries being well represented with works by Karl Spitzweg, Wilhelm Leibl and Lovis Corinth. The museum is also renowned for its fine paintings by artists of the Blaue Reiter group, which was active in Munich from 1911 to 1914 (p33). In 1957 Gabriele Münter, Wassily Kandinsky's partner up to 1914, gave her collection of art from his defining Munich and Murnau period. A building designed by Norman Foster has been added to the gallery. An exhibition hall, which is part of the gallery, can be seen at the Kunstbau space under Königsplatz U-Bahn station.

Museum "Reich der Kristalle"

🔘 H6 🏛 Theresienstr. 41 Ⓤ Theresienstr. 🚌 27 🚌 100 🕐 1–5pm Tue-Sun 🚫 31 Dec & Shrove Tue 🌐 mineral ogische-staatssamm lung.de

The exhibits here are part of the great collection of the Mineralogische Staatsammlung, which originated with collections of rocks and minerals found in the 18th century. The museum owes its valuable collection to Duke Maximilian von Leuchtenberg, who supervised mineral extraction in Siberia. His collection was added to that of the Bavarian Academy of Sciences in 1858.

Artwork on display in the gallery wing of the Städtische Galerie im Lenbachhaus, and (inset) ↓ its vibrant façade

The present museum is in a modern building. Visitors can find colourful mineral formations from all over the world, as well as minerals local to Bavaria. The museum has a few displays as well as a showroom, which hosts special exhibitions.

⑫

Museum Brandhorst

◉H6 ⬧Theresienstr. 35a ⓊUniversität ⬛2, 28, N27 ⬛100 ◷10am–6pm Tue-Sun (until 8pm Thu) ⬤museum-brandhorst.de

Opened in 2009 in the vibrant Maxvorstadt neighbourhood, this spectacular building, covered in multi-hued ceramic tubes, is home to the remarkable Museum Brandhorst. Commissioned by the Bavarian government, it lies adjacent to the Pinakothek der Moderne (p136); visits to both make for a fantastic cultural experience.

The museum features the impressive Udo and Anette Brandhorst collection, which is part of the Bavarian State Painting Collection. An extensive and important collection of modern and contemporary art, the Brandhorst collection has over 1,200 works, including paintings, drawings and sculptures, as well as photos, multimedia pieces and installations. The works of the

Did You Know?

The Museum Brandhorst's multi-coloured façade is made of 36,000 reflective ceramic rods.

leading art figures of the late 20th century – among them Joseph Beuys, Gerhard Richter and Damien Hirst – are on display here. The museum also has the largest collection of works by Andy Warhol in Europe, and more than 60 works by abstract painter Cy Twombly. His *Lepanto* cycle (2001) is on display here.

---

⑬

Lenbachplatz

◉H7 ⑤ⓊKarlsplatz (Stachus) ⬛16, 17, 18, 19, 20, 21, 27, 28, N27

This irregularly shaped square lies between Maximiliansplatz, the Alter Botanischer Garten

and Karlsplatz. The buildings that line it are typical of the late 19th century and are laid out irregularly around the square, creating a set of contrasting perspectives.

On the west side stand the law courts (Justizpalast) and on the south side rises the bizarre outline of the Künstlerhaus. On the north side is the Stock Exchange (Börse). Built in 1868–98, it is an example of pompous Neo-Baroque, its splendour reflecting the power of the financial institution within. The neighbouring Bernheimer Haus, at No. 6, was built in 1889. It was regarded as the ultimate residential building in Munich, a novelty at the time being the exposed iron structure of the ground floor and the huge picture windows.

On the east side of the square is Munich's finest fountain, the Wittelsbacher Brunnen, built by Adolf von Hildebrand in 1893–5 to commemorate the completion of the city's new water-supply system. The fountain symbolizes both charity and the destructive power of water. It is dominated by two allegorical figures – a youth on a steed, and a woman seated on a bull. This square is the perfect place for a short break if you are in the city centre.

The striking, colourful exterior of Museum Brandhorst

↑ Browsing exhibits at the NS-Dokumentationszentrum

⑭
NS-Dokumentations-zentrum

📍G6 🏛Max-Mannheimer-platz 1 🚇Karolinenplatz 🕐10am-7pm Tue-Sun 🌐ns-doku.de

A striking museum, the Munich Documentation Centre for the History of National Socialism (often known simply as the nsdoku) opened to the public in 2015 on the former site of the Braunes Haus (Brown House), the headquarters of the Nazi Party. The Brown House played an important role in Munich as "capital of the movement" during the rise of the Nazi party and the enforcement of Nazism. The building was completely destroyed in 1945.

In its place, this thoughtful museum was built both as an archive of the Nazi regime in Munich and as a warning against the rise of fascism. The building is thoughtfully conceived, with a cube-shaped structure made of a special white concrete; it also features long slit windows designed to create harmony between the vast exhibition spaces and the historical sites around the building.

The museum's permanent exhibition "Munich and National Socialism" is spread across four floors and uses films, period documents, artifacts, photographs and multimedia stations to tell the story of the city's dark 20th-century history. Temporary exhibitions shed light on the role of far-right politics from the 20th century to the present day. Contemporary art is displayed in the exhibition spaces and the centre also hosts workshops and seminars. The museum is a great example of Munich's efforts to reckon with its past through strong education.

SHOP

The Munich Readery
This second-hand bookstore sells an array of titles in English; browse to uncover an old classic or a forgotten cult favourite.

📍H6 🏛Augustenstr. 104 🌐readery.de

Cedon Museum Shop
Cedon has a presence in many famous museums across Munich. The museum shops near the Alte Pinakothek and Pinakothek der Moderne have beautiful books and a selection of stationery on offer.

📍H6 🏛Barer Str. 27/40 🌐cedon.de

Obletter
This expansive, multi-level toy emporium sells many of the world's greatest toys, from nostalgic gems to the latest trends, with over 16,000 toys to choose from.

📍G7 🏛Karlsplatz 11-12 🌐mueller.de

La Belle Epoque
A long-standing antique store with a wonderfully strange selection of ephemera from centuries past. Stock changes regularly, and the owners are happy to take enquiries online.

📍G7 🏛Augustenstr. 41 🌐ankaufantiquitaeten-muenchen.de

EAT

Shandiz

Shandiz is one of the city's best addresses for inventive Persian cuisine. Here you can have a break from Bavarian food and immerse yourself in a world of culinary delights - enjoy delicious dishes including kebabs, served in a traditional dining room with lovely furnishings.

🔢 G6 🏠 Dachauer Str. 50 🌐 shandiz.de

€€€

Justizpalast

🔢 G7 🏠 Prielmayerstr. 7
Ⓢ Ⓤ Karlsplatz (Stachus)
🚋 16, 17, 18, 19, 20, 21, 27, 28, N16, N19, N20, N27

On the northwest side of Karlsplatz stands one of the best-known late 19th-century landmarks in Munich. The law courts, built in 1891–98 by Friedrich von Thiersch, are an example of pure Neo-Baroque architecture, with discreet Neo-Mannerist elements.

The building's great novelty at the time was its vast steel and glass dome, which acted as a skylight. The interior – particularly the main hall and the main stairway, which are directly beneath the dome – has an extraordinary wealth of detail in its design.

↑ The main hall and stairway beneath the huge glass dome inside the Justizpalast

→ Guests drinking in the expansive hall of Löwenbräukeller

West of the Justizpalast are the Neues Justizgebäude (New Law Courts). Built in 1906–08, also by Thiersch, they are in the Neo-Gothic style and have a clocktower and gables.

Alter Botanischer Garten

🔢 G7 🏠 Between Elisenstr. and Sophienstr.
Ⓢ Ⓤ Karlsplatz (Stachus), Hauptbahnhof 🚋 16, 17, 18, 19, 20, 21, 27, 28, N27, N28 🚌 100

Visitors to Munich who find themselves in need of respite from the bustle of the city centre will find a sanctuary in the Old Botanical Garden north of the Justizpalast. Laid out on a semicircular plan in 1804–14, it was designed by Friedrich Ludwig von Sckell, who was also responsible for the Englischer Garten.

The entrance to the garden is through an early Neo-Classical gate built by Emanuel Joseph von Herigoyen in 1811 and bearing a Latin inscription by Goethe. In 1854 the greenhouse was demolished to make space for the Glaspalast. Modelled on London's Crystal Palace, it was built to house the First Industrial Exhibition. The Glaspalast burned down in 1931, destroying at the same time an exhibition of German Romantic painting.

In 1914 a new botanical garden was laid out in Nymphenburg, and the Old Botanical Garden was converted into a municipal park. A restaurant (today the Park Café) was built in

1935–7, as well as an exhibition hall designed by Oswald Bieber. The German sculptor Josef Wackerle created the Neptune Fountain, which has a figure based on Michelangelo's *David*. The café garden, shaded by exotic trees, is an ideal place to relax and enjoy a cold beer.

⓱

Löwenbräukeller

📍G6 🏠Stiglmaierplatz 2/ Nymphenburgerstr.
Ⓤ Stiglmaierplatz
🚋20, 21, 22, N20
🕐11am–11pm daily
🌐loewenbraeukeller.com

Visitors entering the city from the west along Nymphenburgerstraße

will see from afar the marble statue of the lion that crowns the Löwenbräukeller on Stiglmaierplatz. This famous Munich brewery has its own inn, which is large enough to hold 4,000 drinkers.

The picturesque brewery and inn were built in 1883 by Albert Schmidt and were refurbished by Friedrich von Thiersch at the turn of the 19th and 20th centuries. The sides of the Löwenbräukeller's octagonal tower are decorated alternately with the brewery's emblem – a white griffin – and the city's coat of arms. The tower rises above an arcaded entrance hall with a roof terrace.

In summer locals and visitors alike are drawn to the beer garden, which seats

1,000 patrons and is shaded by large chestnut trees. The large garden and inn are also used to host a range of public and private events, from weddings to Christmas parties. Football fans often gather to watch domestic and international games on large screens here.

BEER HALLS

Most commonly associated outside of Germany with the festivities of Oktoberfest, beer halls are an important part of Bavarian culture. The Löwenbräukeller is one of Munich's most popular traditional beer halls. Others include Hofbräuhaus (*p93*), the Augustinerbräu on Landsberger Straße, and the Pschorr at Viktualienmarkt. While some of Munich's central beer halls can be very touristy, venture farther afield to find Spatenhaus (*Residenzstraße 12*) or Andechser am Dom (*Frauenplatz 7*).

The sides of the Löwenbräukeller's octagonal tower are decorated alternately with the brewery's emblem - a white griffin - and the city's coat of arms.

A SHORT WALK
AROUND KÖNIGSPLATZ

Distance 1 km (0.5 miles) **Time** 10 minutes
Nearest U-Bahn station Odeonsplatz

The streets surrounding Königsplatz contain some of Munich's finest gems. On the square itself, Greek and Roman sculpture can be seen in the Glyptothek, with Classical and other prized antiquities in the Antikensammlungen. The Alte Pinakothek, Neue Pinakothek and Pinakothek der Moderne nearby contain some of the richest collections of European painting in the world, while the Lenbachhaus is renowned for works by the Blaue Reiter group. This short walk is a whistle-stop tour past some of central Munich's most iconic locations.

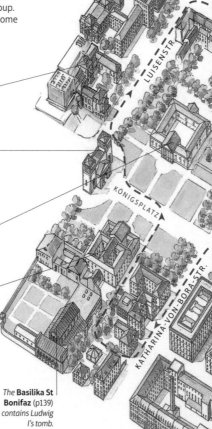

*One of the most impressive exhibits in the **Paläontologisches Museum** (p140) is the cast of a mammoth skeleton from the Tertiary period.*

*The **Städtische Galerie im Lenbachhaus** (p140) is housed in the former home of Franz von Lenbach, the late 19th-century portraitist.*

*The frieze decorating the side towers of the **Propyläen** (p138) features motifs and scenes from the Greek War of Liberation.*

*The **Glyptothek's** (p140) Ionic colonnade is flanked by statues of great artistic figures from Classical antiquity.*

*Among the **Staatliche Antikensammlungen's** (p138) treasures is a collection of ancient art and artifacts.*

*The **Basilika St Bonifaz** (p139) contains Ludwig I's tomb.*

Did You Know?

Lugwig I claimed he wouldn't rest until the whole of Munich looked like Athens.

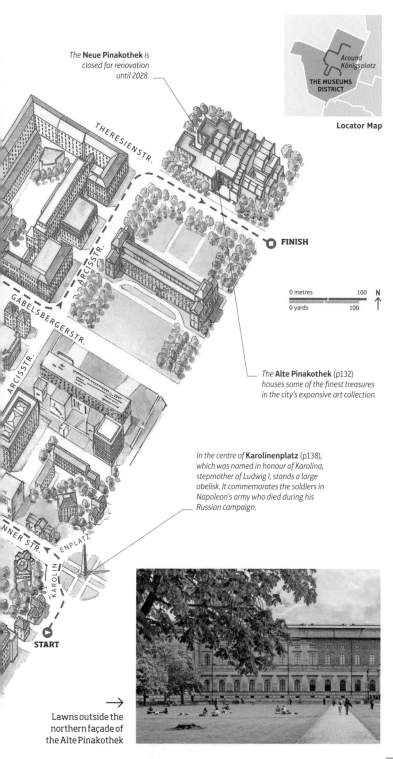

The **Neue Pinakothek** is closed for renovation until 2028.

THERESIENSTR.

ARCISSTR.

GABELSBERGERSTR.

ARCISSTR.

NNER STR.

KAROLIN ENPLATZ

START

FINISH

0 metres	100
0 yards	100

N
↑

The **Alte Pinakothek** (p132) houses some of the finest treasures in the city's expansive art collection.

In the centre of **Karolinenplatz** (p138), which was named in honour of Karolina, stepmother of Ludwig I, stands a large obelisk. It commemorates the soldiers in Napoleon's army who died during his Russian campaign.

→
Lawns outside the northern façade of the Alte Pinakothek

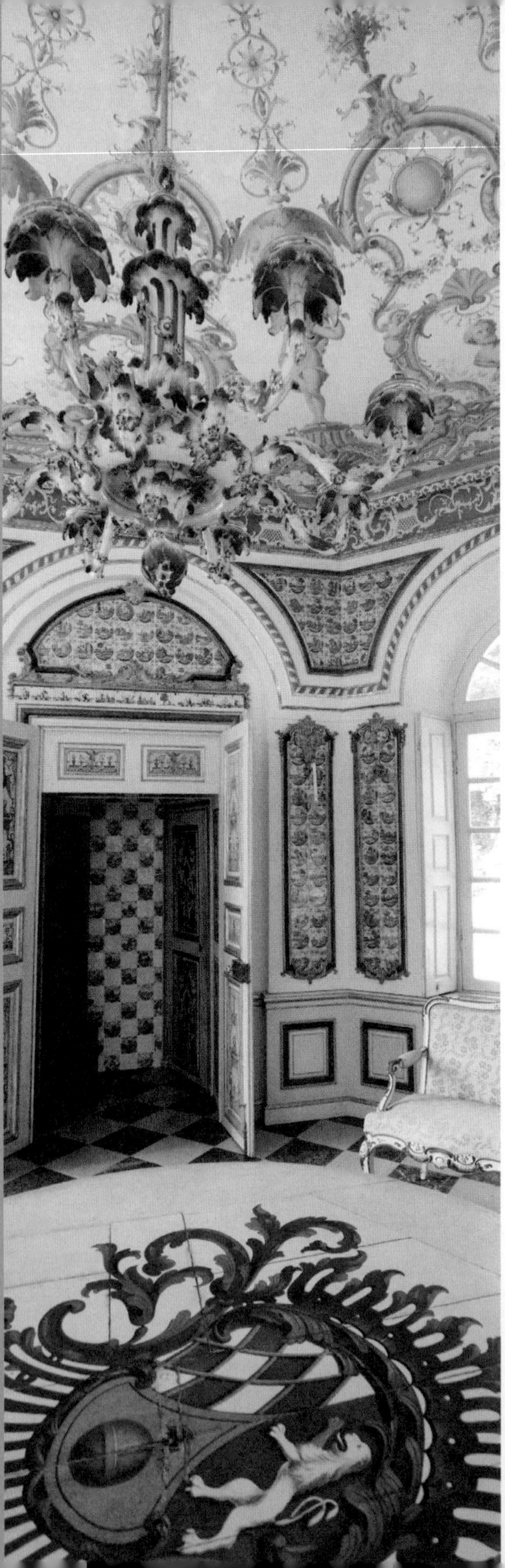

Intricate decoration inside Schloss Nymphenburg

Must See

1 Schloss Nymphenburg

Experience More

2 Neuhausen
3 Olympiapark
4 Botanischer Garten
5 BMW museum and BMW Welt
6 Au
7 Westend
8 Haidhausen
9 Deutsches Museum Verkehrszentrum
10 Sendling
11 Grünwald
12 Tierpark Hellabrunn
13 Asam-Schlössl
14 Bavaria-Filmstadt
15 Theresienwiese
16 Neue Messe München
17 Blutenburg
18 Allianz Arena

BEYOND
THE CENTRE

Munich's expansion began in earnest in the
19th century under Ludwig I, and the city has
grown to form a lively tapestry of districts. The
west of the city was originally farmland, until the
construction of Schloss Nymphenburg initiated
a wave of grand building in what became the
Nymphenburg district. Expansion to the north
of Munich is a more modern phenomenon, with the
famous Olympiapark and the BMW factory's complex
of buildings. Southwest of the Old Town is defined by
theTheresienwiese, where the famous Oktoberfest is
held, and the land to the south of the city includes the
Hellabrunn Zoo in Thalkirchen and the Bavaria Film
Museum in Geiselgasteig. To the east, Munich's pious
history is on display, with architectural masterpieces
including the Mariä Himmelfahrtskirche in Ramersdorf.

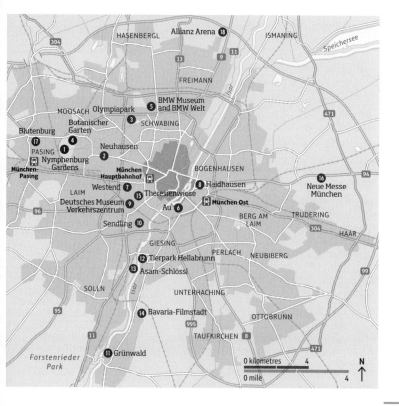

The beautiful palace garden with its stunning variety of plants ↑

1

SCHLOSS NYMPHENBURG

📍A4 🏛Nymphenburg 🚇Rotkreuzplatz, then 🚋12 🚌51 🕐Apr-mid-Oct: 9am-6pm daily; mid-Oct-Mar: 10am-4pm daily 🌐schloss-nymphenburg.de

This palace was designed as a summer residence for the rulers of Bavaria in the 18th century. Its elaborate architectural detailing and grand outlook make it one of the finest Baroque complexes in Central Europe, while its gardens are renowned as a horticultural masterpiece.

After the birth in 1679 of Maximilian Emanuel, the heir to the throne, his father, Duke Ferdinand Maria, presented his wife with a suburban palace. The queen named it Nymphenburg (Nymphs' Castle) and supervised the building work that ensued. Max Emanuel continued his mother's work, creating with architects Joseph Effner and Enrico Zucalli one of the finest palaces and gardens in Europe. Later, buildings were added around the courtyard fronting the palace. In the 1800s the formal French gardens were converted into a landscaped park incorporating the existing canals.

 GREAT VIEW
Monopteros

The gardens feature a Classical monopteros, a circular pavilion popular in French and English garden design. Erected in 1865 at the edge of the Badenburg lake, this charming structure provides stunning views of the garden.

Max Emanuel continued his mother's work, creating with architects Joseph Effner and Enrico Zucalli one of the finest palaces and gardens in Europe.

↑ Lovely location of the Monopteros on the Badenburg Lake

The formal French garden at the rear of the palace forms the main axis of the entire palace and its gardens.

Built by François Cuvilliés, the Amalienburg was a small hunting lodge. Its circular hall was covered with fine shellwork.

Marstallmuseum contains coaches, carriages and sleighs that once belonged to Bavarian rulers.

Badenburg and the first heated tiled pool are surrounded by a viewing gallery.

Pagodenburg was used for receiving visitors and for relaxation.

Magdalenenklause was built as a chapel in a grotto with hermits' cells.

The Porzellanmanufaktur has produced fine porcelain since 1761.

↑ The palace and its beautiful land-scaped gardens

Exploring Schloss Nymphenburg

The palace is an intriguing composite of eras and styles. The central section was built in 1675 in the form of an Italianate villa. In 1702 Maximilian Emanuel commissioned the construction of side pavilions, which were connected to the villa by galleries. Soon after 1715, when Joseph Effner took charge of building work on the palace, the Steinerner Saal (Audience Hall), with stunningly lavish interior decoration, was built, along with the other rooms in the wings, and the stables and orangery.

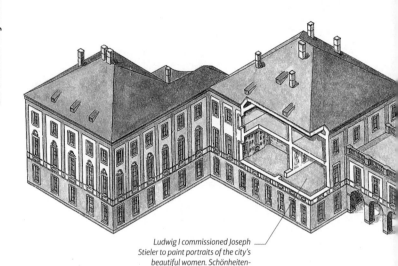

Ludwig I commissioned Joseph Stieler to paint portraits of the city's beautiful women. Schönheiten-galerie houses these portraits.

1 Frescoes are framed by lavish Rococo stucco-work in the Steinerner Saal (Marble Hall).

2 There are many portraits in King Ludwig I's Gallery of Beauties.

3 Johann Baptist Zimmermann's splendid ceiling fresco depicts the Olympian heaven; it adorns the Great Hall.

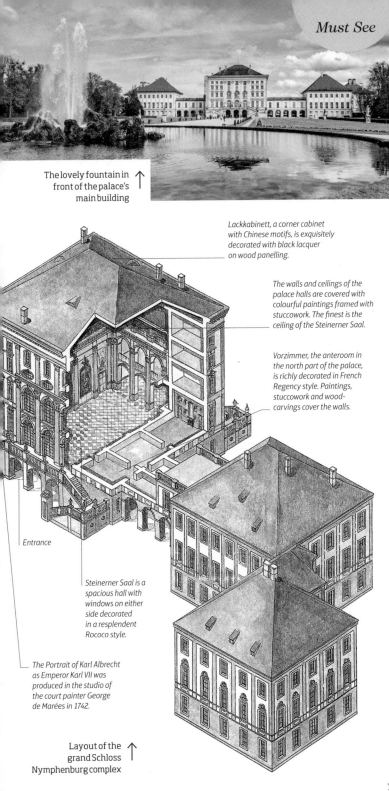

The lovely fountain in front of the palace's main building ↑

Lackkabinett, a corner cabinet with Chinese motifs, is exquisitely decorated with black lacquer on wood panelling.

The walls and ceilings of the palace halls are covered with colourful paintings framed with stuccowork. The finest is the ceiling of the Steinerner Saal.

Vorzimmer, the anteroom in the north part of the palace, is richly decorated in French Regency style. Paintings, stuccowork and wood-carvings cover the walls.

Entrance

Steinerner Saal is a spacious hall with windows on either side decorated in a resplendent Rococo style.

The Portrait of Karl Albrecht as Emperor Karl VII was produced in the studio of the court painter George de Marées in 1742.

Layout of the grand Schloss Nymphenburg complex ↑

EXPERIENCE MORE

② Neuhausen

D5 **Rotkreuzplatz**
12, 16, 17 **53**

Neuhausen is located west of the city centre, between Maxvorstadt and Nymphenburg. It ranges from the railway line in the south across Arnulfstraße and Nymphenburger Straße to Dachauerstraße and the Westfriedhof. The centre of Neuhausen is the Rotkreuzplatz. The district north of the Nymphenburger Schlosskanal is called Gern.

The village of Neuhausen was first mentioned in 1170. Industrialization (especially railway and locomotive manufacturing) led to a growth in population. It was incorporated into Munich in 1890, and in 1992 it fused together with the district of Nymphenburg.

Most of the buildings in Neuhausen date from the Gründerzeit after the Franco-Prussian War of 1870–71 and the Art Nouveau era. Neuhausen is also the setting for Munich's most modern church – Herz-Jesu-Kirche (1997–2000). Other attractions include the large Dantebad pool and spa complex.

③   Olympiapark

E2 **Spiridon-Louis-Ring 21** **Olympiazentrum**
olympiapark.de

Munich's Olympic Park was built for the 20th Olympic Games, which the city hosted in 1972. The modern complex of sports facilities overlies an area formerly used as drill grounds and later as an airfield. The artificial lake is fed by the Nymphenburg Canal and the hills were made from the rubble removed from the city after World War II. The swimming hall here is one of the finest in Europe. The complex comprises five pools, saunas, a jacuzzi and a diving platform, as well as a grassed relaxation area. The whole complex is dominated by the Olympic Tower, which commands a fine view over the city. Note that the tower is undergoing renovation and is closed until 2026.

④ Botanischer Garten

A3 **Menzingerstr. 12**
17 **Hours vary, check website** **botmuc.de**

North of the gardens of Schloss Nymphenburg, new botanical gardens were laid out in 1909–14. Covering 0.22 sq km (0.08 sq miles) and containing over 14,000 species of plants growing in artistic arrangements, this is one of the finest botanical gardens in Europe.

Entry to the garden is through the Botanical Institute, which is fronted by the colourful Schmuckhof (Decorative Yard). Passing through it, visitors see a section on ecology and genetics, followed by a rose garden and a plantation of rhododendrons and protected species, and of medicinal plants and crops. There is also an arboretum with rare

---

DRINK

Cafe Ruffini
A popular spot on weekends, this modern café is known for its range of baked treats and a great selection of Italian wines.

D4 **Orffstr. 22-24**
ruffini.de

Restaurant Broeding
This unassuming building houses one of the best restaurants and wine bars in Neuhausen. The staff are happy to suggest excellent wines to pair with a meal.

D5 **Schulstr. 9**
broeding.de

trees. Beyond this is a section illustrating the vegetation of meadows, plains, swamps and sandy and arctic environments.

The very impressive **greenhouses** shelter tropical plants, cacti and fruit trees, unusual orchids and giant water lilies.

Greenhouses

🏠 Menzinger Str. 65
🕐 9am–5pm

↑ The futuristic structure of the BMW headquarters

BMW Museum and BMW Welt

📍 F1 🏠 Olympiapark 2
Ⓤ Olympiazentrum
🕐 Museum: 10am–6pm Tue–Sun

In the early 1970s, the BMW car manufacturing group built a series of ostentatious structures that went some way to rival the architectural development of the neighbouring Olympiapark.

The designer in charge of the concept, Karl Schanzer of Vienna, used the idiom of architectural symbolism. He envisaged the 19-storey office building that dominates the complex as resembling the four cylinders of a car engine. The building, splendidly clad in silver aluminium, has a unique ground plan in the form of a clover leaf. At the foot of the building, and counterbalancing its imposing structure, is what could be described as a shrine – the BMW Museum. Built in concrete and taking the form of a bowl 41 m (135 ft) across, this window-less, silver-painted structure contains exhibits illustrating the history of the factory's production. A spiral ramp connects five platforms where the first cars, including the famous Dixi, are displayed, along with motorbikes, racing cars of the 1950s and 1960s, the modern BMW range and futuristic prototypes. There are also film and slide shows.

Linked to the museum is **BMW Welt (BMW World)**, an ultra-modern showroom containing exhibitions, a café and the Esszimmer gourmet restaurant.

BMW Welt (BMW World)

🏠 Olympiapark 1
🕐 7:30am–midnight Mon–Sat, 9am–midnight Sun 🌐 bmw-welt.com

> ## BAVARIA'S CAR INDUSTRY
>
> Bavaria's automotive industry has been pioneering for decades. Over 200,000 people are employed in the state's car industry, working at some of the world's largest manufacturers. In a bid to ensure the state remains at the forefront of automotive excellence, the government has announced the Automotive Future Forum, which has contributed €2 billion to pioneer new fields and technologies.

←
Sprawling Olympiapark, dominated by its iconic Olympic Tower

↑ Browsing antiques at a shopping alley in Auer Dult

EAT

Bean Batter

Enjoy a decent cup of coffee and tuck into one of the delicious and decadent waffles at this welcoming spot.

📍E7
🏠Schwanthalerstr. 123
🌐bean-batter.de

___

Yuki Sushi & Bowl

This sushi joint offers a wonderful alternative to Bavarian fare - the varied menu is well curated, with good vegetarian options.

📍E8 🏠Kazmairstr. 29
🌐yuki-sushibowl.de

___

Wirtshaus Eder

This small pub serves excellent dumplings, which pair perfectly with a cold glass of local beer.

📍E8 🏠Gollierstr. 83
🌐ederwirt.de

6
Au

📍J9 🏠17 🚌52

Up until the 15th century, the district of Au was part of the floodplain of the Isar river, and it was only after the river was controlled that people started to settle here. Au was incorporated into Munich in 1854. Until the early 20th century, the poorer population of the city lived in Au, and picturesque cottages typical of old Munich can still be seen here today.

Three times a year, for nine days, the heart of Au transforms into Munich's biggest traditional fair for household articles, antiquities and old books. This local event goes back to the 14th century. The Auer Dult starts on the first weekend in May, at St Jacob's Day and in the week after Kermess. In addition to the many stalls with antiquities, books, pottery and every kind of household stuff, there are some nostalgic shooting galleries, merry-go-rounds, food stalls and a beer tent.

The square with the fair is dominated by Maria-Hilf-Kirche, a Neo-Gothic brick church built by Joseph Ohlmüller and Georg Friedrich Ziebland in 1831–39. It was the first

instance of the Gothic Revival in southern Germany.

___

7
Westend

📍D8
Ⓤ Schwanthalerhöhe
🏠18 🚌53

Picturesque Westend, known locally as Schwanthalerhöhe, is located at the western fringe of the city centre, between Theresienwiese (Oktoberfest), Landsberger Straße, Donnersbergerund Hackerbrücke and the railway line to the south. The name originates from the sculptor Ludwig Schwanthaler, creator of the Bavaria figure (p160).

This densely built district is home to Munich's oldest brewery (Augustiner), the former chief customs office, a branch of the KPMG company and several beautiful green public spaces, such as the Bavariapark with its many statues and figures. After the relocation of the Alte Messe in 1998, parts of the Theresienhöhe were innovatively redesigned, including Steidle-Hochhaus and the Bavaria beer garden. Old Art Nouveau exhibition halls house the Verkehrszentrum of the Deutsches Museum. The old congress hall is now used only for events.

Most of the attractive houses, many in Art Nouveau style with bay windows and sgraffito, were built before 1919. There's a large number of cooperative flats, too. Also remarkable is the 1920s Ledigenheim designed by Theodor Fischer and located near Gollierplatz.

The Westend is one of Munich's most multicultural districts, with one third of residents coming from all over the world. The area is also popular with young Germans. The many dining options include Greek, Italian and Croatian restaurants.

INSIDER TIP
A Westend Stroll

When in Westend, take a leisurely stroll down Kazmairstraße. This street has superb cafés and restaurants, as well as the Büchergalerie bookstore, a Westend institution with a great selection of books.

 8

Haidhausen

📍 K8 🚉 Ostbahnhof/Rosenheimer Platz Ⓤ Rosenheimer Platz/Max-Weber-Platz 🚋 15, 16, 19, 25 🚌 63, 100

Haidhausen is a residential district to the east of the city centre. It is bounded by the Isar, the railway line at Ostbahnhof, Prinzregentenstraße and Rosenheimer Straße. The French quarter, built after 1872, stretches from the Orleansplatz around the bustling Wörthstraße, with Bordeauxplatz as its centre line.

Haidhausen was first mentioned as early as 808 and incorporated into Munich after 1854. It was once thought of as a poor district, but today it is one of the most popular parts of Munich. It offers a multitude of shops, cafés, restaurants and charming squares like the Weißenburger Platz with its beautiful fountain or the Wiener Platz with its daily food market. Excellent beer gardens have been opened here by the Hofbräu and Bürgerbräu breweries.

The Maximilianeum, the state parliament of Bavaria, is located in Haidhausen (p106), as is the Müllersches Volksbad (p108) and the Gasteig Cultural Centre. There is much worth seeing and hearing at the Prinzregententheater and at the Villa Stuck (p107).

 9

Deutsches Museum Verkehrszentrum

📍 E8 🏛 Am Bavariapark 5 Ⓤ Schwanthalerhöhe 🕐 9am–5pm daily 🚫 1 Jan, Good Friday, 1 May, 1 Nov, 24, 25 & 31 Dec 🌐 deutsches-museum.de/verkehrszentrum

The historic exhibition halls on Theresienhöhe house the transport section of the Deutsches Museum. This huge collection ranges from the very first motorcar to the ICE-Experimental train and features interactive displays that illustrate the past, present and future of worldwide travel and mobility.

 10

Sendling

📍 C10 Ⓤ Implerstr./Brudermühlstr.

A charming, leafy neighbourhood to the southwest of the city centre, Sendling is home to some buzzing cultural centres. Bahnwärter Thiel is a creative cultural playground made up of old underground carriages which house club nights, street food and flea markets. Close by, the Alte Utting, next to the former meatpacking district, is an old steam boat that sits atop a bridge, home to a cosy bar and delightful Christmas market. The Isarphilharmonie, too, Munich's new philharmonic concert hall, has moved to the neighbourhood, adding more cultural flair.

↑ Cobbled street lined with cottages in the residential district of Haidhausen

↑ Cycling on the track along the Isar canal dam in Grünwald

⑪ Grünwald

 Burg Grünwald, Grünwald Zeillerstr. 3 Ⓢ Rosenheimer Platz, then tram Ⓤ Silberhornstr. 🚌25 🕐 10am-5pm Wed-Sun 🚫 31 Oct-mid-Mar

Grünwald, on the southern outskirts of Munich, is one of the city's most exclusive villa suburbs. This lovely area is commonly nicknamed "Germany's Hollywood" as it has been home to many famous actors and sporting stars, including English footballer Harry Kane. It is also a good starting point for walking and cycling tours.

The district's greatest attraction is Burg Grünwald, a well-preserved medieval castle whose origins go back to the 12th century. In 1270 the building came into the possession of the Wittelsbachs. In the 15th century a gatehouse was constructed: its stepped gable is set with 11 coats of arms, those of Bavaria at the apex and those of Poland and Jerusalem among the others further down. From 1602 to 1857 the castle accommodated a prison and a small gunpowder store. The archaeological collections housed here illustrate the history of the castle and of Roman art in Bavaria. There are lapidariums and frescoes, a kiln and a reconstruction of a Roman kitchen.

Nearby is the popular Walderlebniszentrum Grünwald (Forest Adventure Centre), a great place for families to explore the surrounding woodland. The small centre is home to a herd of wild boars and an excellent network of guided forest trails.

Did You Know?

The incredibly rare mhorr gazelle, which can be seen at the Tierpark, is the national symbol of Niger.

---

⑫ Tierpark Hellabrunn

 Tierparkstr. 30 🕐 Hours vary, check website 🌐 hellabrunn.de

Established in 1911, Tierpark Hellabrunn is one of the most beautiful zoos in the world. It is home to almost 5,000 animals representing 480 species and covers an area of 3.6 sq km (1.38 sq miles). They are housed in enclosures which are specially designed to re-create natural habitats. The enclosures are organized by continent and by the animals' habitat.

The zoo specializes in breeding animals that are under threat of extinction, with a view to maintaining stable populations in human care. Highlights include an elephant house, a bat cave and a mill village, where you can take a closer look at the local flora and fauna.

Asam-Schlössl

🏠 Thalkirchen, Maria-Einsiedel-Str. 45
🚇 Thalkirchen 🚌 135
🌐 asamschloessl.de

In 1724 Cosmas Damian Asam acquired a 17th-century property in the Isar valley. He intended to use it as an out-of-town residence and studio.

With the help of his brother Egid Quirin Asam, Cosmas Damian rebuilt the house that he had bought, converting the second floor into a spacious studio lit by a huge semicircular window. The house was named Maria Einsiedel in honour of the Swiss pilgrimage church that the brothers had decorated. The artist covered the façade of his new home with paintings. He decorated the third floor with a statue of Moses bearing the Ten Commandments, and a painting of the antique sculpture known as The Borghese Fencer. The building now houses a great

← Beautiful exterior of Asam-Schlössl, decorated with religious paintings

↑ A replica of a German U-boat on display at Bavaria-Filmstadt

restaurant serving interesting takes on local food.

Bavaria-Filmstadt

🏠 Geiselgasteig, Bavariafilmplatz 7
🚇 Rosenheimer Platz (some distance away), then tram 🚇 Silberhornstr, Wettersteinplatz (some distance away) 🚌 25
🕐 Apr-Oct: 9am-6pm daily; Nov-Mar: 10am-5pm daily 🌐 filmstadt.de

Commonly known as Hollywood on the Isar, Bavaria-Filmstadt is one of Europe's major film studios.

Set up in 1919, the studios were originally located in the Stachus district. Among the prominent people who have worked here have been famous directors such as Orson Welles and Ingmar Bergman. Every year scores of films for the big screen and television are made at the Filmstadt ("cinema city"), which opened to the public in 1981.

The 90-minute tour of the studios takes visitors on a delightful miniature railway and on foot, through some fascinating film sets. Entering the 57-m- (187-ft-) reconstruction of the U-boat used in the Oscar-winning film *Das Boot* is an unforgettable experience. Another lasting impression is made by the back-drops used in the production of *Asterix and Obelix*, set in the age of the Romans and Gauls.

To celebrate the studio's 100th anniversary in 2019, a new exhibition space opened which looks back at the studio's history. A 4D cinema room showing a selection of "motion rides" is also a fun attraction for the family.

> ### FILMMAKING IN BAVARIA-FILMSTADT
>
> The Bavaria-Filmstadt was involved in the production of many internationally popular movies. The sets of *Das Boot* (1981), based on Lothar Günther's 1973 novel, and the musical *The Magic Flute* (2022) can be seen here. Contemporary German filmmakers have produced several acclaimed classics in recent years, including *Good Bye Lenin* (2003), *Balloon* (2018), *The Baader Meinhof Complex* (2008) and *The Lives of Others* (2006).

15

Theresienwiese

F8 **Theresienwiese**

The events that took place in Munich on 17 October 1810 had far-reaching consequences. This was the day on which the marriage of Therese von Sachsen-Hildburghausen and Ludwig I, the future king, took place. To mark the occasion, horse races, a cattle fair and a folk festival were held in meadows outside the city. The folk celebrations were repeated in following years, and this custom continued to grow and eventually became the Oktoberfest, the largest folk festival in the world. The festival grounds were named Theresienwiese in honour of the bride.

The folk festival is not, however, the only attraction of Theresienwiese. On an elevated ridge with a grand stairway stands the Neo-Classical **Ruhmeshalle**

(Hall of Fame), built by Leo von Klenze in 1848–53. It is an open hall fronted by 48 Ionian columns and containing the busts of 77 prominent Bavarians. In front of the hall stands a gigantic figure of Bavaria as a Germanic goddess carrying a sword and an oak wreath and accompanied by a lion. This unusual work by Leo von Klenze and Ludwig Schwanthaler, which stands 18 m (59 ft) high, was the first monumental cast iron figure to be made – it even predates New York's Statue of Liberty by some 30 years, though the pose is similar. Visitors can view the city from a platform in the figure's head.

Ruhmeshalle
Theresienhöhe 16
Apr–mid-Oct: 9am–6pm daily

→ Bronze statue at Ruhmeshalle, Theresienwiese

16

Neue Messe München

Am Messesee 2
Messestadt-West, Messestadt-Ost
messe-muenchen.de

In 1992 the international airport at Riem was closed and the site, where building work took place from 1995 to 1998, was transformed into a huge exhibition area.

This was the Neue Messe München, which came to stand as an example of modern functional yet elegant architecture. It was designed by Bystrup, Bregenhoj & Partners, architects from Copenhagen, the winners of the international competition that was announced in 1991.

A sequence of 17 halls is arranged along the Atrium, an arterial axis 600 m (1,968 ft) long. The main entrance is

---

OKTOBERFEST

This famous folk festival, the world's largest, began in 1810 when Princess Therese von Sachsen-Hildburghausen married King Ludwig I. Horse races and cattle fairs were organized in a meadow on the edge of Munich, which was named Theresienwiese in honour of the bride. Over time this became a regular event; agricultural shows were hosted alongside equestrian events and shooting contests. The event was expanded with the addition of beer tents and fireworks, giving rise to Oktoberfest. Today, the festival attracts over seven million global visitors.

↑ Blutenburg reflected in the waters of the River Würm

flanked by the multi-functional ICM (International Congress Centre Munich) building. The entire covered area of 200,000 sq m (50 acres) stands in front of a large lake. Major international events that are held in the Neue Messe include an information and telecommunications fair, a fashion show, a crafts show and a mineralogy congress.

 17

Blutenburg

⌂ Blutenburg
Ⓢ Obermenzing (some distance away) 🚌 143, 160 🌐 blutenburg.de

On an artificial island in the River Würm stands Blutenburg, a small hunting lodge. From 1425 the lodge belonged to the Wittelsbachs and its residents included Duke Albrecht III, his son Sigismund, the later Princess Henriette Adelaide, Therese Kunigunde Sobieska and Maximilian I Joseph.

The lodge now houses the **Internationale Jugendbibliothek**. Containing over 500,000 volumes in 110 languages, the library is the largest collection of children's and young people's literature in the world and is under the patronage of UNESCO.

The only original part of the lodge that still stands is

St Sigismund's Chapel (1488), built by the architects of Munich's Frauenkirche. The frescoes on its exterior walls are among the few surviving examples of late Gothic mural painting. The interior of the chapel, covered with intricate rib vaulting, contains some treasures of religious art, including altarpieces of 1491 by Jan Polack and late Gothic sculptures and stained glass.

Internationale Jugendbibliothek

⌂ Blutenburg Ⓒ 2-6pm Mon-Fri 🌐 ijb.de

  18

Allianz Arena

⌂ Werner-Heisenberg-Allee 25 Ⓤ Fröttmaning Ⓒ 10am-6pm daily (except match days) 🌐 allianz-arena.com

Since May 2005 the Allianz Arena has been home to the two Munich football clubs – FC Bayern München and TSV 1860 München. The stadium was designed by the Swiss architects Jacques Herzog and Pierre de Meuron and can now house more than 75,000 visitors. The distinctive exterior consists of 2,760 rhombic air cushions, which can be illuminated in red, blue or white, depending on

whether Bayern (red), TSV (blue) or the German national team (white) are playing. The arena covers 6,000 sq m (64,600 sq ft), has a partial roof that shelters all seats, and includes a fan shop and various catering options.

DRINK

Das Bad

Munich's smallest pub, Das Bad is a former public washhouse that has been converted into a cosy little space. It serves fresh beer and solid Bavarian food.

📍 F8 ⌂ Bavariaring 5 🌐 dasbad089.de

Hotel Mariandl

Close to the Theresienwiese, the Hotel Mariandl is an old *belle époque* hotel famous for its cocktails and brunches. It also hosts great art exhibitions.

📍 G9 ⌂ Goethestr. 51 🌐 mariandl.com

EXPERIENCE
THE BAVARIAN ALPS

Admiring Königssee and the nearby Alps

GETTING TO KNOW
THE BAVARIAN ALPS

Bordered to the north by the mighty Danube and to the south by the verdant Bavarian Alps, southern Bavaria is among Germany's most beautiful and diverse regions. We've broken the region down into six areas to help you get the most out of your Bavarian adventure.

PAGE 168

UPPER BAVARIA (NORTH)

Nature lovers and royal history buffs have plenty to admire in the northern stretches of Upper Bavaria, a region defined by its verdant valleys, vast hop plantations and romantic castles. A particular highlight is the Baroque Neues Schloss at Schleißheim, one of many examples of Bavaria's ostentatious royal structures. Equally interesting is the town of Freising, with its cathedral and its museums containing fine collections of religious art.

Best for
Scenic valley walks

Home to
Eichstätt, Ingolstadt, Neuburg an der Donau, Schleißheim Palace

Experience
A stroll around the beautiful streets and squares of Neuburg an der Donau

LOWER BAVARIA

Religious architecture and stunning landscapes combine to beautiful effect in Lower Bavaria. Many visitors begin their exploration in the region's capital, Landshut. Every four years tourists come for the Landshut Wedding, a great historical spectacle held at the foot of Trausnitz Castle. Away from the capital, Passau, at the confluence of the Danube, Inn and Ilz rivers, is especially picturesque, with beautiful trails and cycle routes leading into the region's green wilderness. Lovers of architecture can follow the "Asam Trail", taking in the region's best churches.

Best for
Ornate churches

Home to
Landshut, Straubing, Passsau, Bayerischer Wald

Experience
A ride along the Danube Cycle Path from Passau

UPPER BAVARIA (EAST)

Lying between the rivers Inn and Salzach, this region draws crowds for its breathtaking beauty and plethora of historic churches and castles. The little churches of Maria Gern and St Bartholomä have a delightful charm, while Burghausen boasts the world's longest castle. The town of Rosenheim on the river Inn could be regarded as the capital of eastern Upper Bavaria; it becomes especially busy in late summer, when the town's folk festival takes place – imagine a more intimate version of Oktoberfest.

Best for
Enjoying intimate folk festivals

Home to
Altötting, Burghausen

Experience
A boat trip across Königssee

$\rightarrow$

PAGE 234

UPPER BAVARIA (SOUTH)

Upper Bavaria's southern region is defined by its snow-capped mountains, glittering lakes and rolling farmland. Many come here for outdoor excursions; in the winter, Garmisch-Partenkirchen is a haven for skiers and snowboarders, while Starnberger See and Ammersee offer great water sports. Away from the water, Landsberg am Lech, the largest town in the region, is home to winding streets, cobbled alleys and pretty squares. Traditional festivals and holidays are celebrated across the region, making for a perfect rural break.

Best for
Skiing and snowboarding

Home to
Landsberg am Lech

Experience
The cable car to the summit of the Zugspitze, Germany's tallest mountain

PAGE 256

THE ALLGÄU

The Allgäu is one of the least industrialized regions of Bavaria. Its capital is Kempten, a beautiful town with a history stretching back to the Romans. The town of Memmingen also has many historic monuments, but visitors to the region typically head beyond the towns. Most are here to admire the iconic fairytale castles of Hohenschwangau and Neuschwanstein, at the foot of the Alps; both are reached by the Romantische Straße (Romantic Road). Equally splendid are the Renaissance castles of the wealthy Fugger family in Babenhausen and Kirchheim, and the lovely Ottobeuren Abbey.

Best for
Swooning over castles

Home to
Memmingen, Lindau, Kempten, Schloss Neuschwanstein

Experience
A drive along the Romantische Straße

NORTHERN SWABIA

Northern Swabia, historically under separate governance from the rest of Bavaria, is today among the most diverse regions of southern Bavaria, both in its landscapes and its cultures. Each valley has its own crops and pastures; each town its own architectural style. The main city is Augsburg, the third largest city in Bavaria after Munich and Nuremberg. Within easy reach to the north are the Ries Basin, a huge crater nestling the town of Nördlingen, and the impressive Harburg Castle, as well as historic towns such as Donauwörth and Dillingen.

Best for
Historic towns

Home to
Nördlingen, Augsburg

Experience
The Fuggerei of Augsburg, one of the world's oldest social housing projects

UPPER BAVARIA (NORTH)

During the Jurassic period, a lagoon existed at the northern edges of Upper Bavaria. This became what is today the valley of the meandering River Altmühl – Jurassic fossils unearthed here testify to the abundance of prehistoric fauna in the region. Northern Upper Bavaria has been marked for centuries by its fertility, with its rolling green expanse used primarily as farmland. Extensive asparagus plantations stretch out around Schrobenhausen, while in the area known as Hallertau, vast forest-like plantations indicate the large-scale production of beer hops.

From the 17th century, the landscapes of Upper Bavaria were used as a backdrop to the architectural ambitions of religious and political rulers. The imposing outlines of castles tower over towns such as Beilngries, Eichstätt, Ingolstadt and Neuburg. There is also a wealth of ecclesiastical buildings, the most prominent being the grand churches and abbeys at Scheyern, Indersdorf and Fürstenfeldbruck. In the 20th century, the charming town of Dachau became synonymous with one of the earliest concentration camps to be set up in Germany. The camp is still surrounded by barbed wire and functions as a sobering museum.

Though the region is not quite as varied as the land to the south, the north today attracts plenty of visitors for its distinctively Bavarian landscapes and grand royal history.

LOWER BAVARIA p191

UPPER BAVARIA (NORTH)

Must Sees
1 Eichstätt
2 Ingolstadt
3 Neuburg an der Donau
4 Schleißheim Palace

Experience More
5 Beilngries
6 Pfaffenhofen
7 Freising
8 Scheyern
9 Fürstenfeldbruck
10 Erding
11 Sankt Wolfgang
12 Oberschleißheim
13 Dachau
14 Kloster Indersdorf

UPPER BAVARIA (EAST) p216

↑ Traditional Baroque buildings lining the Marktplatz

1

EICHSTÄTT

C2 🏠110 km (68 miles) N of Munich city centre
🚉🚌Bahnhofplatz 17 ℹ️ Domplatz 8; eichstaett.de

Eichstätt is among the prettiest towns in Bavaria, nestled in the scenic valley of the River Altmühl. The town has been a centre of religious life in the region since 741, and the influence of Catholicism remains strong, with a small Catholic university and numerous ornate churches. The town makes for a wonderful base for exploring the wild trails and rolling hills of the wider Altmühl valley.

①

Marktplatz

Marktplatz, north of the cathedral, is the focal point of the burghers' district, and is surrounded by the houses of prominent merchants; these magnificent abodes alternate with modest crafters' houses. On the west side of the square stands the town hall, whose tower dates from 1444. The façade and upper part of the tower were built in 1823–4.

Eichstätt's other squares – Residenzplatz, Domplatz and Leonrodplatz – were also key elements in the urban planning of the town. Residenzplatz is one of the finest squares in the whole of Germany. It lies south of the cathedral and has a trapezoid shape.

The two-storey buildings that line the square were originally part of the chapterhouses that were designed by Gabriel de Gabrieli.

Domplatz, with the cathedral on its southern side, is laid out on the site of the former cemetery.

On Leonrodplatz stands the church and former Jesuit abbey, as well as the former cathedral deaconry.

---

②

Dom St Salvator und St Willibald

Domplatz

Eichstätt's cathedral is a key monument in Bavaria, which dates from the medieval era. It features a late-Gothic nave and presbytery. The latter is flanked by twin Romanesque towers, which feature a collection of 18

> Marktplatz, north of the cathedral, is the focal point of the burghers' district, and is surrounded by the houses of prominent merchants.

bells. The Baroque façade was added by Gabriel de Gabrieli in 1716–18.

The Gothic cloisters on the south side of the cathedral adjoin the presbytery. The west wing of the cloisters contains a double-naved moratorium containing the Gothic tombs of priests, chaplains and benefactors of the cathedral. Distinctive among the many works of art to be seen in the cathedral is the statue of St Willibald, who became the first bishop of Eichstätt in the 8th century. The statue, carved in the late Gothic style, was made in 1514 by Loy Hering. In 1745 Matthias Seybold built the two-sided Pappenheimer altar with a canopy to cover the statue of the saint and the tomb containing his relics. This altar is located on the elevated part at the west end of the cathedral.

↑ Rococo staircase at the Fürstbischöfliche Residenz

③
Schutzengelkirche

⌂ Ostenstr.

This former Jesuit church was built in 1617–20 under the direction of Hans Alberthal. Having suffered destruction in 1634, in the course of the Thirty Years' War, it was rebuilt in 1660. The interior was lavishly decorated by Franz Gabriel and Johann Rosner, among others, in the first half of the 18th century. To the south of the church are the buildings of the former Jesuit College, dating from the 17th and 18th centuries, with two courtyards and cloisters. The college is now used as a seminary.

④
Fürstbischöfliche Residenz

⌂ Residenzplatz 1
☏ (08421) 6001
🕘 8am–noon Mon–Wed & Fri, 2–4pm Thu

The former bishop's residence was built in 1700–27 around a central courtyard. The building, with its large Baroque three-wing complex, adjoins the cathedral on its southern side. The interior has decorative stuccowork and Rococo frescoes. It also features a fine Rococo staircase and Hall of Mirrors. The Residenz houses the district administration.

JÖRG MAGER

Born in Eichstätt, music theorist Jörg Mager was a pioneer of electronic music. He worked as a school teacher to fund his research into electronic music, inventing a handful of instruments in his lifetime. After he took part in the 1918 failed Communist coup in Bavaria, he left for Berlin to develop his theories further.

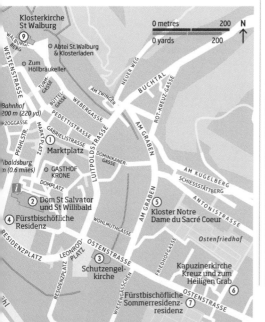

EAT

Zum Höllbräukeller

This friendly pub serves delicious *Kaiserschmarrn* (Bavarian fluffy pancakes), steaks, homemade lamb sausages and potato dumplings. It also offers exceptional desserts like apple strudel and tiramisu. Book ahead.

⌂ Pedettistr. 38
◷ Mon & Tue
w zumhoellbraeukeller.de

€€€

Gasthof Krone

Set in the heart of Eichstätt, this popular traditional inn serves hearty Bavarian favourites. It offers a separate kids' menu and one for group travellers, too. You can bring your own reusable containers to take dishes away; inform the restaurant in advance.

⌂ Domplatz 3
w krone-eichstaett.de

€€€

SHOP

Abtei St Walburg

The St Walburg Abbey and Klosterladen has a lovely little gift shop, selling herbal liqueur made in the abbey grounds, homemade jams and preserves, and lavender-filled cushions.

⌂ Walburgiberg 6
w abtei-st-walburg.de

---

⑤

Kloster Notre Dame du Sacré Coeur

⌂ Notre Dame 1 **◷** Apr-Oct: 9am-5pm daily (to 5pm Sat & Sun); Nov-Mar: 9am-noon Mon-Fri (also 2-4pm Mon-Thu) **ℹ** Informationszentrum Naturpark Altmühltal; (08421) 98 760

This convent was built for a foundation established in 1711 for the education of young girls. Work on the convent began in 1712, and on the church in 1719, both to designs by the architect Gabriel de Gabrieli.

The façade is divided by huge pilasters and decorated with a sculpture of the Immaculate Conception above the portal. The headquarters of the information centre for Altmühl Valley National Park are housed in the church.

---

⑥

Kapuzinerkirche Kreuz und zum Heiligen Grab

⌂ Kapuzinergasse 2 **☎** (08421) 6001 400 **◷** Daily during daylight

This modest church of the Capuchin monks was built in 1623–5 and enlarged in 1905. To the south of the nave stands an oval stone-built Romanesque rotunda crowned by an open gallery and a dome supported on tall, slender columns. It was built in 1160 in imitation of the Church of the Holy Sepulchre in Jerusalem.

---

⑦

Fürstbischöfliche Sommerresidenz

⌂ Ostenstr. 24

The former bishop's 18th-century summer residence was designed by Gabriel de Gabrieli. The ground and upper floors and narrow side galleries now house the offices of the Catholic university. The residence is set in geometrically laid out parkland that merges into a landscaped park descending in terraces to the River Altmühl.

---

⑧

Willibaldsburg

⌂ Burgstr. 19 **w** Jura-Museum: jura-museum.de; Museum für Ur- und Frühgeschichte: histver.de/museum

This castle, on a hill northwest of the town centre, overlooks

Did You Know?

Willibaldsburg's garden is inspired by *Hortus Eystettensis,* a classic 17th-century botanical guide.

the Altmühl river valley. It can be reached by car through a 63-m- (206-ft-) long tunnel. The castle is surrounded by 17th-century fortifications. From 1353 to 1725 it was the seat of bishops but was partly demolished in the 19th century. The present approaches to the castle were built in the first half of the 17th century. The castle walls contain the ruins of a residence built for Bishop Martin von Schaumberg.

The western section of the hill is occupied by a three-winged building with central cloisters, and a main building with small towers. Both were built by architect Elias Holl. Together with Augsburg town hall, they are regarded as Germany's most important late Renaissance buildings.

The north wing houses the Jura-Museum, with a collection of fossils from the Jurassic period. The south wing contains the Museum für Ur- und Frühgeschichte (Museum of Prehistory and Early History), with fascinating displays.

FOSSILS FROM THE JURASSIC ERA

About 150 million years ago, the region of the Altmühl river valley in northern Upper Bavaria and southern Franconia lay beneath a shallow lagoon that was separated from the open Jurassic sea by a reef of corals and sponges. Today, collectors search quarries for fossils of ammonites, small crustaceans, insects and marine plants. A rich collection of fossils is on view in the Jura-Museum.

⑨

Klosterkirche St Walburg

 Westenstr.

This church was built on the spot where the relics of St Walburg were buried in 875. The present monastery dates from 1629–31. In the chapel behind the high altar is St Walburg's tomb, the church's most holy feature and the object of pilgrimages. The chapel, which contains numerous votive images placed there in gratitude to the saint, is decorated with intricate wrought-iron grilles. The altarpiece consists of Gothic carvings depicting St Walburg, his parents and his brother, St Willibald.

↑ Klosterkirche St Walburg overlooking the tranquil River Altmühl

2

INGOLSTADT

⬛D3 🏛Moritzstr. 19 🌐ingolstadt-tourismus.de

The small city of Ingolstadt is where Ludwig the Rich founded Bavaria's first university in 1472. Today, the city is known principally for the Audi cars manufactured here, but Ingolstadt is also home to a charming array of gabled houses, ancient city gates, imposing towers and an impressive fortress.

①

Asamkirche Maria de Victoria

🏛Neubaustr.
🕐 Mar-Oct: 9am-noon & 1-5pm Tue-Sun (May-Oct: daily); Nov-Feb: 1-4pm Tue-Sun

This hall was built in 1732–6 as the meeting place of the Marian students'

association. The stuccowork is by Egid Quirin Asam, and the painting by his brother Cosmas Damian Asam, who exploited the various points of perspective as he covered the ceiling with extensive frescoes. The sacristy contains a famous monstrance of 1708 by the Augsburg goldsmith Johannes Zeckl, depicting the defeat of the Turks at the Battle of Lepanto in 1571.

②

Kreuztor and City Walls

The city walls, together with their semicircular towers,

were built from 1362 to 1440. Of the four original city gates, only the western one, known as the Kreuztor, survives. It is considered to be one of the finest of its kind in Germany.

The Taschenturm, a tower with stepped gables, also survives. Of the fortification towers, built from 1539 to 1579 and demolished in 1800,

---

DRINK

Das "Mo" Neue Galerie

This Bavarian bar and restaurant, located close to the beautiful Kreuztor city gate, has good food and an even better beer garden. It is advisable to make a reservation if you're visiting at the weekend.

🏛Bergbräustr. 7
🌐dasmo.de

Rosengasse 2

A rustic hangout serving good beers and a selection of cocktails. Live music on some weekends.

🏛Große Rosengasse 2
📞(0841) 9017 643

↑ Charming town of Ingolstadt straddling the Danube

only the ruins of casemates and bastions still stand today. Fortifications begun in 1823 are dotted around the town.

---

③

Alte Anatomie

◎ Anatomiestr. 18/20
◎ Deutsches Medizinhistorisches Museum: 10am–5pm Tue-Sun ⓦ dmm-ingolstadt.de

This fine Baroque building, completed in 1723, originally housed the university's Department of Medicine and is now home to a museum of medical history. The pleasant courtyard has a garden where medicinal herbs are grown.

---

④

Museum Mobile

◎ Audi Forum Ingolstadt, Ettinger Str. 60 ⓒ 10am–5pm Mon-Fri, 10am–4pm Sat & Sun ⓦ audi-media center.com

With its "Museum Mobile", the Audi Forum is a delight

for car enthusiasts. The museum opened its doors in 2000. More than 80 Audi cars, motorbikes and bicycles are on display and the history of the automobile is documented in fascinating detail.

---

⑤

Museum für Konkrete Kunst

◎ Tränktorstr. 6-8
ⓒ 10am–5pm Tue-Sun ⓒ 1 Jan, Shrove Tue, Good Friday, 1 Nov, 24-25 Dec, 31 Dec
ⓦ mkk-ingolstadt.de

Opened to the public in 1992, the Museum für

Konkrete Kunst was inspired by Dutch artist Theo van Doesburg's Concrete Art movement from the 20th century. The movement sought to prioritize abstract expression over objective depictions of reality. Set in the former Danube Barracks, this is the first and only museum in Germany dedicated exclusively to the form. Its airy galleries, spread across three floors, feature exhibits from the private collection of acclaimed German Concrete poet Eugen Gomringer; the museum also hosts workshops for children and a number of temporary exhibits. It is scheduled to move to the foundry hall in Ingolstadt in late 2025.

ORIGINS OF AUDI

In 1909, automobile engineer August Horch established the August Horch Automobilwerke GmbH in Zwickau. The name Audi is based on a Latin translation of Horch's surname. In 1932, Audi merged with Horch, DKW and Wanderer, to form the Auto Union AG. The iconic four interlocking rings of the brand symbolized the merger of the brands. The company has had its headquarters in Ingolstadt for over 70 years.

Intricately carved cannons at the Neues Schloss ↑

⑥
Neues Schloss

🏠 Paradeplatz 4
Bayerisches Armee-
museum 🕐 9am–5:30pm
Tue–Sun (from 10am Sat &
Sun) 🌐 armeemuseum.de

The Neues Schloss (New Castle) was built in the first half of the 15th century. Set with corner towers, the two-storey castle appears to be an impregnable stronghold. A Renaissance gateway leads into an inner courtyard. The castle houses the Bavarian Army Museum, displaying items from the wars against the Turks.

⑦
Altes Rathaus

🏠 Rathausplatz 2

The origins of a civi building in this spot date back to the 14th century, though Ingolstadt's town hall was lavishly remodelled in the Neo-Renaissance style by German architect Gabriel von Seidl in 1882–3. Its decoration was designed by Lorenz Gedon. The building incorporates a former residence.

⑧
Herzogskasten

🏠 Hallstr. 4

This ancient castle, standing on the southeastern corner of the city walls, was built in 1255. The oldest secular building in Ingolstadt, it was a ducal residence until it got superseded by the Neues Schloss, which was built in the 15th century. It was then converted into a granary. Rising two storeys high, it has a very tall roof with a Gothic stepped gable. It now houses a library.

⑨
Moritzkirche

🏠 Hieronymus Str. 3

Begun in the mid-14th century and completed in 1489, this

Did You Know?

On 1 May 1776, the secret society of the Bavarian Illuminati was founded in Ingolstadt.

church is dedicated to St Maurice. It has a Gothic basilica with a 14th–15th-century watchtower known as the Pfeifturm.

The hospital nearby, completed in 1434, served as the main university building from 1472 to 1800.

⑩
Liebfrauenmünster

🏠 Bergbräustr./
Kreuzstr. 1

This great 15th-century church with diagonally set twin towers is one of the largest Gothic brick buildings in Bavaria. The church was built on the site of an already existing wooden church. Construction began in 1425, with funding provided by Duke Ludwig VII. The Duke planned for this to be his burial church, but he did not see its completion. The construction was finally completed in 1525, a hundred years after work had begun.

The high altar, completed in 1572, commemorates the centenary of the foundation of Ingolstadt's university. The altar, 9 m (30 ft) high,

incorporates 91 paintings by Hans Mielich. Other features of the interior are the Renaissance stalls and pulpit, the Gothic and Renaissance stained glass, and the monument to Johannes Eck, Martin Luther's greatest opponent, who died in 1543.

Klenzepark

 Brückenkopf 4

South of the Old Town and just across the Danube (accessible via footbridge), the Klenzepark housed the former Ingolstadt state fortress. It was also the site

of the 1992 State Garden Show and remains an important green oasis in Ingolstadt today. The park has something for everyone: in the warmer summer months, it gets around 100,000 visitors in a month. The rose garden is a delightful spot for a stroll, and the park's adventure playground and fountains are a hit with children. Events often take place in the park: at the start of the summer holidays (the end of July in Bavaria), the TUMULTimKLENZE festival provides youngsters with live music, arts and crafts and a graffiti wall to decorate and free concerts take place regularly. German architect Leo von Klenze (after whom the park is named) designed the park's centrepiece, Turm Trivia, a striking, classical fortress that now houses the Bavarian Police Museum.

Glorious high-lofted vaulting of the Liebfrauenmünster, and *(inset)* the church's distinctive Gothic towers

EAT

Hamburgerei Ingolstadt
This hip all-day burger restaurant serves up a delicious menu of mouthwatering meat and vegetarian burgers, with beers to wash it down.

Theresienstr. 11
hamburgerei.de

€€€

Weissbräuhaus zum Herrnbräu
Run by a German-Scottish couple, this traditional restaurant has existed since 1894. The time-honoured menu is consistently excellent; try the superb schnitzel.

Dollstr. 3
weissbraeuhausin.de

€€€

❸

NEUBURG AN DER DONAU

🗺C3 🅿 🛈 Ottheinrichplatz A118; neuburg-donau.de

Situated on the River Danube (Donau), Neuburg is a picturesque historic town that has been continuously inhabited since the Bronze Age. The town flourished in the 16th century, when the Wittelsbach family turned the town's historic castle into an ornate Renaissance palace. Neuburg is now renowned for its narrow, winding streets and its architecturally varied churches, as well as for the lush lowland forest and rolling hills which surround it. Its tranquil setting makes Neuburg a perfect base for exploring wider Upper Bavaria.

①

Karlsplatz

There are few town squares in Bavaria more charming than Karlsplatz. Surrounded by trees, it has a Mariensäule (Column of the Virgin) and a fountain in the centre. The square is dominated by the façade of the Hofkirche, which occupies its entire eastern side. The square has exquisite proportions and fine, elegant buildings. On the northern side of the square stands the Renaissance town hall of 1603–09. Its double exterior stairway leads to the grand entrance on the first floor. Beside it stands the Taxishaus (named after the von Thurn und Taxis family). It was completed in 1747 and its façade is decorated with elaborate polychrome stuccowork. Further on is the Zieglerhaus, with fine wrought-iron grilles and an elegant gate. On the west side of the square is the pleasantly proportioned and decorated Lorihaus and the library building, its Rococo façade facing onto Amalienstraße. Built in 1731–2, it was furnished in 1802 with furniture from the Kaisheim monastery library.

②

Oberes Tor and Town Walls

In the 14th century Obere Stadt was enclosed by walls, towers and galleries. Considerable vestiges of the upper

---

Did You Know?

Karlsplatz was officially named after the 18th-century Elector of Bavaria, Karl Theodor.

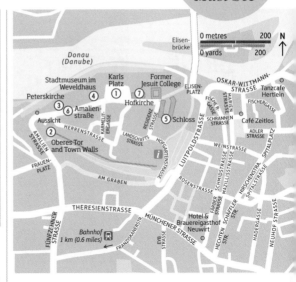

THE DANUBE

The Danube is Europe's second-longest river. It starts from the confluence of the Breg and Brigach rivers in the Black Forest and flows into the Black Sea, 2,850 km (1,770 miles) away. It has been an important waterway throughout history – the Greeks sailed it, Alexander the Great advanced along it and the nomadic Avars used it as a border.

town remain, notably Oberes Tor, the main gate. It was rebuilt in 1530, when it was flanked by towers and topped with a Renaissance gable.

③
Peterskirche

◪ Amalienstr. 40

The church stands on the site of the oldest church in

Neuburg, first mentioned in 1214. It was designed by Johann Serro of Graubünden and built in 1641–6. The triple-nave open interior is decorated with Baroque painting and stuccowork.

④
Stadtmuseum im Weveldhaus

◪ Amalienstr. A47
◷ Mar–Dec: 10am–6pm Tue–Sun ◷ Jan–Feb

The two-storey late Gothic Weveldhaus was built in the 16th century, and was redecorated in 1715 by Gabriel de Gabrieli, who added a fine Baroque portal. The building houses a museum that contains many artifacts relating to the history of the town and the surrounding area. Visitors can also explore the interesting items on sale at the museum shop on the ground floor.

←

Karlsplatz, with charming buildings and the Mariensäule in the centre

DRINK

Hotel & Brauereigasthof Neuwirt

Carefully renovated, this homely hotel and bar is famous for its hearty Bavarian dishes and great local beer.

⌂ Färberstr. 88
🌐 neuwirt-neuburg.de

Tanzcafe Hertlein

Enjoy great views from the terrace of this lovely bar, which offers a selection of good local beers. Visitors can also relax in the beer garden.

⌂ Oskar-Wittmann-Str. 14 🌐 tanzcafe-hertlein.de

Café Zeitlos

This popular drinking spot with terrace seating commands excellent castle views. Try the coffee and tea specialities with a delicious cake or tart on the side.

⌂ Schrannenpl. 45
🌐 zeitlos-neuburg.de

Schloss Neuburg

⌂ Residenzstr. 2
📞 (08431) 64430
🕐 10am–5pm Tue–Sun

The history of the Neuburg Castle stretches back to Roman times, when the fort of Venaxamodorum stood here. It has been in the possession of the Wittelsbach family since the 13th century. The present-day castle, built

Picturesque view of Schloss Neuburg across the River Danube ↑

in 1530–45, was redecorated in the Renaissance style in 1667–70.

The residential and state rooms of the castle are home to an impressive display of artifacts that offer a fascinating insight into Bavarian history, with over 550 works of art and craft spanning portraits, tapestries, furniture and weapons.

The west wing of the castle features one of the most recent galleries of the Bayerische Staatsgemälde-sammlungen (Bavarian State Painting Collection): the State Gallery of Flemish Art. Here you can see a selection of masterworks that define the Flemish Baroque, including works by Peter Paul Rubens, Anthony van Dyck and Jan Brueghel.

There's also a Renaissance chapel here with galleries and ceiling frescoes painted by Hans Bockberger in 1543. These were plastered over

> **The west wing of the castle features one of the most recent galleries of the Bayerische Staats-gemäldesammlungen (Bavarian State Painting Collection).**

in 1616, when Protestant fervour celebrated its triumph over Catholicism, but they were uncovered again in 1934–51. The attractive Renaissance courtyard is surrounded by a double tiered gallery. The west side of the courtyard has sgraffito decorations and two stone figures of dukes, probably dating from the second half of the 17th century. An underground passage beneath Neuer Bau, the north wing, leads from the Danube to Obere Stadt. The Baroque grottoes are open to visitors.

⑥ Amalienstraße

Of the many fine gabled houses that line this street, two are especially worthy of note. One is the Eybhaus, the old post office, built in 1720 and located next to Weveldhaus, and the other the Court Pharmacy, first mentioned in 1713. Both have ornamental gables. Equally elegant are the 17th- and 18th-century houses that can be seen in Herrenstraße.

> 💬 INSIDER TIP
> **Neuburg's Medieval Festival**
>
> Every two years at the end of June, Neuburg an der Donau celebrates a lavish medieval festival. There are jousting tournaments for knights, parades and musical performances.

⑦ Hofkirche

🏠 **Karlsplatz 10**

The former Hofkirche (Court Church) was founded by the Protestant rulers of Neuburg in reaction to the building of the Jesuit Michaelskirche in Munich. Work began in 1608 but was interrupted by the death of Philip Ludwig. In 1617 his Catholic successor brought the Jesuits to Neuburg and donated the church to them. It was completed in 1627 and was the preferred church of the royal family and the college church of the Jesuits. The late Renaissance building, with a flat façade and a central octagonal domed tower, was decorated with fine stuccowork in 1616–18. The beautiful paintings by Peter Paul Rubens that once graced the altar are now in the Alte Pinakothek in Munich.

Some particularly interesting features of the presbytery are the ducal loggia and the stairway to the crypt, the dukes' final resting place. A passage connects the church to the neighbouring castle.

↑ Ornately carved pulpit and altarpiece in the Hofkirche

4 🏛 🍴 🖥

SCHLEISSHEIM PALACE

📍D4 🏛Oberschleißheim ⏰Apr-Sep: 9am-6pm Tue-Sun; Oct-Mar: 10am-4pm Tue-Sun 🌐schloesser-schleissheim.de

Situated within a grand Baroque park, the Schleißheim complex is home to three palaces – Altes Schloss, Schloss Lustheim and the Neues Schloss – constructed on the site of a humble manor house in the 18th century. The complex, which became one of the Wittelsbachs' summer residences, is an ornate highlight of the German Baroque.

Originally intended to rival the splendour of Versailles, the palace at Schleißheim was the architectural setting for the imperial ambitions of Maximilian Emanuel. Work started in 1701, led by architect Enrico Zucalli. It was then interrupted, but restarted in 1717 under the direction of Joseph Effner, who deviated from

the original plans. The 330-m (1,082-ft) long Neues Schloss has a lavish interior, which was decorated by artists Cosmas Damian Asam and Johann Baptist Zimmermann. Today, as well as admiring the elaborate interior decoration, visitors can see the palace's outstanding gallery of Baroque painting.

Did You Know?

Almost the entire roof and several rooms of the Altes Schloss were destroyed during World War II.

In the late 16th century Wilhelm V built himself Altes Schloss. Heinrich Schön the Elder remodelled it in 1616–23, with mouldings and paintings by Peter Candid. It was rebuilt after World War II.

The doors leading into the vestibule were carved by Ignaz Günther in 1736 and are counted among his masterpieces.

A gateway with a clock tower built in about 1600 leads into the courtyard in front of the Altes Schloss.

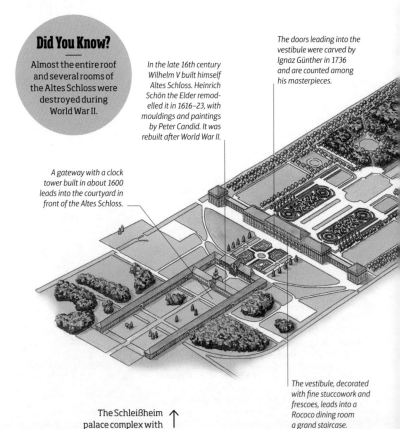

The vestibule, decorated with fine stuccowork and frescoes, leads into a Rococo dining room a grand staircase.

The Schleißheim palace complex with its three palaces ↑

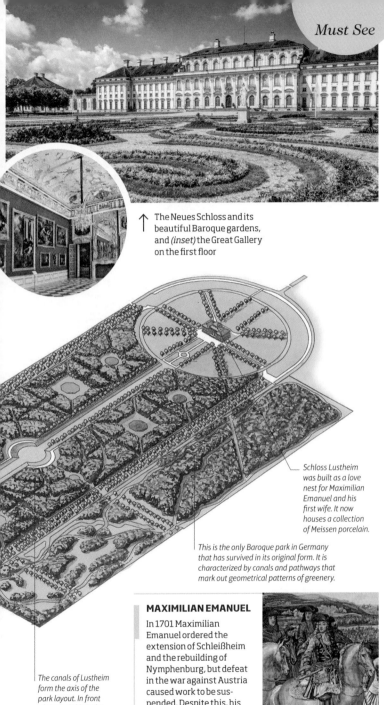

↑ The Neues Schloss and its beautiful Baroque gardens, and *(inset)* the Great Gallery on the first floor

Schloss Lustheim was built as a love nest for Maximilian Emanuel and his first wife. It now houses a collection of Meissen porcelain.

This is the only Baroque park in Germany that has survived in its original form. It is characterized by canals and pathways that mark out geometrical patterns of greenery.

The canals of Lustheim form the axis of the park layout. In front of Neues Schloss the water flows into a basin with a tall cascade and fountains.

MAXIMILIAN EMANUEL

In 1701 Maximilian Emanuel ordered the extension of Schleißheim and the rebuilding of Nymphenburg, but defeat in the war against Austria caused work to be suspended. Despite this, his patronage brought Bavaria into the mainstream of the high Baroque, giving the Wittelsbach family a name for splendour and prestige.

Historic buildings lining a street in Beilngries

EXPERIENCE MORE

5

Beilngries

 D2 🚍🚃 *i* Hauptstr. 14; beilngries.de

The best way to reach Beilngries is by road or boat from Kelheim along the scenic Altmühl valley. The town still has a section of its defensive walls, which are set with nine towers and reinforced by a *fosse* (moat). Among the buildings on Hauptstraße is the late 16th-century house at No. 25, known as the Kaiserbeckhaus, which has a cantilevered upper storey supported on corbels.

The imposing Neo-Baroque Pfarrkirche St Walburga was built in 1912–13 to a design by Wilhelm Spannagl. The span of its vaulting and its circular windows are impressive.

On a hill outside the town once stood a medieval castle, vestiges of which are two tall Romanesque towers flanking the gatehouse. In 1760–64 the castle was converted into the Bishop's hunting lodge. Its main motifs are deer, which led to its being called Schloss Hirschberg ("Deer Mountain"). The Imperial Hall and the Knights' Hall are decorated with paintings by Michael Franz and have Rococo stuccowork. The palace chapel, built with

material from the walls of the Romanesque castle chapel, was designed by Alexander von Branca in the 1980s.

6

Pfaffenhofen

 D3 🚍🚃 *i* Hauptplatz 47; pfaffenhofen.de

The town, situated on the River Ilm, lies at the western end of the hop-growing region. It was once surrounded by fortifications set with 17 towers and pierced by four gates. Around the square stands the Gothic St Johannes-Baptist-Kirche and a Neo-Gothic town hall. The Mesnerhaus, a house dating from 1786, contains a **museum** with a sizeable collection of art dating from the 16th to the 19th centuries.

Museum im Mesnerhaus

🏠 Scheyrer Str. 5 🕐 Only by prior arrangement

7

Freising

 D3 🚍🚃🚏 *i* Rindermarkt 20; freising.de

The seat of a bishopric from 720, the town was for centuries the residence of the bishops of Freising and Munich. The hill on

which the cathedral stands is known as Mons Doctus (Learned Mount). The cathedral dates from the mid-13th century, with the cloisters added in the 15th century. It was remodelled in 1723–4 with the involvement of the Asam brothers *(p63)*.

An outstanding feature of the interior is a Pietà of 1492 by Erasmus Grasser and Gothic stalls dating from 1485–8. The Romanesque crypt contains an elaborately carved column known as the Bestiensäule. Beside the crypt is the Maximilianskapelle, with stuccowork and paintings by Hans Georg Asam.

The late Gothic cloisters feature paintings by Johann Baptist Zimmermann of 1717 and tombstones dating from the 15th to the 18th centuries. The cloisters are linked to the Gothic Benediktuskirche of 1345, and a cathedral library designed by François Cuvilliés.

The Gothic Johanniskirche, in front of the cathedral, is linked to the bishop's residence, which has fine Renaissance cloisters. On the hill is the **Diözesanmuseum**, Germany's largest museum of religious art.

In the town at the bottom of the hill are the church of St Peter und Paul, designed in the early 18th century by Giovanni Antonio Viscardi, with paintings by Johann Baptist Zimmermann, and the late Gothic St-Georg-Kirche,

---

 INSIDER TIP
Brewery Tours

You can book a tour of the Weihenstephan brewery in the cloisters of Freising (*www. weihen-stephaner. de/en*). Tours must be booked in advance.

---

as well as the Neo-Renaissance town hall of 1904–5.

On Weihenstephan hill stands the world's oldest brewery, founded in 1040. The Benedictine monastery now houses departments of Munich's Technical University.

Diözesanmuseum

🅐 Domberg 21 🕐 Hours vary, check website 🆆 dimu-freising.de

---

⑧ Scheyern

🅐 D3 🚌🚆 Pfaffenhofen 🛈 Ludwigstr. 2; (08441) 80 640

In 1119, when the seat of the Scheyern family was converted into a monastery, it was occupied by monks of the Benedictine order. After the dissolution of the monasteries,

the Benedictines left but returned in 1837 at the request of Ludwig I.

The triple-nave basilica of Mariä Himmelfahrt was remodelled in the Baroque style in 1768–9, with mouldings by the Wessobrunn stuccoists. The Chapel of the Holy Cross contains a late Renaissance crucifix of 1600.

---

⑨ Fürstenfeldbruck

🅐 C4 🚇🚆 🛈 Hauptstr. 31; fuerstenfeldbruck.de

The most important building in the town is the former Cistercian abbey, situated on the way to Augsburg and built in 1263–90. In 1691–1754, after it was remodelled by Giovanni Antonio Viscardi, it became one of the largest Baroque abbeys in Bavaria.

The façade of Klosterkirche Mariä Himmelfahrt conceals a stuccowork interior by Pietro Francesco Appiani, with

Benedictine monastery in Scheyern and *(inset)* the high-vaulted nave ↓ of its abbey

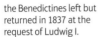

EAT

Klosterstüberl, Fürstenfeldbruck
This spot serves a fantastic *Zwiebelrost-braten* - roast beef with crispy fried onions. Don't miss the creamy pastry puffs (*windbeutel*).

🅐 C4 🛈 Fürstenfeld 7C, Fürstenfeldbruck 🆆 klosterstueberl.de

€€€

vaulting painted by Cosmas Damian Asam and a high altar of 1760–62 designed by his brother Egid Quirin Asam.

The monastery now houses a police college and museum. Many historic townhouses line the main street. The old town hall, refurbished in 1866–8, features paintings dating from 1900.

On St Lucy's Day, in memory of the flood of 1725, children float model houses illuminated with candles across the Amper.

↑ Erding's Landshuter Tor, crowned by a Baroque dome

Erding

⚑D3 🚌🚉🔄 ⓘLandshuter Str. 1; erding.de

This town is bounded by the rivers Fehlbach and Sempt, which join to its south. The buildings are grouped along two intersecting axes: Landshuterstraße, which culminates in the Schrannenplatz, and the streets of Lange Zeile.

West of Schrannenplatz is the Gothic Johanneskirche, built in the late 14th to early 15th centuries. It has an unusual layout, with the presbytery facing the square. Outside the presbytery stands a 10-storey belfry. Inside the church is a larger-than-life figure of Christ on the Cross, carved by Hans Leinberger in about 1525.

THERME ERDING

Just outside Munich, Therme Erding (thermeerding.de) is Europe's largest thermal bath complex, which accommodates thousands of visitors each day. The complex features a kids' water park, 24 steam rooms, saunas, sunbeds, a pool bar and several restaurants. Concerts and events are held in summer, too.

Opposite Landshuterstraße stands the Gothic Landshuter Tor, or Schöner Turm. At Landshuterstraße 1 is the 17th-century former residence of the counts of Preysing, which is now the town hall.

Erding is also known for the Therme Erding water park, one of the best in Bavaria, and the Erding Weissbier which is exported around the world from the local brewery.

Sankt Wolfgang

⚑E4 🚌🚉St Wolfgang. Hauptstr. 9 **🌐**st-wolfgang-ob.de

The town is named in honour of St Wolfgang, the Bishop of Ratisbon (Regensburg), who was canonized in 1052. According to legend, the saint, while on his way to Mondsee monastery, discovered a spring with miracle-working waters here.

In the early 15th century a chapel was built over the spring. Wolfgangskirche, an outstanding example of late Gothic Bavarian architecture, was built to the south of the chapel in 1430–77.

The foundations contain the Stone of St Wolfgang, a piece of red marble bearing what is said to be the saint's footprint. Ruins of the original Gothic altar remain. There is a carving of St Wolfgang with St George and St Sigismund by Heinrich Helmschrot of

Landshut (or his studio), and paintings of scenes from the life of St Mary. In the northern nave, and a few steps higher up, is the original chapel with the miracle-working spring, which attracts pilgrims. In the early 18th century it was decorated with fine stuccowork. The figure of St Wolfgang that stands on the Rococo altar was made in 1470 and is said to have miraculous powers. Before the altar is a deep covered well. Visitors can lie down beside it and drink its curative water using a ladle.

The town hall is another interesting building. It was originally a presbytery, built by Johann Baptist Gunetzrhainer.

Oberschleißheim

⚑D4 🔄 ⓘMittenheimer Str. 56; tourismus-schleissheim.de

This town is best known for its three impressive palaces (p184), set in the gardens of the Hofgarten. But also of interest is the Flugwerft Schleißheim, a museum located on one of the oldest aerodromes in Germany. Part of the Deutsches Museum (p102), the museum is located in restored buildings dating from 1912–19, in an exhibition hall and on the apron. Some 50 aircraft and helicopters are on display. There is also an exhibition illustrating the

Aircraft on display at the Flugwerft Schleißheim, Oberschleißheim

development of flight and of space flight.

Dachau

D4 🚉🚏 *i* Konrad-Adenauer-Str. 1; dachau.de

A pretty town on the River Amper with panoramic views of Munich, this was once one of the sites of the Holocaust.

In 1933 the first Nazi concentration camp was set up here and it was in use up until 1945, during which time 30,000 prisoners perished here. The site of the camp was opened to the public as a place of remembrance in 1965.

One of the buildings contains the KZ-Gedenkstätte Dachau, a museum which documents the history of

 ←

The lovely gardens and grounds of the Renaissance palace in Dachau

the concentration camps. On the hill at the edge of the town, a palace was built on the site of a 15th-century castle as a summer residence for the Wittelsbachs. Of the original four wings constructed in 1558–77, only the southwest wing remains. The ceremonial hall on the first floor, which survives, was decorated in 1564–5 by Hans Wissreuter.

The focal point of the town is a triangular plaza on which the town hall and the church stand. Hans Krumpper's late Renaissance Jakobskirche was built in 1624–5. It incorporates an earlier presbytery with a fine tower dating from about 1425 and extended in 1676–8 with the addition of a dome.

Kloster Indersdorf

C3 🚉🚏 *i* Markt Indersdorf, Marktplatz 1; markt-indersdorf.de

This former Augustinian abbey built in the early 11th century stands on the north bank of the River Glonn. Vestiges of a 12th-century Romanesque basilica

with a twin-towered façade and Gothic remodelling are discernible in the later Klosterkirche Mariä Himmelfahrt. The latter was lavishly furnished during the 18th century. Franz Xavier Feichtmayr the Elder added the interior Rococo stucco-work in 1754–6, and the paintings of scenes from the life of St Augustine were executed by Matthäus Günther, assisted by Johann Georg Dieffenbrunner.

The abbey buildings of 1694–1704 are set around two courtyards south and east of the church.

LOWER BAVARIA

Lower and Upper Bavaria's early history was defined by division and reunification. The Duchy of Lower Bavaria was created with the first Bavarian partition in 1255 under Duke Henry. Reunification came almost a century later in 1340, but Bavaria was divided yet again in 1349. Today, Lower Bavaria (Niederbayern) remains both a distinct cultural entity and a separate administrative area.

Lower Bavaria borders Austria and the Czech Republic in the east, with its capital in Landshut. The region is noted for its agriculture-intensive south and wild mountainous north and east. This part of Bavaria encompasses most of the Bayerischer Wald (Bavarian Forest), Germany's first national park, and is intersected by the River Danube which flows through many of Lower Bavaria's towns and villages. The rural people of the region are traditionally noted for their piety, with a glorious selection of pilgrimage churches dotted across the landscape, including Bogenberg, known as the Mount Athos of Lower Bavaria, and Geiersberg, near Deggendorf. A range of 20th-century initiatives to industrialize Lower Bavaria resulted in the construction of two modern factories in Dingolfing, where BMW cars are produced.

LOWER BAVARIA

Must Sees

1. Landshut
2. Straubing
3. Passau
4. National Park Bayerischer Wald

Experience More

5. Rohr
6. Weltenburg
7. Bogenberg
8. Metten
9. Museumsdorf Bayerischer Wald
10. Ortenburg
11. Fürstenzell
12. Osterhofen
13. Aldersbach
14. Vilshofen
15. Sammarei

↑ Sunset over the Old Town of Landshut, as seen from across Isar river

LANDSHUT

⚑ E3 ℹ Altstadt 315; landshut.de

Landshut, the capital of Lower Bavaria, grew up around Trausnitz Castle and flourished in the 14th and 15th centuries. The town is now a popular destination for day trips from Munich, and a good base from which to explore Lower Bavaria.

① Jesuitenkirche

⚑ Spiegelgasse

The Church of St Ignatius was formerly part of a Jesuit monastery. Designed by the Jesuit architect Johannes Holl, it was built from 1631 to 1641. The interior features a fine Baroque high altar dating from 1663.

② Jodokskirche

⚑ Jodoksgasse

This Gothic triple-nave brick basilica, built in 1338–1450, was dedicated to St Jodok, the son of a Breton duke who lived in the 7th century and who became a pilgrim and hermit. In the mid-19th century the church was restored to its original Gothic appearance and was furnished in Baroque style.

③ Martinskirche

⚑ Altstadt 68
🕐 7:30am-6:30pm daily (Oct-Mar: to 5pm)
🔔 10:30am-3pm Mon & Fri

Three architects collaborated on the building of this Gothic church. One of them was

Hans von Burghausen, whose tombstone, dated 1432, is built into its southern wall. At 131 m (430 ft) high, the brick church tower is the tallest in the world; the steeple was added in 1500. The tower commands a splendid view of the town and of the castle and its gardens, while the interior of the church abounds in many extravagant Gothic furnishings.

④

Dominikanerkirche

 Regierungsplatz

The Church of St Blasius was built in 1271–1384 in the form of a triple-nave Gothic basilica. The interior was remodelled in the Rococo style by Johann Baptist Zimmermann and decorated with lavish stucco-work. The Neo-Classical façade was added in 1805.

---

⑤

Stadtresidenz

Altstadt 79
(0871) 92 41 10
Apr–Sep: 9am–6pm Tue–Sun; Oct–Mar: 10am–4pm Tue–Sun

This residence consists of two adjacent buildings. The Deutscher Bau, built in 1536–7, has a Neo-Classical façade dating from about 1780. A museum of local history was laid out here in 1935. The Italienischer Bau has a fine arcaded courtyard. The building's façade, looking onto Ländgasse, is decorated with a large cartouche bearing the coat of arms of Ludwig X of Bavaria. Inside visitors can see

the fine reception halls, which occupy two floors, and admire the beautiful Renaissance frescoes depicting mytho-logical scenes.

---

⑥

Burg Trausnitz

burg-trausnitz.de

This castle, whose history began in the year 1204, was

the seat of the von Bayern-landshut branch of the Wittelsbach family. It was extended in the 14th and 15th centuries, and was converted into a residence in 1568–79. In 1961 a fire destroyed the northwest wing, but painstaking restoration has allowed it to reopen to visitors. The late Romanesque chapel and the original staircase were spared.

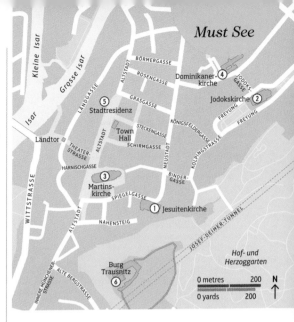

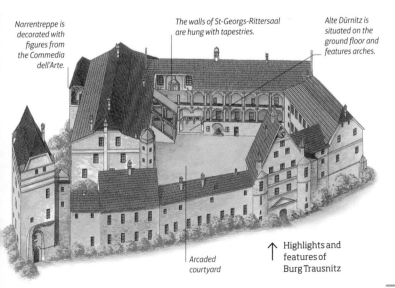

Narrentreppe is decorated with figures from the Commedia dell'Arte.

The walls of St-Georgs-Rittersaal are hung with tapestries.

Alte Dürnitz is situated on the ground floor and features arches.

Arcaded courtyard

↑ Highlights and features of Burg Trausnitz

A SHORT WALK
LANDSHUT

Distance 1 km (0.5 miles) **Time** 15 minutes
Nearest Station Banhofplatz

hLandshut, like Munich, lies between a fork
in the Isar river. It stretches out between
Trausnitz castle, which is set on a vantage
point, and the Cistercian Seligenthal Abbey.
The central conurbation is concentrated
around two wide parallel streets that
function as squares lying on a north-
south axis. They are known as Altstadt
and Neustadt. This walk reveals some
of the highlights of this quintessentially
Bavarian town, including the charming
town hall and the Gothic town gates.

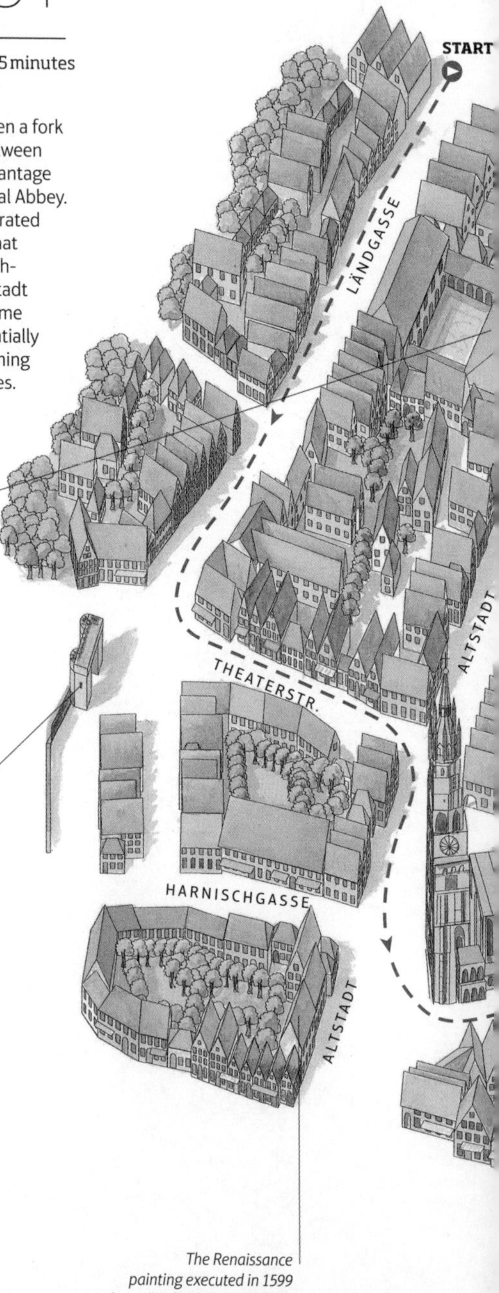

Stadtresidenz (p195),
*built for Duke Ludwig X in
1536–43, was the first
Renaissance palace
in Germany.*

Ländtor, *the Gothic
gateway leading into the
town from the side on
the Isar is a vestige of the
old town fortifications.*

START

LÄNDGASSE

THEATERSTR.

ALTSTADT

HARNISCHGASSE

ALTSTADT

Did You Know?

Landshut is so called
because of its early
status as the protector,
or "hut", of the region.

*The Renaissance
painting executed in 1599
on the walls of **Landschaftshaus**
is a good example of this
kind of exterior decoration
in Landshut.*

Locator Map

The **Gothic Town Hall** *has a fine Renaissance oriel window. The interior paintings and stained-glass windows on the theme of the Landshut Wedding date from 1860.*

FINISH

STECKENGASSE

It was in **Grasbergerhaus**, *a late Gothic house with stepped gables and a street-level arcade, that the betrothed Polish Princess Jadwiga stayed in 1475.*

SCHIRMGASSE

The spacious interior of **Martinskirche** *(p194), which took more than a hundred years to build (1389–1500), impresses with its height, its forest of columns and its fine vaulting.*

KIRCHGASSE

INSFRIEDHOF

SPIEGELGASSE

BALSGÄSSCHEN

0 metres 50
0 yards 50

N

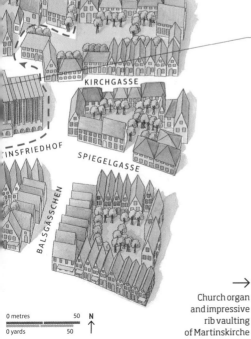

→ Church organ and impressive rib vaulting of Martinskirche

②
STRAUBING

 E2 **🛈** Fraunhoferstr. 27; straubing.de

Standing on the south bank of the Danube in the fertile Gäuboden, Straubing is a pretty, historic town. The medieval appearance of the Old Town has survived basically unchanged, bearing a faithful resemblance to the wooden model made in 1568 by Jakob Sandtner and now on view in the Bayerisches Nationalmuseum in Munich. Every year in August the town holds the Gäubodenvolksfest, a folk festival.

①
Ludwigsplatz and Theresienplatz

The pedestrianized market square resembles a long, wide avenue cutting through the heart of the Old Town. It is pleasant to wander through the large garden between closely packed stalls and crates full of colourful flowers, fruit and vegetables, and admire the historic buildings. The Stadtturm, or tower, offers a sweeping panorama of the town, the Gäuboden and the Bavarian Forest.

Ludwigsplatz and Theresienplatz have two fountains dedicated to the town's patron saints, St Jacob (1644) and St Tiburtius (1685).

On Theresienplatz stands a column built in 1709, featuring gilt figures of the Holy Trinity.

Opposite the town gates on the south side of the square is the two-storey town hall, its two wings enclosing a courtyard. The town hall was created in 1382, when two Gothic houses were conjoined behind a single façade. The stepped gable, however, dates from the 19th century.

②
Gäubodenmuseum

🏛 Fraunhoferstr. 9
🕐 10am–4pm Tue–Sun
🌐 gaeubodenmuseum.de

This local history museum was founded in 1845. Its most renowned exhibit is

> The town hall was created in 1382, when two Gothic houses were conjoined behind a single façade. The stepped gable, however, dates from the 19th century.

↑ Trinity column with the Stadtturm in the background at Theresienplatz

the Römerschatz, or Roman Treasure, which was discovered in 1950 and which caused a sensation among academics. It is the largest collection of Roman parade armour to have been found anywhere in the former Roman Empire.

③
Karmelitenkirche

🏠 **Albrechtsgasse 20**

This spacious triple-nave Gothic church with a tower was partly remodelled in about 1700 by Wolfgang Dientzenhofer. The lavish 17th- and 18th-century furnishings successfully harmonize with the later Baroque decoration. In the church is the tomb of Duke Albrecht II. His son, Albrecht III, secretly married Agnes Bernauer, who was the beautiful daughter of a barber from Augsburg. When he found out Albrecht II ordered the drowning of Agnes in the Danube in 1435. Every four years in June/ July amateur actors re-create this historical tragedy in the Agnes-Bernauer-Festspiele.

④
Ursulinenkirche

🏠 **Burggasse 9**

This church, which forms part of an Ursuline convent, was built

THE GÄUBODEN

Straubing is at the centre of the Gäuboden, a geographical region marked by its loess sediment, soil that is especially good for agriculture, in particular for growing sugar beet. During the last Ice Age, storms from landscapes largely devoid of vegetation blew dust into the Gäu soil, from which loess up to 6 m (20 ft) thick was formed. The Gäuboden was populated around 5500 BCE and has been used for agriculture since the 1st century BCE.

and decorated by the Asam brothers in 1736–41. In their inspired collaboration, Egid Quirin Asam created the architectural design and Cosmas Damian Asam painted the frescoes and the altarpieces.

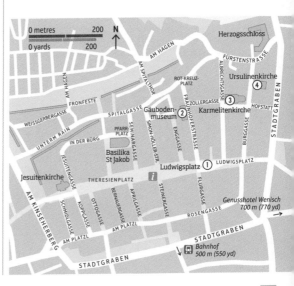

❸

PASSAU

G3 **ℹ**Rathausplatz 2; tourismus.passau.de

Passau is one of the oldest cities in Bavaria. Also known as the Dreiflüssestadt (City of Three Rivers), it nestles at the confluence of three rivers. These waterways divide Passau into three separate districts interconnected by 15 bridges. The Old Town lies on a peninsula between the Danube and the Inn, while Innstadt lies beside the Inn and Ilzstadt beside the Ilz. Passau's fine buildings and squares give it its unique Bavarian charm.

①
Domplatz

In 1155 the cathedral chapter acquired a plot of land between the cathedral and the western section of the city walls with the aim of building on it chapterhouses arranged around a large square. What were the originally modest chapterhouses were later remodelled in a more ostentatious Baroque style.

Distinctive among them is the Lamberg Chapterhouse, at No. 6 Domplatz, on the west side of the square. Rebuilt in 1724, the chapterhouse is also known as Lamberg Palace for its magnificent façade, which is decorated with fine mouldings. The old chapterhouses at Nos. 4 and 5, known as the Barbarahof and Kanonikatshof Starzhausen, today accommodate the presbytery and the seminary.

The square itself features a monument to the first Bavarian king, Maximilian I Joseph, and was created by Christian Gorhan the Younger in 1824.

②
Dom St Stephan

Domplatz 1

The original cathedral was destroyed in the Great Fire of 1662. It was rebuilt in 1668–77 by Carlo Lurago, , incorporating the surviving Gothic presbytery and transept into the new renovation scheme.

The towers can be seen from afar. The interior contains a stuccowork and other ornamentation added in 1677–85 by Giovanni Battista Carlone, and paintings by Carpoforo Tencalla. The burial chapels on the north side of the cathedral feature the Gothic Herrenkapelle, which was built in about 1300. It contains an enormous Romanesque Crucifix dating from about 1190.

Passau Cathedral is famous for its organ, one of the largest in the world. It was built in 1924–8 and refurbished in 1979–81. Organ recitals take

---

 PICTURE PERFECT
Capturing a Confluence

The Dreiflüsseeck is where the Ilz flows into the Danube from the left and the river Inn flows in from the right, leading to spectacular colours. It can be snapped on the left bank of the Danube in the Old Town.

← The city of Passau at dusk, with boats lining the Danube

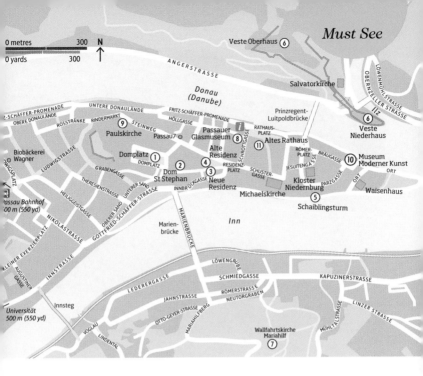

Map labels:

Veste Oberhaus ⑥
Salvatorkirche
ANGERSTRASSE
Donau (Danube)
Prinzregent-Luitpoldbrücke
LÖWENMÜHLSTRASSE
OBERNZELLER STRASSE
Ilz
Veste Niederhaus ⑥
2-SCHÄFFER-PROMENADE
OBERE DONAULÄNDE
UNTERE DONAULÄNDE
FRITZ-SCHÄFFER-PROMENADE
RÖSSTRÄNKE   RINDERMARKT
STEINWEG ⑨
HÖLLGASSE
RATHAUS-PLATZ
Passau7
Paulskirche
Passauer Glasmuseum ⑧
Altes Rathaus ⑪
RÖMER-PLATZ
BRÄUGASSE
Museum Moderner Kunst ⑩
Biobäckerei Wagner
LUDWIGSTRASSE
Domplatz ①
DOMPLATZ
Alte Residenz ④
SCHROTTGASSE
RESIDENZ-PLATZ
JESUITENGASSE
ORT
GRABENGASSE
Dom St Stephan ②
SCHUSTER-GASSE
Kloster Niedernburg
PARZGASSE
ORT
NIGSPLATZ
THERESIENSTRASSE
UGASSE
Neue Residenz ③
Waisenhaus
Passau Bahnhof 00 m (550 yd)
HEILIGGEISTGASSE
UNTERER SAND
INNBRÜCKGASSE
Michaelskirche
Schaiblingsturm ⑤
NIKOLASTRASSE
OBERER SAND
GOTTFRIED-SCHÄFFER-STRASSE
Inn
KLEINER EXERZIERPLATZ
INNSTRASSE
Marien-brücke
MARIENBRÜCKE
AUGUSTINER GASSE
LÖWENGRUBE
SCHMIEDGASSE
KAPUZINERSTRASSE
Universität 500 m (550 yd)
Innsteg
LEDERERGASSE
JAHNSTRASSE
RÖMERSTRASSE
NEUTORGRABEN
LINZER STRASSE
VOGLAU
LINDENTAL
OTTO-GEYER-STRASSE
MARIAHILFBERG
MÜHLTALSTRASSE
Wallfahrtskirche Mariahilf ⑦

0 metres 300   N
0 yards 300

---

place every day at noon from May to October.

---

③

Neue Residenz

🏛 **Residenzplatz 8 Treasury and Diocesan Museum** 📞 (0851) 39 30 🕐 **2 May–31 Oct: 10am–4pm Mon–Sat**

The new bishop's residence, which occupies the south side of Residenzplatz, was built in 1713–30 to plans by Domenico d'Angeli and Antonio Beduzzi. It was refurbished in 1764–71 by Melchior Hefele of Vienna, with stuccowork by members of the local Modler family, the addition of a Neo-Classical façade and interior decoration in the late Baroque style.

The design and decoration of the vestibule and staircase are particularly successful. The reception rooms contain large collections of artifacts from the Diocesan Museum and Cathedral Treasury, some

---

of which can also be seen in the cathedral.

---

④

Alte Residenz

🏛 **Theresienstr. 18.**

The Old Residence is an important landmark visible from the River Inn. The residence probably stands on the site of a bishopric mentioned in 1188. The medieval buildings have been remodelled over the ages, and their present uniform appearance dates from 1680.

The reception rooms were decorated in the 18th century, but soon afterwards the bishopric was moved to the New Residence. The buildings now house the Landgericht, or provincial court.

---

⑤

Schaiblingsturm

The 14th-century Schaiblingsturm, on the

---

bank of the River Inn, is a vestige of the old city fortifications. The pointed dome of the tower looks over the Innkai. In centuries gone by, the tower protected the port on the important salt route. It also functioned as a mooring point for the boats.

SHOP

Passau7

From postcards to beautifully deco-rated beer steins, puzzles to Christmas baubles, this delightful shop sells high-quality gifts in a pleasant and well-curated space.

🏛 **Steinweg 4**
🌐 **passau7.shop**

↑ Covered stairway adorned with numerous votive tablets in the Wallfahrtskirche Mariahilf

Veste Oberhaus and Veste Niederhaus

🏛 Oberhaus 125. Oberhausmuseum Passau 🕐 Mid-Mar-mid-Nov: 9am-5pm Mon-Fri, 10am-6pm Sat-Sun & public hols; 26 Dec-6 Jan: 10am-4pm

Work on the imposing Oberhaus (Upper Castle) began in 1219, initiated by the bishop Ulrich II. It is set on a rocky outcrop known as St Georgsberg, on the bank of the Danube opposite the Old Town. The main castle consists of Gothic buildings and a chapel. The Niederhaus (Lower Castle) is connected to the Oberhaus by a gallery descending from the polygonal tower. Work on the Niederhaus, on a spit of land between the rivers Danube and Ilz, began in 1250. Both castles, which have been extended and fortified over time, symbolize the power of the church over the town.

The Oberhaus now houses a historical museum. On the route to the Observatoriums-turm (observatory tower) is the Passauer Tölpel (Fool of Passau), a huge head with a mocking expression. This is the remains of a statue of St Stephen of about 1370 that fell from the cathedral during the Great Fire of 1662.

The Niederhaus, whose appearance dates from about 1444, was the home of the painter Ferdinand von Wagner from 1890 to 1907. He filled the interior with antique furniture and his own paintings. A private residence, it is closed to visitors.

Wallfahrtskirche Mariahilf

🏛 Mariahilfberg 3

This pilgrimage church, set on the hill known as Mariahilfsberg, dominates the River Inn and Passau's Innstadt district. It commands a fine view of the city and the Dreiflüsseeck – the confluence of the three rivers.

The Capuchin church and monastery, completed in about 1630, are reached by a covered flight of 321 steps. The object of pilgrimage is a copy of a painting of the Madonna and Child by Lucas Cranach the Elder which has been venerated since 1622. The original painting was acquired from a gallery in Dresden by Leopold, Bishop of Passau in 1611. In 1650 the painting was moved to the

---

EAT

Biobäckerei Wagner
This popular, family-run organic bakery is known for its fantastic German loaves, rolls, gateaux, cakes, desserts, roulades and a wide range of shortcrust pastries. It's also worth stopping here to enjoy a morning cappuccino.

🏛 Nordendstr. 34
🌐 wagner.bio

€€€

Jacobskirche in Innsbruck, where it remains to this day.

The austere interior of the church has a silver eternal lamp presented by the Emperor Leopold I in 1676 during his marriage in Passau.

---

(8)

Passauer Glasmuseum

⌂ Höllgasse 1
☎ (0851) 35 071
🕐 9am-5pm daily

Housed in the Wilder Mann hotel, this museum of glass contains over 30,000 pieces of decorative and household glassware from the 18th to the 20th centuries.

The large collection of Bohemian glassware and the glass made in the workshops of the Bavarian Forest are remarkable. There is also an interesting section on Art Nouveau glass.

Over the years the museum has attracted some eminent visitors, from Neil Armstrong to Mikhail Gorbachev.

---

(9)

Paulskirche

⌂ Rindermarkt

The parish church of St Paul was built in 1663–78 on the site of a medieval church that was destroyed by the Great Fire of 1622. The stuccowork in the interior was executed in 1909. The façade's tall, picturesque tower is a Passau landmark.

---

(10)

Museum Moderner Kunst

⌂ Bräugasse 17
🕐 10am-6pm Tue-Sun
🚫 24, 25, 31 Dec & Good Friday 🌐 mmk-passau.de

Located in one of the Old Town's most beautiful houses, Passau's Museum of Modern Art exhibits art from the 20th and 21st centuries. There are regular international exhibitions of different modern artists.

---

(11)

Altes Rathaus

⌂ Rathausplatz
☎ (0851) 39 60 🕐 Apr-6 Jan: 10am-5pm daily

The Town Hall stands on the site of the former Fish Market alongside the Danube. With the annexation of houses standing between Schrottgasse and Marktgasse, the town hall was constantly enlarged, a process that was in progress up until the 19th century. The original tower, which was demolished in 1811, was replaced in 1890–91 by a fine Neo-Gothic tower designed by Heinrich von Schmidt. It is encircled by a gallery and has a steep sloped roof. Floodmarks on the façade show the high levels reached by the Danube at various times. Entering the building from the side facing Schrottgasse, visitors pass through a late Gothic carved portal of 1510.

The Town Hall's interior and three courtyards date from the 16th and 17th centuries. The halls, open to the public, contain a collection of paintings by world-renowned artist Ferdinand von Wagner.

→ The striking Altes Rathaus with its Neo-Gothic tower

④ Ⓜ Ⓠ Ⓨ

NATIONAL PARK BAYERISCHER WALD

🔒 G2 🏠 Information Point: Bahnhofstr. 54
🌐 www.nationalpark-bayerischer-wald.bayern.de

Founded in 1970 as Germany's first national park, the Bavarian Forest is a 60,000-acre (24,000-ha) wonderland of uninterrupted wilderness. It forms one of the largest areas of woodland in Central Europe and is home to a stunning mosaic of wildlife habitats.

Running along the border of Germany and the Czech Republic, this vast area of ancient forest conjures images of a bygone Europe, when woodland ecosystems dominated the region. The park's glades, rolling mountainsides and vast lakes like Rachelsee have seen some of Europe's most successful wildlife reintroduction schemes, with lynx and grey wolves roaming the landscape once more. Since the park was established, it has been a policy to keep interference to a minimum, allowing an abundance of spruce, beech and fir trees to thrive. One of the most popular ways to experience the landscape is the tree-top walk, the Baumwipfelbad in Neuschönau, which offers a barrier-free walkway leading to a dome-shaped observation tower. A 200-km (120-mile) cycle network runs through the forest – though cycling off of these trails is strictly prohibited.

> 💬 INSIDER TIP
> **Public Transport**
>
> The Baumwipfelbad in Neuschönau is a perfect starting point for your forest adventure, and it is accessible by public transport. Visit *bayer-waldticket.com* for local train and bus times to the park from stops throughout Bavaria.

The rising walkways of the Baumwipfelbad ↑

1 Bikepacking along the forest's trail network.

2 Hiking to a lookout over Rachelsee.

3 Pair of Eurasian lynx in the park in winter.

TOP 4 ANIMALS IN THE PARK

Capercaillie
This huge, striking woodland grouse can be seen in the park's higher reaches.

Eurasian lynx
The park is one of the few places in Europe where wild breeding lynx can still be seen.

Grey wolf
Packs of wolves prowl the forest since their reintroduction, though they can be hard to spot.

Ural owl
In Germany, Ural owls became extinct in 1926, but a reintroduction project in 2007 saw them return.

LANDSCAPES OF THE BAVARIAN ALPS

Southern Bavaria is one of Germany's most picturesque and scenically varied regions. The Alpine ecosystem is a mosaic of habitats forged over thousands of years by the region's volatile geology. To the south, Bavaria is bordered by the Alps, with their breathtaking limestone peaks and verdant slopes, while to the north flows the Danube, with its marshy floodplains. The region's landscapes consist of undulating hills dotted with mountain streams and lakes formed by glaciers during the Ice Age. Much of the terrain takes the form of pasture and fields, or is covered in ancient forests.

FOREST HABITATS

Southern Bavaria is home to the largest forest landscape in Central Europe, much of it within the Bayerischer Wald *(p204)*. At higher altitudes, remarkable mountain spruce trees stretch across the undulating terrain, their branches decked in snow even in early summer. At lower elevations, fir, copper beech and sycamore comprise the mixed forests, their extensive canopies bursting into shades of gold and amber come autumn.

RESPECTING WILD BAVARIA

Swimming
Swimming in the Isar river or in the clean waters of Chiemsee are popular pastimes for Bavarians. Note, however, that the Isar's water level varies greatly, and it's strongly recommended that swimmers refrain from entering the Isar when its water is above 1 m (3 ft) in Munich.

Wild camping
Bavaria has some of the strictest wild camping rules in all of Germany and pitching up in wild spaces can lead to hefty fines. Thankfully, there are a host of excellent campsites throughout the state which can be booked in advance online.

Hiking
Stick to designated hiking trails when exploring the wilds. Many of the best routes are adequately waymarked, but it's highly recommended that you map your route in advance.

Wildlife
Though wolves have been reintroduced to the Bavarian countryside, you're highly unlikely to encounter them in the wild. In any case, it's recommended that you stick to the trails to avoid damaging habitats or encountering predators.

THE LAKES

Bavaria's beautiful patchwork of waterways was formed centuries ago as glaciers melted towards the end of the last Ice Age. From secluded mountain reservoirs to the huge Chiemsee (nicknamed the "Bavarian sea"), these bodies of inland water are one of the region's greatest calling cards. Though lakes like Tegernsee attract vast numbers of visitors, the water remains of excellent purity; 97 per cent of Bavaria's bathing waters have been classified as "excellent" or "good" in terms of their hygiene.

THE PEAKS

Forming a jagged natural border with Austria to the south, Bavaria's southern Alps are among the country's most impressive natural features. The chiselled peaks aren't particularly high; the Zugspitze, Germany's tallest mountain, only rises to 2,960 m (9,700 ft). But the way the mountain range appears sharply from

BAVARIAN CONSERVATION

Bavarians are proud of their ecological diversity, and the state government has been proactive in implementing conservation policies. In 2023, it launched The Open Land Contract Nature Conservation Programme which rewards land managers for dealing with ecosystems in a sustainable manner. The wider Bavarian Biodiversity Strategy uses EU funding to protect ecologically valuable Alpine grassland, arable land and ponds.

the surrounding Bavarian farmland gives the impression of far greater heights. Ski resorts in these mountains tend to be less developed than their French counterparts, but the epic pistes in areas like Garmisch-Partenkirchen have a distinct and quieter charm for winter sports lovers.

↑ Looking out over the towering Bavarian Alps and *(inset)* a stream in the Bayerischer Wald

Benedictine monastery of Weltenburg on the edge of the Danube

EXPERIENCE MORE

5

Rohr

D3 Abensberg
Marienplatz 1; (08783) 96 080

The town of Rohr is built around a 12th-century abbey, the **Kloster Rohr**, remodelled in the first half of the 13th century after its ownership transferred to Benedictines.

The abbey's Asamkirche is famed for its stuccowork and the 1723 high altar by Egid Quirin Asam. The altar was built like a theatrical stage with wings. The sculptural group on the altar depicts the Assumption of the Virgin. It embodies the idea of a *theatrum sacrum (p63)*.

Kloster Rohr

Abt-Dominik-Prokop-Platz 1 6am–8pm daily kloster-rohr.de

6

Weltenburg

D2 Kelheim

This small town is located in a picturesque setting on a terrace beside the Danube. It is home to the vast Benedictine **Kloster Weltenburg**, a historic

← Statue of the Virgin in the high altar of Kloster Rohr

WELTENBURG BREWERY

Weltenburg houses the oldest monastic brewery in the world. First started in 1050, it produces many excellent beers, the most popular being the pitch-black Kloster Barock Dunkel. It's best sipped in the abbey's beer garden, accompanied by roast *schweinshaxe* (pork knuckle) and Bavarian dumplings. Bottles can also be purchased.

---

complex that dates from the early 7th century.

The Asam brothers added to the complex the Baroque Georgs- und Martinskirche, which was completed in 1716. Cosmas Damian Asam was responsible for the designs and the paintings, and Egid Quirin Asam built the high altar and the statue of St George slaying a dragon.

There is a beer garden in the cloisters where visitors

EAT

Hotel Burgwirt
This guesthouse serves traditional home-cooked food, with an array of salads paired with local sausage.

F2 Deggendorfer Str 7, Metten Sun
whotel-burgwirt.de

€€€

can sample the monastery's beer. Boat trips through the Danube Gorge to Kelheim also depart from a quay nearby.

Kloster Weltenburg

 Asamstr. 32 9-11am & 12:30-4:30pm Mon-Sat, 12:30-4:30pm Sun & public hols wklosterschenke-weltenburg.de

---

7

Bogenberg

F2 Bogen Stadt platz 56; www.bogen.de

Rising above the small town of Bogen, the imposing Bogenberg, or "Mount Athos" of Lower Bavaria, was once a Celtic sacred place. Since the Middle Ages it has been a place of pilgrimage. Standing on the top is the Gothic Hl. Kreuz und Mariä Heimsuchung, which commands an excellent view over the Danube valley.

Pilgrims come here to honour the miraculous statue of the pregnant Virgin Mary, dating from around 1400. Dozens of votive candles flicker in the presbytery.

According to an ancient custom, at Pentecost the

strongest man from the nearby village of Holzkirchen brings to the church a great candle – *Die lange Stang*, up to 100 kg (220 lb) in weight and 13 m (40 ft) long.

8

Metten

F2 Krankenhausstr. 22; www.markt-metten.de

Metten's Benedictine **abbey** was founded in about 766. In 1830, after it had been appropriated as a result of the dissolution of the monasteries, it was returned to its industrious owners.

The Michaelskirche in the monastery, which has been rebuilt many times since its foundation, was remodelled in 1712–29. The church's twin-towered façade outlines two circular chapels. The interior features stunning paintings and a high altar by Cosmas Damian Asam.

The most exquisite part of the abbey is the library, built in 1722–9 and decorated with stuccowork by Franz Josef Holzinger. It is one of the finest library buildings in the world. A remarkable pair of Atlases support the vaulted ceiling.

Kloster Metten

Abteistr. 3 Daily
wkloster-metten.de

↑ Admiring the Baroque stuccowork in the library at Kloster Metten

Museumsdorf Bayerischer Wald

G3 **Am Dreiburgensee** **Tittling** **Week before Easter-Oct: 10am-5pm daily; Nov-Mar: 9am-5pm daily (museum grounds only)** **museumsdorf.com**

Near Tittling, on the west side of the road from Grafenau to Passau, this open-air museum is one of the largest in Europe. Here over 140 buildings dating from the 18th and 19th centuries have been erected on a 200,000-sq-m (50-acre) site. As well as traditional cottages with all their furnishings, visitors can see forges, sawmills and also the oldest public school building in Germany.

In the buildings, you'll find informative exhibitions on everyday life in 17th–19th century Bavaria, with an array of interactive elements to ensure younger visitors are engaged throughout.

Near the museum, in a pretty inn dating from 1829, traditional Bavarian specialities are on offer. Visitors to the inn include prominent German figures, including the former chancellor Helmut Kohl and the Swiss writer Friedrich Dürrenmatt.

The museum is located in the Dreiburgenland, which is so named after three castles, Saldenburg, Fürstenstein and Englburg. They are well-preserved but are not open to the public.

Ortenburg

F3 **Vilshofen or Passau** **Marktplatz 11; ortenburg.de**

This old market town in Passau was established by the Counts of Ortenburg, who built a Renaissance palace here. The palace is set on a ridge and was constructed in about 1567 on the site of a medieval castle belonging to the Bavarian von Krailburg-Ortenburg family. Joachim, one of the family members, brought the Reformation to the town in 1563, and ever since then Ortenburg has been a Protestant enclave within Catholic, Counter-Reformation Lower Bavaria.

The palace is today in private ownership, but it contains a **museum** that is open to the public. Visitors can also see such features as a fine late Renaissance panelled ceiling dating from around 1600 in the castle chapel, the remnants of trompe l'oeil frescoes on the wall of the Knights' Hall and a torture chamber. The well outside the palace, which descends to a depth of 55 m (180 ft), supplied the townspeople with water until 1927.

The presbytery of the late Gothic church, which has been a Protestant church since 1563, contains the splendid tombs of the owners of the Ortenburg palace in the 16th and 17th centuries.

> The Ortenburg palace is set on a ridge and was constructed in about 1567 on the site of a medieval castle belonging to the Bavarian von Krailburg-Ortenburg family.

Twin-towered exterior of the Marienkirche in Fürstenzell abbey, and *(inset)* its Baroque high altar and nave

Schlossmuseum Ortenburg

 🅐 Vorderschloss 1 🅒 Apr–Oct: 10am–5pm Tue–Sun 🆆 schloss-ortenburg.de

---

⓫

Fürstenzell

🅐 G3 🚋🚌 Passau
🅘 Marienplatz 7; fuerstenzell.de

Founded in 1274, the quaint Cistercian abbey in Fürstenzell reached the height of its artistic development in the 18th century. Barring the church, the abbey is closed to the public.

The abbey's **Marienkirche**, built in 1738, was designed by Johann Michael Fischer, with stuccowork by Johann Baptist Modler and Johann Georg Funk and ceiling paintings by Johann Jakob Zeiller. The interior features Baroque and Rococo altars, the high altar by Johann Baptist Straub, and a fine Rococo pulpit. The Gothic tombs of the Cistercian abbots and the abbey's founders are also of interest.

←

Picturesque setting of the open-air Museumsdorf Bayerischer Wald

The monastery, situated south of the church, was remodelled in 1674–87, and extended after 1770. The Festsaal (State Room), with frescoes of 1773 in the late Viennese Neo-Classical style, is outstanding.

The monastery library was decorated in about 1760. Together with the monastery library in the town of Metten nearby, it is arguably the finest example of artistic patronage by the Cistercian order in Germany. The interior is lined with a gallery supported on alternating Tuscan columns and herms (the head of Hermes on a stone pillar). The bookcases are decorated with Rococo putti and stunning Atlases by Joseph Deutschmann.

Marienkirche

 🅐 Marienplatz 15
📞 (08502) 91 150 🅒 8am–6pm daily (via advance booking only, call ahead)

STAY

Landhotel Tannenhof
This cosy country hotel, in the resort town of Spiegelau, is a restorative spot for hikers in the Bavarian forest. Surrounded by mountains, it includes a wellness area with an indoor swimming pool, a spa, a sun terrace and a sauna.

🅐 Auf der List 27, Spiegelau 🆆 landhotel-tannenhof.de

€€€

↑ Lavishly decorated high altar at the Asambasilika in Osterhofen

12
Osterhofen

⚑F3 🚍🚃Altenmarkt
ℹ Stadtplatz 13;
osterhofen.de

This small Bavarian town, whose history goes back almost six centuries, is home to a jewel of Baroque architecture, the **Asambasilika**.

The church was built in 1726 on the site of a medieval Premonstratensian church. Its appearance is the result of a collaboration between the architect Michael Fischer and the Asam brothers. While its exterior is somewhat austere, with the façade merging with a wing of the monastery, the decorative scheme of the interior is phenomenal.

The unusual shape of the single-nave interior is created by its oval side chapels and serpentine walls. The architecture, painting and stuccowork are fused into a single entity.

While the extensive ceiling frescoes by Cosmas Damian Asam create an illusion of extensive space, Egid Quirin Asam's stuccowork blurs the boundaries between reality and illusion. Absorbing the superb artistry and admiring the artists' skill can take some time.

The Asambasilika made a profound impression on Pope John Paul II, who visited Osterhofen during his pilgrimage to Germany in 1980.

Asambasilika
♿🕙 ⚑Hauptstr. 59
🌐asambasilika.de

13
Aldersbach

⚑F3 🚍🚃Vilshofen
ℹ Klosterplatz 1; alders bach.de

Work on the Cistercian monastery in the town of Aldersbach began at the end of the 17th century. It was remodelled by Dominikus Magzin in the first half of the 18th century, when it became the exquisite church of **Mariä Himmelfahrt**.

The interior, which is lit by large windows, is decorated with exquisite paintings and stuccowork executed by Egid and Cosmas Damian Asam in 1718–20, the first time that the brothers had collaborated on a project *(p63)*. Among the most outstanding features are the choir borne by angels in wide flowing garments, and the trompe l'oeil paintings on the ceiling over the nave.

The high altar, dating from 1723, is Matthias Götz' masterpiece. The pulpit, of 1748, and the stalls, of 1762, are by Joseph Deutschmann.

Mariä Himmelfahrt
⚑Ritter-Ortolf-Str. 1A
🌐asamkirche-aldersbach.de

14
Vilshofen

⚑F3 🚃 ℹStadtplatz 27;
vilshofen.de

Founded in 1206 where the Vils, Wolfach and Pfudrach meet the Danube, Vilshofen

centres around Stadtplatz. This long street is lined with colourful houses that were built after the great fire that destroyed the town in 1794.

The 14th-century parish church of **St Johannes der Täufer** was rebuilt in 1803–4. Its Baroque decoration was executed in the 18th century, and was originally intended for the Nikolakirche in Passau.

The town is also home to the late Gothic Barbarakirche, built in the second half of the 15th century, and the Mariähilfskirche, a former pilgrimage church built in 1611 by Antonio Riva. The Mariähilfskirche is decorated with stuccowork and frescoes executed by northern Italian artists, including Giovanni Pietro Camuzzi.

The gate tower was built in 1643–7 and designed by Bartholomäus Viscardi in the Mannerist style. It has greyish-white tones and an onion dome. It has come to symbolize the town.

Vilshofen's most prominent building is the Benedictine **abbey** of Schweiklberg, designed by Michael Kurz and built in 1909–11. The church has two Art Nouveau steeples.

St Johannes der Täufer

🏛 Kirchplatz 21
🌐 bistum-passau.de

Kloster Vilshofen

🏛 Schweiklberg 1 ⏰ 8am–5pm daily 🌐 schweiklberg.de

🄯 Sammarei

🗺 F3 🚆🚌 Vilshofen or Passau 🛈 Markt-platz 11, Ortenburg; (08542) 16 421

Sammarei has one of the most remarkable pilgrimage churches in the whole of southern Germany.

An old wooden chapel miraculously survived the fire that destroyed the neighbouring house of Cistercian monks from Aldersbach. The chapel was subsequently enclosed within the late Renaissance church of Mariä Himmelfahrt, occupying part of the presbytery. The ambulatory that was created between the walls of the chapel and the presbytery of the church are covered with Baroque votive images, as are the walls of the chapel itself.

The chapel is separated from the nave by a fine high altar of 1645, which acts as a kind of iconostasis.

The chapel's late Rococo altar contains the miraculous image that is venerated by pilgrims to the church: a copy of the original *Madonna and Child* ascribed to Hans Holbein the Elder.

← Yellow steeple of St Johannes der Täufer towering over Vilshofen

THE DANUBE CYCLE PATH
PASSAU TO SCHLÖGENER

Distance 40 km (25 miles) **Stopping-off points** Obernzell, Engelhartszell **Terrain** Flat, paved **Nearest station** Passau

The Danube Cycle Path is one of Europe's most popular cycling routes. Hugging the river, with paved stretches on both the north and south bank, the path makes for beautiful, flat riding, with no cars in sight for much of the route. This stretch starts in Passau and heads off north of the river into the Upper Danube Valley, before crossing the border into Austria. Along the way, you'll pass delightful monasteries, verdant valleys and quaint towns. The route can be followed all the way to the city of Vienna, making for a perfect two-week cycling holiday. Note that public transport options are limited on this stretch of the route.

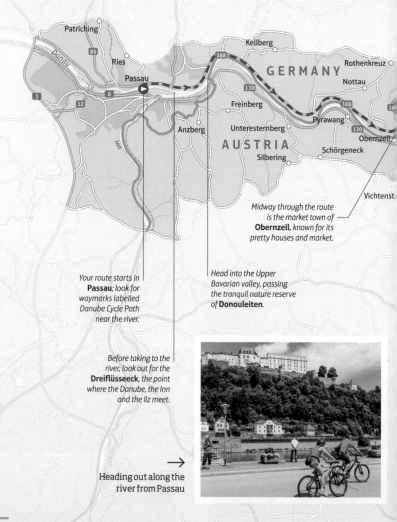

Midway through the route is the market town of **Obernzell**, known for its pretty houses and market.

Your route starts in **Passau**; look for waymarks labelled Danube Cycle Path near the river.

Head into the Upper Bavarian valley, passing the tranquil nature reserve of **Donouleiten**.

Before taking to the river, look out for the **Dreiflüsseeck**, the point where the Danube, the Inn and the Ilz meet.

→
Heading out along the river from Passau

Locator Map

LOWER BAVARIA
(GERMANY)

Passau to Schlögener

AUSTRIA

→
The Schlögener
Schlinge river loop
in the Danube

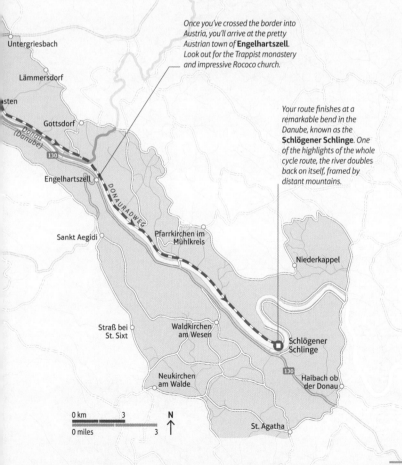

Untergriesbach

Lämmersdorf

...sten

Gottsdorf

*Donau
(Danube)*

130

Engelhartszell

DONAURADWEG

Sankt Aegidi

Pfarrkirchen im
Mühlkreis

Niederkappel

Straß bei
St. Sixt

Waldkirchen
am Wesen

Schlögener
Schlinge

130

Neukirchen
am Walde

Haibach ob
der Donau

St. Agatha

*Once you've crossed the border into
Austria, you'll arrive at the pretty
Austrian town of* **Engelhartszell***.
Look out for the Trappist monastery
and impressive Rococo church.*

*Your route finishes at a
remarkable bend in the
Danube, known as the*
Schlögener Schlinge*. One
of the highlights of the whole
cycle route, the river doubles
back on itself, framed by
distant mountains.*

0 km   3
0 miles   3

N
↑

UPPER BAVARIA (EAST)

Lying between the rivers Inn and Salzach, eastern Upper Bavaria has long been prized for its natural beauty. The region's snow-covered Alpine slopes, lush green valleys and lakes such as Chiemsee and Königssee were coveted by the Romans, who frequented the region for its health springs. In the following centuries, the region was favoured by Bavarian rulers, who dotted the landscape with fine castles, churches and palaces. The churches of Maria Gern and St Bartholomä are among Bavaria's most beautiful, while Burghausen is home to the world's longest castle. It wasn't only Bavaria's royal rulers who favoured the region's beautiful landscapes. During the reign of the Nazis, Hitler prized his "Eagle's Nest" residence, which was located high on Mount Kehlstein; the spot was used to entertain a number of visiting dignitaries.

Eastern Upper Bavaria today attracts travellers looking to experience the charms of rural Bavarian life, with the historic towns on the River Inn – particularly Rosenheim, Wasserburg and Rott – especially popular with tourists and outdoor enthusiasts in summer.

UPPER BAVARIA (EAST)

Experience

1. Altötting
2. Tittmoning
3. Laufen
4. Burghausen
5. Berchtesgaden
6. Anger
7. Maria Gern
8. Bad Reichenhall
9. Ruhpolding
10. Reit im Winkl
11. Ramsau
12. Königssee
13. Aschau
14. Herrenchiemsee
15. Stein an der Traun
16. Fraueninsel
17. Amerang
18. Bad Aibling
19. Kloster Seeon
20. Rott am Inn
21. Wasserburg am Inn
22. Neubeuern

EXPERIENCE

❶ Altötting

🅰E4 🚉 ℹ️ Kapellplatz 2a; altoetting.de

This town, established in the 8th century, is one of the earliest Christian sites in Europe. It is also the earliest place of pilgrimage in Bavaria, and is called the Heart of Bavaria by some. Every year about half a million pilgrims come here to pay their respects to the Black Madonna. This 66-cm- (26-in-) tall statue was carved from wood in the early 13th century. It is kept in the Heilige Kapelle (Holy Chapel), which stands in the centre of a large square. The chapel, with a Carolingian apse and a Gothic nave, is surrounded by an ambulatory whose walls are covered with votive images. Pilgrims holding crosses inch up to it on their knees. Pope John Paul II paid a visit to the shrine during his pilgrimage to Germany in 1980.

The treasury of the late Gothic Stiftskirche contains valuable votive offerings from the Holy Chapel. The most highly prized of these is the Goldenes Rössl (Golden Steed) of 1404, a masterpiece of French goldwork. There's also a crypt containing the mortal remains of Johann Tilly, the renowned military leader in the Thirty Years' War.

Another feature of interest is the **Panorama** re-creating the view from the hill of Golgotha in Jerusalem. It is located in a building dating from 1902–3.

Some 2 km (1.5 miles) north, on the River Inn, is Neuötting. Notable buildings here include Nikolauskirche, a 15th-century Gothic church designed by Hans von Burghausen, and the late Gothic Annakirche, completed in 1515.

Panorama

 🅰 Gebhard-Fugel-Weg 10 🕐 Mar–Oct: 10am–5pm daily; Nov–Feb: 11am–2pm Sat & Sun 🌐 panorama-altoetting.de

---

❷ Tittmoning

🅰F4 🚌 🚉 Laufen, Burghausen ℹ️ Stadtplatz 1; tittmoning.eu

The entrance to this little town on the River Salzach is through a gate in the town walls. The market square is lined with colourful houses with bay windows and woodcarvings. Among them is the tall town hall, its tower and façade dating from 1711–12. The hill above Tittmoning, the summit crowned by a 13th-century castle, gives a fine view of the surrounding countryside and the Alps. The castle is home to the Rupertiwinkel Museum, which features excellent

collections of folk art and antique tools once used by local crafters and farmers.

The Maria Ponlach pilgrimage chapel of 1617 is reached by a road round the castle that follows a ravine overlooking the River Ponlach.

Laufen

🅰 F4 🚇 ℹ️ Rathausplatz 1; stadtlaufen.de

Set on a bend in the River Salzach, this town has a southern, almost Italian feel. It was originally a Roman settlement, and flourished during the Middle Ages. Entry into the town is through two medieval gates. The streets are lined with arcaded houses with oriels and concave roofs typical of the region.

The 14th-century parish church is the oldest single-nave Gothic church in southern Germany. With its huge roof and late 12th-century Romanesque tower, it dominates the town.

North of the church is the Dechantshof, the old archbishop's castle, which contains plaques from the church. Its staircase is decorated with the

The decorative chapel at Heilige Kapelle, and *(inset)* the church's elegant exterior in Altötting

↑ The Gothic castle, perched on a ridge above Berghausen

portraits of bishops. The four-winged castle, with an inner courtyard, was built in 1606–8 by Vincenzo Scamozzi.

Burghausen

🅰 F4 🚇 ℹ️ Stadtplatz 99; burg-burghausen.de

Situated on the River Salzach, which forms the border with Austria, Burghausen is famous for having the longest castle in Europe. With its six courtyards, the castle stretches some 1,050 m (3,500 ft) along a ridge between the river and Wöhrsee. The castle was built in 1025 and rebuilt in 1490. The main castle (Hauptburg) contains several museums, including a local history and a photographic museum. In the rooms that are open to the public, German paintings and furniture are on display.

In 1180, the Wittelsbach family took possession of the castle, which lay on the salt trade route between Austria and Passau. Duties were collected here, making the town a commercial hub. This was reversed in the late 16th century when a monopoly

was imposed, and the town experienced an economic decline. This continued for centuries, until the town flourished again in the 20th century.

The Old Town, between the castle and the river, has an old-world atmosphere. The market square is surrounded by what are Burghausen's finest buildings: the Gothic Jakobskirche, with a Baroque tower, the town hall, the mid-16th-century old Bavarian government building, with a Renaissance courtyard, the Schutzengelkirche of 1731–46, and many historic houses.

On the north side of the square is the Jesuit Josefskirche of about 1629 and the Marienbrunnen, a mid-17th-century fountain.

 PICTURE PERFECT
Burghausen Castle

The Burg Burghausen, which stretches for 1,050 m (3,500 ft), is set high on a narrow ridge overlooking the town of Burghausen. Climb the stairs to the top of the walls to take a photo looking over the town.

⑤

Berchtesgaden

△F5 🚌🚉
ℹ️ **Maximilianstraße 9; berchtesgaden.de**

The area known as Berchtes-gadener Land enjoys an excellent climate. The town is set in beautiful Alpine scenery on the River Ache at the foot of the Watzmann, which at 2,713 m (8,900 ft), is the second highest peak in Germany.

The town is an ideal base for hikes throughout the region but with its old-world charm it also has plenty to offer. Here you'll find houses with walls decorated with *Lüftlmalerei*. One of them, the Gasthof zum Hirschen, an inn dating from about 1600, has small paintings depicting monkeys parodying a range of human vices.

Another interesting building is the Gothic Franziskanerkirche, while a major attraction is the nearby saltworks – the **Salzbergwerk und Salzmuseum**. A little way from the town is the Kehlsteinhaus, also known as Hitler's Eagle's Nest. A scenic excursion follows the Roßfeld-Panoramastraße, which winds its way along hairpin bends to a height of 1,600 m (5,249 ft).

The **Königliches Schloss**, formerly an Augustinian monastery and now owned by the Wittelsbach family, contains a museum with an interesting collection of furni-ture, paintings and Gothic woodcarving. The adjoining church was remodelled in the Gothic style, although it retains its original Romanesque portal. The façade, with its rose window and two towers, was added in 1864–68. The Romanesque cloisters, unusual in southern Germany, date from the 12th century.

Salzbergwerk und Salzmuseum
🏛️ Bergwerkstr. 83 🕐 May-Oct: 9am-5pm daily; Nov-Apr: 11am-3pm daily
🌐 salzbergwerk.de

Königliches Schloss
🏛️ Schlossplatz 2 🕐 16 May-15 Oct: 10am-noon & 2-4pm Sun-Fri; 16 Oct-15 May: 11am-2pm Mon-Fri
🌐 schloss-berchtesgaden.de

⑥

Anger

△F5 🚌🚉 ℹ️ **Dorfplatz 4; anger.de**

Ludwig I deemed Anger the prettiest village in Bavaria. Much of its charm has been eroded by the arrival of a motorway and commercial

KEHLSTEINHAUS – "THE EAGLE'S NEST"

Set atop the Kehlstein, this stone building resembling a mountain shelter is known as the Adlerhorst (Eagle's Nest). It was given to Hitler by Martin Bormann in 1939 and became the Führer's favourite residence. On the way up, a road with superb views passes through five tunnels, after which there is an elevator whose shaft is cut into the rock. The Eagle's Nest offers one of the best Alpine outlooks.

Idyllic location of the
Maria Gern church, with
Alpine peaks behind

EAT

Grillstüberl Berchtesgaden

A popular food counter
serving decadent
currywurst, burgers
and an array of vegan
takeaway options.

F5 ⬛ Marktplatz 24,
Berchtesgaden ⬛ grills
tuberl.de

€€€

Pizzeria Einkehr

Overlooking
Berchtesgaden's
central square, this
family-friendly Italian
restaurant serves great
pizzas and pasta.

F5 ⬛ Maximilian-str.
2, Berchtesgaden
⬛ speisekartenweb.de

€€€

development, but it still has a
delightfully situated late
Gothic church. The large
square, which is lined with
interesting houses, has a
column with the statue of
St Mary in the centre.

Two km (1.5 miles) to the
north is Höglwörth, a tiny
former Augustine abbey built
in the 12th century on an
island in a lake covered with
water lilies.

The interior is decorated
with stuccowork by Joseph
Schmidt. The walls of the
presbytery are hung with
votive images spanning the
12th to the 20th centuries,
and the altar has a beautiful wooden carving of the
Madonna by Wolfgang
Huber before which the
faithful pray for forgiveness.

The Ölbergkapelle below
the church dates from 1710.

which features two lions
supporting the columns.

Gradierwerk, the inhalation
house in the Kurpark built
in 1909–10, gives visitors an
idea of how salt used to be
produced by evaporation.
In the **Alte Saline**, the old
saltworks, which date from
1836–51, Ludwig I ordered
a salt museum to be built.
The fascinating exhibits
here include old salt-making
equipment. The saltworks'
marble enclosures date from
1524–36 and, together with
an underground tunnel system, were designed by the
leading German sculptor
Erasmus Grasser.

7

Maria Gern

⬛ F5 ⬛⬛ Berchtesgaden
⬛ Berchtesgaden,
Königsseer Str. 2; (08652)
96 70

This pilgrimage church is
in a serene and picturesque
setting among woodland
pastures. Built in 1708–10, its
pink pilasters on the exterior
make a pleasing contrast with
the white walls and the steep
polygonal roofs harmonize
with the Baroque onion dome
of the tower.

8

Bad Reichenhall

⬛ F5 ⬛ ⬛ Wittelsbacherstr.
15; bad-reichenhall.de

The town has been known
for its salt since Celtic and
Roman times, and in the mid-
19th century it became an
important spa. Noteworthy
buildings include the St Zeno
former Augustinian monas-
tery dating from the first half
of the 12th century. Although
it was remodelled after the
Gothic period, it retains its
original Romanesque portal,

Alte Saline mit Salzmuseum

⬛ An der Salinenstr.
⬛ May-Oct: 10am-11:30am
and 2-4pm daily; Nov-Apr:
2-4pm Tue-Fri and the
first Sunday in the month
⬛ alte-saline.de

↑ Nave with ceiling frescoes depicting scenes from the Bible at Georgskirche in Ruhpolding

⑨ Ruhpolding

 E5 🚌🚉
ⓘ Bahnhofstrasse 8; ruhpolding.de

Ruhpolding attracts a high volume of tourists. It is over-looked by the Georgskirche, built in 1738–54 with highly decorated altars and a pulpit dating from the same period. The right-hand altar features a small Romanesque figure of the Virgin Enthroned, with large almond-shaped eyes, dating from about 1200. Above the church is the old cemetery, which has a Baroque chapel and tombstones dating from the 18th and 19th centuries.

The old Renaissance hunting lodge houses the **Heimatmuseum**, which has a collection of furniture, glass and jewellery spanning the 17th to the 19th centuries. Also on display in the museum is a collection of fossils and interesting minerals that were found in the surrounding mountains. Among the displays at the **Museum für Bäuerliche und Sakrale Kunst** (Museum of Folk and Religious Art) is a fine collection of church ornaments, as well as

royal jewels and crowns. There is also an extensive collection of weapons on display.

Heimatmuseum
🏠 Schlossstr. 2 📞(08663) 41 230 🕐10am–noon Tue–Fri 🚫Nov–Dec

Museum für Bäuerliche und Sakrale Kunst
🕙 🏠 Roman-Friesinger-Str. 1 📞(08663) 5078 🕐9:30am–noon & 2–4pm Tue–Sat, 9:30am–noon Sun 🚫25 Oct–25 Dec

⑩ Reit im Winkl

 E5 🚌🚉 Marquartstein
ⓘ Dorfstraße 38; reitimwinkl.de

This small town, at an altitude of almost 700 m (2,296 ft), may not have any buildings of historic interest, but it is still a very popular tourist resort. Set in the middle of the forest, with its colourful storybook houses and narrow streets, it is easy to see why the place is so appealing. Many people flock here, especially in winter, as the area has the best snow cover in the Bavarian Alps. In summer hikers use it as a base for day trips into the surround-ing area or into the whole Berchtesgadener Land. The road to Ruhpolding, 24 km (15 miles) in length, is excep-tionally scenic. Forming part of the Alpine Route, it winds among lakes which, when seen from above, resemble a necklace of green beads strung on either side of the wooded road.

→ Passengers aboard an electric motorboat on scenic Lake Königssee

Ramsau

F5 Berchtesgaden
Tal 2; ramsau.de

This resort town, nestling amid beautiful mountain slopes, has one of the most photographed churches in the world – the 16th-century Pfarrkirche St Sebastian. Inside you'll find wooden figures of Jesus and the twelve apostles, dating back to 1430. Its picturesque cemetery, which was laid out in 1658, houses tombstones spanning the 17th to the 20th centuries. The church is situated above a stream, and stands out wonderfully against the magnificent backdrop of the Reiteralpe. Malerwinkel (Painters Corner), across the Holzbrücke Bridge, is the perfect spot from which to photograph the church.

12

Königssee

F5 Berchtesgaden, Maximilianstr. 9; national park-berchtesgaden.de

With its crystal-clear water and fjord-like setting between mountain ridges, Königssee is Bavaria's loveliest lake. The area also forms part of a national park.

The electric-powered boats that are used on the 8-km (5-mile) lake take visitors to the pilgrimage church of St Bartholomä, built in about 1700 and set on a peninsula below the eastern escarpment of the Watzmann. Nearby is a well-frequented inn. The boat trip offers views of awesome rock formations, enchanting little spots, waterfalls and echoing cliffs that throw back the sound of the boat's horn. The trip goes all the way to the northern end of Königssee, from where Obersee can be reached on foot.

INSIDER TIP
Boat Trip on Königssee

Germany's deepest and cleanest lake, the Königssee is breathtaking to sail across. The boat fleet *(www. seenschifffahrt.de/en/ koenigssee)* is entirely electric, and the driver plays a trumpet along the way so the sound echoes off the cliffs.

The famous Latona-Brunnen fountain in the garden of Schloss Herrenchiemsee, and *(inset)* the palace's interior

13
Aschau

 E5

 Kampenwandstr. 38; aschau.de

In the centre of this small town, set against fine mountain backdrops, stands a magnificent twin-towered church. Originally built in the Gothic style, it was rebuilt in the Baroque period and in the early 18th century was decorated with stuccowork and captivating paintings of scenes of the life of St Mary.

Beside the church is the small Kreuzkapelle, built in the mid-18th century, while opposite, at Kirchplatz 1, is an old inn, built in 1680 and today named the Post Hotel.

From Aschau a road leads south towards **Schloss Hohenaschau**, which, set on a height, is visible from a distance. This imposing 12th-century fortress was decorated in the Baroque style in the 17th century,

although its medieval walls still survive. The vast reception hall on the second floor was decorated in 1682–4 with Baroque mouldings. The historic grounds are also worth exploring; the castle is home to a falconry and there are regular birds of prey demonstrations. The castle is only accessible via a guided tour.

You can also reach Hohenaschau from Aschau on the Kampenwand Cable Car *(kampenwand.de)*. The 15-minute ride offers an excellent vantage point to take in views of Lake Chiemsee and the Alps. The mountain station at Hohenaschau is also the starting point for a number of hiking trails.

Schloss Hohenaschau

 Hours vary, check website aschau.de/schlosshohenaschau

14
Herrenchiemsee

 E5 To Stock
 herrenchiemsee.de

The largest island in Chiemsee, Herreninsel has been settled since prehistoric times. Thanks to Ludwig II, it is among the region's main tourist attractions. The king aimed to build a huge palace set in a vast park filled with statues, fountains and a canal along its axis. It was to be the Versailles of Bavaria.

The imposing **Schloss Herrenchiemsee**, based on Louis XIV's great Palace of Versailles, was built to satisfy Ludwig II's absolutist leanings. Built in 1878–86, it was to

> The largest island in Chiemsee, Herreninsel has been settled since prehistoric times. Thanks to Ludwig II, it is among the region's main tourist attractions.

outdo all previous royal palaces, but its construction was never completed.

Ludwig II spent a mere nine days in it, and at the time of his death only 20 of the 70 rooms that were planned for the three wings were ready. They show an astonishing lavishness and splendour. Particularly spectacular are the Große Spiegelgalerie (Hall of Mirrors), and the Chambre de Parade. The palace also houses the König Ludwig II Museum dedicated to Ludwig II.

There are also the remains of a church and an Augustinian monastery on the island. These are known collectively as **Altes Schloss**.

Schloss Herrenchiemsee, König Ludwig II Museum and Altes Schloss

⊘ ⊘ 🕒 Apr–Oct: 9am–6pm daily; Nov–Mar: 9:40am–3:50pm daily 🖥 herren chiemsee.de

Stein an der Traun

🅰E4 🚌🚆 ℹ Rathausplatz 3, Traunreut; traunreut.de

One of Upper Bavaria's most distinctive buildings is **Höhlenburg**, a castle set 50 m (160 ft) above the River Traun. It forms part of a system of three castles. Torch in hand, visitors pass through a series of caves and tunnels. This is said to be the home of the fearful Heinz von Stein, a legendary giant knight who abducted girls. Casemates lead between the medieval upper castle, the lower castle and the new castle, which dates from the 15th century and was rebuilt in the Neo-Gothic style in 1885–9.

Höhlenburg

⊘ ☎ (08621) 25 01 🕒 Apr–third Sun in Oct: 2pm Tue–Sun; mid-Jul–mid-Sep: 2 & 4pm Tue–Sun

Fraueninsel

🅰E5 🚢

The Fraueninsel is the second-largest of the three islands on Lake Chiemsee. It offers a microcosm of wider Bavarian life, with a twelve-hundred-year-old monastery and an old fishing village. About a third of the island to the south is taken up by the 8th-century Frauenwörth Abbey, one of the oldest abbeys in Bavaria. The northern part of the island is dominated by the old fishing village and the large village green, with delightful rural houses. Once home to a thriving community of fishers and craftspeople, today the island houses a convent of Benedictine nuns as well as about 300 permanent residents. Ferries from towns around Chiemsee can be found online (www. chiemsee-schifffahrt.de).

CHIEMSEE'S ECOSYSTEM

The largest lake in Bavaria, Chiemsee's water is of excellent quality, making the region's ecosystem one of the most diverse in Germany. It is home to 30 species of fish, 300 types of birds and 1,300 varieties of plant. The lake's delicate reed beds, mudflats, wooded shores, moorlands and wetlands are part of the larger Chiemsee conservation area; the shallow shore zones around the protected wildlife areas, known as the Achendelta, are an important retreat for wading birds. During migration,

wood sandpiper, spotted redshank, dunlin and common greenshank can be spotted here. You may also catch a glimpse of beavers on the lake, though they are furtive and tend to only appear around sunset. At Hirschauer Bucht, a pristine bay on the lake's eastern shore, there's an observation tower that is frequented by birders and wildlife watchers. Though the lake's waters are home to an abundance of trout and carp, fishing around Lake Chiemsee is heavily regulated and isn't usually open to visitors.

EAT

Restaurant Dionysus

Only the freshest ingredients are used to prepare dishes at this popular Greek restaurant. The extensive menu offers a full range of favourites, from loaded gyros to decadent moussaka. It also serves Mediterranean delicacies.

🅰D4 🅰Kirchzeile 13, Bad Aibling dionysos-badaibling.de

€€€

Gasthof Kriechbaumer

Perhaps the best traditional Bavarian restaurant in Bad Aibling, this cosy spot has perfected its schnitzel and dumplings. The pink roasted lamb rump served with herb butter, bacon beans and roast potatoes is also excellent. The food is best enjoyed in the large beer garden.

🅰D4 🅰Ebersberger Str., Bad Aibling gasthof-kriechbaumer.de

€€€

CafélotteBar

Bad Aibling's most esteemed café, CafélotteBar prides itself on decadent Bavarian breakfasts. It is also home to one of the region's best homemade cheesecakes.

🅰D4 🅰Kirchzeile 2, Bad Aibling cafelottebar.de

€€€

Bauernhausmuseum's inner courtyard and pigeonry, Amerang ↑

🔟 Amerang

🅰E4 🚌🚆 Wasserburger Str. 11; amerang.de

Schloss Amerang, the Renaissance palace in this small town, was built by several Italian architects, including members of the Scaligeri family of Verona. Its large cloistered courtyard is a venue for open-air concerts. There is also a museum.

At the other end of the town is the **Bauernhausmuseum** (open-air museum) with farmhouses, a bakery, a mill and a forge. Car enthusiasts will enjoy exploring the fascinating **EFA-Automobil-Museum** (Museum of German Automobile History), featuring more than 200 cars dating from 1886 to the present.

Schloss Amerang
🅾Easter-mid-Oct
🌐schlossamerang.de

Bauernhausmuseum
🅰Hopfgarten 2 🅾Mid-Mar-Oct: 9am-6pm Tue-Sun
🌐bhm-amerang.de

Did You Know?

For many years, Bad Aibling was home to a monitoring station that provided surveillance data to the US.

EFA-Automobil-Museum
🅰Wasserburger Str. 38
🅾10am-5pm Wed-Sun
🌐efaautomuseum.de

1️⃣8️⃣ Bad Aibling

🅰D4 🚌🚆 Wilhelm-Leibl-Platz 3; bad-aibling.de

Bad Aibling is known for its mud baths, which were in use as far back as Roman times. However, it was only in the mid-19th century that it acquired its present status as a spa town.

There is much of architectural interest here. On

Kloster Seeon

⚠E4 🚌🚉 Bad Endorf or Traunstein 🛈 Kultur- und Bildungszentrum des Bezirks Oberbayern, Klosterweg 1; kloster-seeon.de

On the edge of Klostersee stands Kloster Seeon, a monastery that was taken over by Benedictine monks. The original Romanesque church was built in stages in the 11th and 12th centuries. Remodelled by Konrad Pürkhel, it acquired its Gothic appearance in 1425–33. The ceiling was decorated by Salzburg painters in 1579. Also worth seeing are the impressive Renaissance frescoes depicting scenes from the lives of Christ and the Virgin Mary.

St Barbara's Chapel contains the magnificent tomb of Aribo I dating from about 1400 and ascribed to the Salzburg sculptor Hans Heider.

South of the church is a cloistered courtyard built from 1428 to 1433, which has Gothic tombstones.

In 1993, the premises was reopened as a cultural and educational centre. Since then, it has served as a venue for numerous conferences, seminars, concerts and exhibitions. You can also spend a night in one of its hotel rooms.

a hill stands the church of Mariä Himmelfahrt, built in the late Gothic style but later remodelled in the Rococo style by Abraham Millauer to plans by Johann Michael Fischer. Sebastianskirche was built on the site of a 16th-century votive chapel after the plague epidemic of 1634, which decimated the local population. After a series of fires that destroyed most of the town only a few houses survived. One is the 17th-century house at Kirchzeile 13 (today the Hotel Ratskeller), which has painted exterior walls and three oriel windows. The **Heimatmuseum** is also worth a visit.

Some 6 km (4 miles) southwest of Bad Aibling is Berbling, with an authentic Bavarian village atmosphere. The charming Rococo church, the old houses, the barns, the maypole and the fields that stretch right up to the houses are quintessentially Bavarian. The painter Wilhelm Leibl once stayed here, while he was living in Bad Aibling from 1882 to 1889.

The Renaissance Maxlrain Palace, with its award-winning palace brewery, lies on the other side of Bad Aibling, approximately 4 km (2.5 miles) to the north. It was built in 1580–88 and has a steeply pitched roof and four onion-domed towers. At the neighbouring 18th-century inn, beer from the palace brewery is served.

Heimatmuseum

🏠 Wilhelm-Leibl-Platz. 📞 (08061) 46 14 🕒 3–5pm Fri, 2–5pm Sun

↑ Crucifix at the Romanesque Pfarrkirche St Lambert in Kloster Seeon

20
Rott am Inn

⚠ E4 🚌 🚉

This small village on the River Inn is home to a number of scenic cycling and hiking trails. The highlight, however, is the former Benedictine church of Sts Marinus und Anianus. The church was rebuilt in 1759–63 to plans by Johann Michael Fischer, preserving the pre-existing 12th-century Romanesque tower. Once part of the monastery dedicated to Sts Marinus and Anianus, the church has one of the finest Rococo interiors, decorated by some of the greatest artists of the time: the stuccoist Jakob Rauch, the fresco-painter Matthäus Günther and the sculptor Ignaz Günther. The church has undergone extensive restoration work and is now open to the public.

Franz Josef Strauß, the former leader of Bavaria's ruling conservative party, is buried in the cemetery of the church, which is regularly visited by members of his CSU party.

21
Wasserburg am Inn

⚠ E4 🚌 🚉 ℹ Marienplatz 2; wasserburg.de

Wasserburg is set on a promontory on a bend in the Inn, and is one of the best-preserved historic towns on the river. The best view of it is from the bridge across the Inn, which leads to a picturesque Gothic gate which in turn leads into Bruckgasse. At No. 25 in this lane is the Mauthaus, the ducal customs office, dating from about 1400, with stepped gables and three Renaissance oriel windows, added in 1539.

The street leads to Marienplatz, which is lined with houses. Among them is the Kernhaus, which once belonged to the patrician Kern family. The façade features decorative mouldings by Johann Baptist Zimmermann. Opposite stands the Gothic town hall, which occupies

💬 INSIDER TIP
Boating on the River Inn

You can explore the Isar and the Inn rivers in inflatable boats, but taking a ferry is far more relaxing. The ride offers breathtaking views of Wasserburg from the water (chiemseealpenland.de).

two buildings with stepped gables. The Frauenkirche was built in 1368 and is attached to the watchtower.

The large Jakobskirche was begun in the early 15th century by Hans von Burghausen. The castle, with its covered staircase, can be reached from the church. Remaining parts of the castle include the residential wing, which was converted into a granary during the Renaissance, and a 15th-century chapel.

Gothic façade of the town hall in Wasserburg am Inn ↓

 House decorated with trompe l'oeil paintings in Neubeuern

The streets of the town are lined with old houses with typical gateways, courtyards, oriel windows and arcades.

㉒

Neubeuern

⬛E5 🚌🚋 Raubling or Rohrdorf **ℹ** Marktplatz 4; kulturdorf-neubeuern.de

This small town situated in the valley of the River Inn is held to be one of the prettiest in Bavaria, if not in the whole of Germany. It owes its present appearance to Gabriel von Seidl, who rebuilt the town and the medieval castle after two devastating fires in 1883 and 1893. Today it is often used by filmmakers. With its town gates, houses and church, all of which are covered with trompe l'oeil paintings, it possesses everything that a director needs to re-create an old-style Bavarian town.

Above the houses, decked with greenery and colourful window boxes, towers the castle with its tall keep, built in the local historical style in 1904–8. On fine days there is a good view of the Alps from the castle terraces.

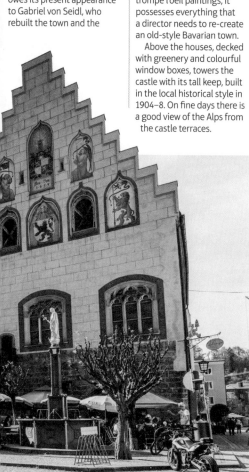

A CYCLE TOUR
AROUND CHIEMSEE

Distance 23 miles (37 km) **Stopping-off points** Gstadt, Seebruck
Terrain Flat and paved **Nearest train station** Prien am Chiemsee

Chiemsee, also known as the Bavarian Sea, covers an area of 80 sq km (30 sq miles) and reaches a depth of 73 m (240 ft). Bavaria's largest lake, it is a favourite place for holiday-makers, and its shores are dotted with towns and holiday villages. This cycling tour starts just outside Prien am Chiemsee and traces the northwestern stretch of the lake, passing divine Alpine landscapes and quaint Bavarian towns. A train runs from Munich to Prien am Chiemsee, though you will need to book bike spaces in advance. While some hotels around the lake offer bike rentals, you're advised to rent a bike in Munich or Prien an Chiemsee.

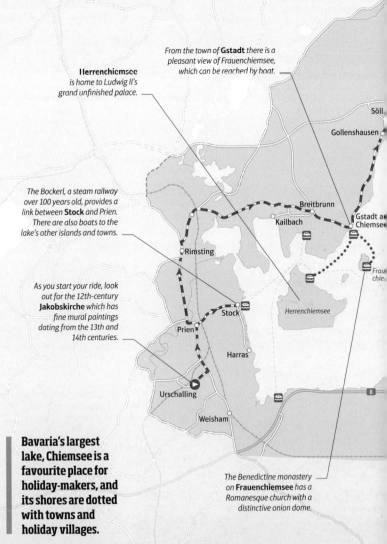

*From the town of **Gstadt** there is a pleasant view of Frauenchiemsee, which can be reached by boat.*

Herrenchiemsee *is home to Ludwig II's grand unfinished palace.*

*The Bockerl, a steam railway over 100 years old, provides a link between **Stock** and Prien. There are also boats to the lake's other islands and towns.*

*As you start your ride, look out for the 12th-century **Jakobskirche** which has fine mural paintings dating from the 13th and 14th centuries.*

Söll

Gollenshausen

Breitbrunn

Kailbach

Gstadt am Chiemsee

Rimsting

Frauenchiemsee

Stock

Herrenchiemsee

Prien

Harras

Urschalling

Weisham

*The Benedictine monastery on **Frauenchiemsee** has a Romanesque church with a distinctive onion dome.*

> **Bavaria's largest lake, Chiemsee is a favourite place for holiday-makers, and its shores are dotted with towns and holiday villages.**

The Benedictine monastery on the island of Frauenchiemsee

Alz

Seebruck

The small Roman town of **Seebruck** *today has a watersports centre and a large marina.*

Ising

Egerer

Lake Chiemsee

Chieming

Finish in the town of **Chieming**; *attractions here include the beach, with a 7-km- (4-mile-) long promenade and houses with lavish floral displays.*

Hirschau

ambach

Feldwies

0 km   2
0 miles   2

N ↑

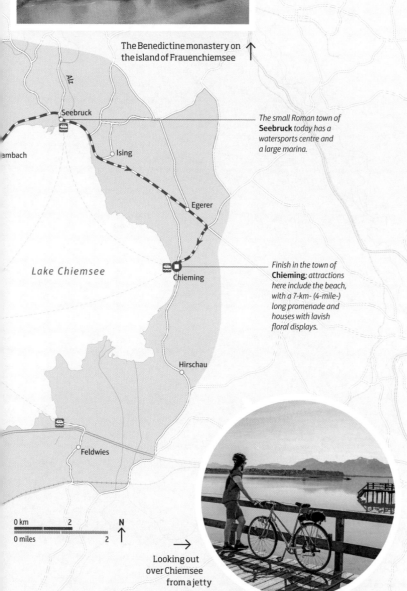

→
Looking out over Chiemsee from a jetty

UPPER BAVARIA (SOUTH)

The Werdenfelser Land, the southernmost region of the Bavarian Alps, stretches from Murnau to Garmisch-Partenkirchen, with a dramatic sub-Alpine backdrop formed by the imposing Karwendel, Wetterstein and Ammergauer mountain ranges. In the Iron Age the fertile Werdenfelser Land was first settled by Illyrians, before the Celts and then the Romans conquered the region. Historically, southern Upper Bavaria benefited economically from close trade links with Italy, but this part of the region only truly prospered in 1889 with the opening of a railway link with Munich. Southern Upper Bavaria quickly became the city's natural recreation ground.

This continued into the 20th century, when the route between Munich and Garmisch-Partenkirchen, the area's largest winter sports and hiking centre, was linked by a faster railway line. The journey now takes less than an hour and a fast suburban train also connects the Bavarian capital with the large Starnberger See and the Ammersee. These lakes, together with the Weßlinger See, Wörthsee and Pilsensee, make up the Fünfseenland (Land of Five Lakes), also popularly known as Munich's baths.

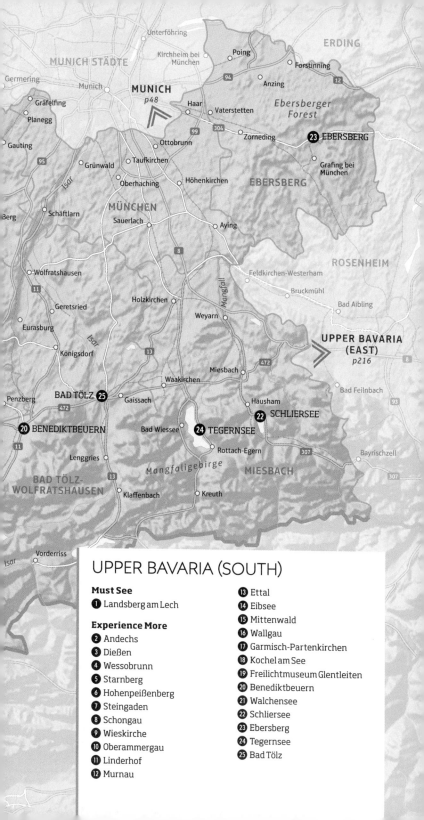

UPPER BAVARIA (SOUTH)

Must See

1. Landsberg am Lech

Experience More

2. Andechs
3. Dießen
4. Wessobrunn
5. Starnberg
6. Hohenpeißenberg
7. Steingaden
8. Schongau
9. Wieskirche
10. Oberammergau
11. Linderhof
12. Murnau
13. Ettal
14. Eibsee
15. Mittenwald
16. Wallgau
17. Garmisch-Partenkirchen
18. Kochel am See
19. Freilichtmuseum Glentleiten
20. Benediktbeuern
21. Walchensee
22. Schliersee
23. Ebersberg
24. Tegernsee
25. Bad Tölz

LANDSBERG AM LECH

C4 🛈 Hauptplatz 152; landsberg.de

Landsberg rises in terraces up the elevated banks of the River Lech. Enclosed by walls set with towers and pierced by gateways, the town largely retains its medieval character with steep narrow streets, hidden alleys, a charming market square and steep-roofed houses. The town's delightful corners and squares, such as the Hexenviertel, Seelberg and Blattergasse, are best explored on foot.

① Historisches Rathaus

📍 Hauptplatz 152
📞 (08191) 12 82 68
🕐 8am-noon & 2-5pm Mon-Thu, 8am-12:30pm Fri

The Historisches Rathaus, or town hall, stands on the west side of the square. The façade and rooms on the second floor have fine mouldings executed by Dominikus Zimmermann in 1718-20. Outside the Rathaus is the Marienbrunnen, a fountain with a statue of the Madonna, dating from 1783.

② Lechwehr

This weir was built in the 14th century at the point where the Mühlbach stream branches off from the River Lech. Over the centuries, the weir has been repeatedly washed away by floods and rebuilt.

③ Klosterkirche der Dominikanerinnen Hl. Dreifaltigkeit

📍 Peter Dörfler Str.

The church, with its uniform Rococo decoration, was built in 1764-6. It stands in the same street as the Dominican convent, whose façade was painted with murals in about 1765. This entire group of buildings was the last work that Dominikus Zimmermann executed before his death.

④ Bayertor and Town Walls

🕐 May-Oct: 10am-noon & 2-5pm daily

One of the best-known gateways in Bavaria is Landsberg's colourful Bayertor. Built in 1425, it has a 36-m (118-ft) high crenellated tower whose interior contains a stone sculpture of the Crucifixion and armorial cartouches. The other surviving gates

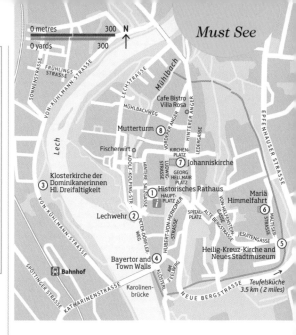

0 metres 300 N

0 yards 300

Hitler was sentenced to prison following the failed coup attempt in Munich in 1923. He ended up in Landsberg am Lech in 1924, and it was here, in prison, that he wrote the first half of *Mein Kampf*. In an effort to address this dark chapter in the history of the town, the council erected information boards and opened an information centre in the town hall.

in Landsberg am Lech are the Mannerist Sandauertor, dating from 1625–30, the Bäckertor of about 1430, and the Färbertor, built in the later 15th century. The Sandauertor is crowned by the tall, circular Luginsland tower, which functioned as a watchtower during the Middle Ages. Except for those on the west side, the medieval town walls have been preserved almost in their entirety.

The earliest parts of the fortifications, built in the 13th century, can be seen on Vordere Mühlgasse and Hintere Salzgasse. The colourfully tiled Schmalzturm, or Schöner Turm, also dates from the 13th century. The most recent section of the walls was built in the early 15th century.

↑ The Marienbrunnen fountain in front of the Historisches Rathaus

Heilig-Kreuz-Kirche

🏛 Von-Helfenstein-Gasse 426 ☎ (08191) 12 83 60 🕐 2pm–5pm Tue–Fri, 10am–5pm Sat, Sun & public hols

The Heilig-Kreuz-Kirche was built in 1752–4 to a plan by Ignaz Merani, replacing the previous building of 1580. It was the first Jesuit church in southern Germany. Set high up on a slope overlooking the town, it has a flat façade flanked by belfries with Baroque roofs. The ceiling is decorated with two trompe l'oeil paintings by Thomas Scheffler, a pupil of the Asam brothers. The paintings create the striking illusion of the Holy Cross falling from above. The high altar painting by Johann Baptist Baader, dating from 1758, depicts the crucifixion of Christ. There are also monastery buildings standing beside the church.

Opposite the Heilig-Kreuz-Kirche, a little farther down the hill, is the former Jesuit college, built in 1688–92 in a refined but simple style.

> **Opposite the Heilig-Kreuz-Kirche, a little farther down the hill, is the former Jesuit college, built in 1688–92 in a refined but simple style.**

Baroque appearance in about 1700. The windows of the presbytery have late Gothic stained glass, although this is unfortunately obscured by the high altar. Also in the presbytery, in the Altar of the Rosary made by Dominikus Zimmermann in 1721, is a Gothic figure of the Madonna and Child, an outstanding work executed by Hans Multscher of Ulm in about 1440. Since 1989 the building has housed the local history museum, which chronicles Landsberg's past from pre-history to the late 20th century.

Mariä Himmelfahrt

🏛 Georg-Hellmair-Platz

The church, built in 1458–88 and retaining its Romanesque tower, was given its present

Richly decorated altar of the Mariä Himmelfahrt parish church

↑ Eye-catching Mutterturm (Mother Tower)

⑦
Johanniskirche

🏠 Vorderer Anger

Built by Dominikus Zimmermann in 1750–52, this brick Gothic church features an impressive 108-m- (354-ft-) tall spire. It has an oval plan, four semicircular external corner niches and a separate circular presbytery. Zimmermann, working with Johann Luidl, was also responsible for the decoration of the interior, which features a magnificent high altar. The imaginative rocaille structure depicts the baptism of Christ, in front of a painted landscape background, in pastel tones.

---

⑧
Mutterturm

🏠 Von-Kühlmann-Str. 2
📞 (08191) 12 83 60
🕐 Apr-mid-Oct: 1-6pm Tue-Sun

The Mother Tower, built in 1884–7 in a wooded glade

on the side of the river opposite the town, was the summer residence and studio of Hubert von Herkomer, the Bavarian-born British painter and dramatist, who died in 1914. Dedicated to his mother, the house was built in the style of a Norman castle keep and stands 30 m (98 ft) high. The museum in the tower has objects from the artist's studio, including an array of his early drawings and etchings, and some of his renowned social realist paintings which depicted the life of the working classes in rare detail. Note that the tower is sometimes closed even within its stated opening hours.

JOHNNY CASH IN LANDSBERG

Between 1951 and 1954, famous American singer-songwriter Johnny Cash was stationed at Landsberg am Lech's air base. His squadron specialized in intercepting Soviet morse messages. Though unconfirmed, Cash even claimed he was the first person to break the news of Stalin's death to his colleagues back in the US.

EXPERIENCE MORE

② Andechs

🅰C4 🏠Andechser Str.16 🚌🚆Herrsching 🌐gemeinde-andechs.de

Andechs is home to one of the oldest churches in Germany. The main part of the building dates from 1420. The church was remodelled in the Baroque style in 1669–1751. The stuccowork and painting are the work of Johann Baptist Zimmermann.

The church attracts some 200,000 pilgrims every year.

Did You Know?

The internationally famous Andechser Doppelbock Dunkel beer is a whopping 7.1 per cent ABV.

Because of its situation almost 180 m (590 ft) above the level of Ammersee, together with the Rococo decoration of its late Gothic church, the Benedictine monastery draws large numbers of visitors.

Another reason for the monastery's popularity with visitors is the strong beer that is brewed here. It is served at the monastery's inn and on the terrace, from which there is a breathtaking view over the lake.

③ Dießen

🅰C4 🏠Bahnhofstr.15 🚌🚆 🌐diessen.de

This small fishing town is located on Ammersee, Bavaria's third-largest lake. The area is very popular with people from nearby Munich. Although large

↑ Beautiful ceiling fresco at the Marienmünster in Dießen

numbers of tourists come here, their presence is not especially noticeable. It is pleasant to walk along the lakeside promenade, and especially to visit one of the homely restaurants and to sample Ammersee's speciality, the salmon-like *Renken*.

A few old houses survive here, including the oldest wooden peasant cottage

Famous 15th-century church in Andechs, surrounded by greenery ↑

in Upper Bavaria, dating from 1491. The most exquisite historic building is the early Rococo Marienmünster, a church built for the Augustinian monastery in 1732–9 to a design by Johann Michael Fischer. The fine ceiling paintings, executed by Johann Georg Bergmüller in 1736, depict the saints and blessed members of the von Andechs family. The side altars feature depictions of St Sebastian by the renowned Venetian painter Giovanni Battista Tiepolo and of St Stefan by Battista Pittoni.

THE DEATH OF LUDWIG II

On 13 June 1886, King Ludwig II, Bavaria's Fairy Tale King, died in Starnberger See. The hugely ostentatious expense of the castles he had built meant that he had his critics, and rebelling ministers sought to depose Ludwig. In early June, 1886, he was deemed psychologically unfit to rule. Shortly afterwards, he died in the lake. His death was officially ruled a suicide, but it has been speculated that he was murdered by his political opponents.

Wessobrunn

C5 Zöpfstr. 1
Weilheim
wessobrunn.de

The exterior of the former Benedictine abbey here conceals a fine courtyard, lavish stuccowork in the monastery and Rococo decoration in the church,

which was built in 1757–9. Of the original Romanesque buildings, all that remain are the defence tower and the crucifix in the church. The stuccowork and trompe l'oeil painting in the cloisters and on the monastery staircase were executed by the workshop of Johann Schmuzer in 1680–96.

It was here in 814 that the *Wessobrunner Gebet* was written. This two-part poem describing the Creation is the oldest extant document in the German language. It is today preserved in the Bayerische Staats-bibliothek in Munich *(p121)*.

Starnberg

C4

Linked to Munich by a railway since 1854, the picturesque town of Starnberg is home to luxury villas and has a large marina. It sits on Starnberger See, Germany's second-largest freshwater lake. Originally a small village of fishers, Starnberg developed into the most important settlement on the lake when Bavarian rulers built a lavish palace there in the 16th century. Later, in the second half of the 19th century, steam shipping became the real impetus for the village's rapid development.

The Italian Renaissance palace was redesigned in the 19th century in the Neo-Gothic style. Ludwig II chose the manor as his summer palace during this period; it was the ruler's last residence before his tragic drowning in Starnberger See in 1886. The palace can still be seen, and the gardens are open to the public, though the building itself is closed.

The area around Starnberg has long enjoyed great popularity: wealthy citizens build expensive villas here, while outdoor lovers visit to swim and boat on the lake. Popularly known as "Munich's summer swimming pool," the lake has become one of Munich's favourite destinations in the summer. The area offers a range of watersports around the lake such as sailing and rowing, as well as ample cycling and hiking opportunities. Visitors can also stop at one of the many restaurants here for a delicious meal or sample local ales at a beer garden.

↑ Road leading past the Gnadenkapelle at Hohenpeißenberg

6

Hohenpeißenberg

🅰C5 🄰Blumenstr. 2 🚌🚋Peißenberg or Peiting 🌐hohenpei ssenberg.de

The mountain known as Hoherpeißenberg rises east of the town of Peißenberg. The summit, at a height of 988 m (3,241 ft) above sea level, is reached by a scenic winding road and offers an extensive panorama of Upper Bavaria, from Ammersee and Starnberger See to the Alps. The height of the peak and the superb views it affords have led to the mountain being nicknamed the Bavarian Mount Parnassus.

On the summit stands the Gnadenkapelle, built in the late Gothic period and remodelled in the Baroque style, the church of Mariä Himmelfahrt, built in 1616–19, and a former chapterhouse of 1619. The small chapel contains a miracle-working image of the Madonna Enthroned dating from 1460–80

and brought here from the nearby town of Schongau in 1514.

7

Steingaden

🅰C5 🄰Krankenhausstr. 1 🚌🚋Peiting 🌐stein gaden.de

This town has the well-preserved Romanesque Pfarrkirche St Johannes der Täufer, built in the second half of the 12th century and partially rebuilt in the 15th century. The columned basilica has a triple apse and twin towers above the west front. The interior was decorated with Rococo mouldings and paintings in 1771–4.

In 1147, the Premon-stratensians built an abbey here, of which the western cloisters, dating from the early 13th century, survive. The architect Dominikus Zimmermann was buried in the Romanesque chapel of St John in 1766.

8

Schongau

🅰 C5 🚌🚋 🄰Münzstr. 1-3 🌐schongau.de

Schongau is picturesquely located on the river Lech and surrounded by idyllic fields and pastures. The town is enclosed by almost completely preserved town walls with wooden walkways

and towers. They were built in the 14th century and later reinforced in the 17th century. The main street in Schongau is the wide Münzenstraße, which is lined with shops and restaurants.

One of the town's finest buildings is the church of Mariä Himmelfahrt, which was built by Dominikus Zimmermann in 1751–3 on the site of a Gothic church. Also of interest is the former castle of the Wittelsbachs, dating from the 15th century and refurbished in 1771–2, and the late Gothic Ballenhaus, whose ground floor with open-beamed ceiling houses the town hall. The **Stadtmuseum Schongau**, a local history museum, is to be found in Erasmuskirche, a former hospital church, established in the 15th century and rebuilt in the 17th century.

SCHONGAU'S FORESTS

Schongau is famous for its *märchenwald (www. schongauer-maerchenwald.de),* a forest trail with playgrounds and themed areas that relate to characters and stories from the Brothers Grimm fairy tales. There are several of these *märchenwald -* or fairytale forests - dotted around Bavaria. The *Märchenwald im Isartal* (south of Munich) and the *Märchenwald Sambachshof* (northern Bavaria) are also popular Grimm-themed outdoor amusement parks.

Some 3 km (2 miles) northwest is Altenstadt, which has Michaelskirche, the finest surviving monumental Romanesque basilica in Upper Bavaria. Dating from about 1200, it is surrounded by a wall. It is decorated with Gothic frescoes and contains the Great God of Altenstadt, a crucifix 3 m (10 ft) tall, and a carved Romanesque font.

Stadtmuseum Schongau

 Christophstr. 55
☎ (08861) 25 46 05
🕐 2–5pm Wed, Sat, Sun & public hols

---

❾

Wieskirche

🅰 C5 🚪 Krankenhausstr. 1, Steingaden 🚌
🚉 Füssen or Peiting
🌐 wieskirche.de

The attractive pilgrimage church of Zum Gegeißelten Heiland, nestling in the sub-Alpine scenery, is not only the most resplendent example of South German Rococo, but probably the finest Rococo church in the world. UNESCO listed it as a World Heritage Site in 1983.

In 1738, the figure of Christ in a small chapel in the fields southwest of the present church is said to have wept genuine tears, and soon afterwards pilgrims began to flock to the site of the miracle. In 1743–4, the Premonstratensian abbot of Steingaden commissioned Dominikus Zimmermann to design a church here.

Built in 1754 and decorated in 1765, the

> **The nave of the Wieskirche is built to an oval plan and the ceiling is supported by eight pairs of columns, with an elongated presbytery.**

church represents the work of Dominikus and Johann Baptist Zimmermann at its peak. The nave of the Wieskirche is built to an oval plan and the ceiling is supported by eight pairs of columns and there is an elongated presbytery. The entire building displays an extraordinary fusion of painting, woodcarving and stuccowork and an almost mesmerizing interplay of colour and light. The many windows, in fantastic and varied shapes, enliven the exterior and contribute to the bright, airy space of the interior. Not surprisingly given this attention to detail, the church has been fondly nicknamed the Lord God's Ballroom.

→

Stunning stuccowork and frescoed ceiling of Wieskirche, and *(inset)* its oval, Rococo exterior

11

Linderhof

📍C5 🚌🚶Ettal ⏰Hours vary, check website
🌐schlosslinderhof.de

Of all Ludwig II's many fairy-tale residences, the palace at Linderhof best shows his great fondness for France and his regard for the Bourbons and Louis XIV. The smallest of Ludwig II's castles and the one he visited most often, it was built by Georg von Dollmann in 1870–86 and is surrounded by an extensive park. The extravagant luxury of the interior decoration is based on French Baroque style. Although it was intended as a private residence, the palace still has an ornate royal audience chamber. The other rooms in the palace are no less extravagantly decorated.

The palace is surrounded by French-style formal gardens and by Italianate terraced gardens with cascades, which in turn are surrounded by landscaped grounds. There is an artificial grotto dating from 1876–7 with a lake, a stage and a throne with colourful lighting that brings to mind the Venus Grotto in Wagner's opera *Tannhäuser*. Ludwig II would take rides on the lake in a conch-shaped boat.

Another attraction of the park surrounding the palace is the Moorish kiosk, made by Karl von Dibitsch in 1850 and purchased by the king in 1876. Inside it is a lavish Peacock Throne. Just as resplendent is the Moroccan House of 1878–9.

Did You Know?

Linderhof is the only palace Ludwig II saw completed in his lifetime.

10

Oberammergau

📍C5 🏠Eugen-Papst-Str. 9a
🚌🚶 🌐oberammergau.de

Oberammergau is one of the best-known towns in Upper Bavaria. Its renown rests on its painted houses, and it is the centre of the colourful style of trompe l'oeil house-painting known as *Lüftlmalerei*, which is typical of the region.

The town also has an international reputation for its Passion play, which has been performed here at Easter ever since 1633, when an epidemic of the plague finally passed. Originally an open-air event, the play has been performed in a purpose-built theatre since 1930.

The spectacle, which last for six hours, is per-formed by 1,400 amateur actors, all of whom must be local people or their family members. The play attracts an audience from all over the world.

12

Murnau

📍C5 🏠Untermarkt 13
🚌🚶 🌐murnau.de

Murnau is situated on an elevation between

←
Ludwig II's Neo-Rococo Schloss Linderhof set in terraced gardens

SHOP

Susanne Bosse
Packed with handpicked home and lifestyle products, this stylish shop has Murnau's prettiest window display. It's a great place to visit for gifts.

A C5
Obermarkt 5, Murnau W bosse-conceptstore.de

two lakes, Staffelsee and Riegsee, north of the marsh known as the Murnauer Moos, on what was once the Roman road to Augsburg. During World War II an officers' prisoner-of-war camp existed here. Today Murnau is famous for its two breweries.

The Nikolauskirche is an interesting building. It was designed by Enrico Zucalli and was completed in 1734, after 17 years' work. The small Baroque Maria-Hilf-Kirche stands on Marktstraße, the main street, which commands a view of the Alps to the south.

There are numerous inns and guesthouses, a Neo-Gothic town hall, houses with oriel windows and decorative signboards, and narrow, winding alleys which give the town a unique charm. The monument to Ludwig II, on Kohlgruber Straße, was erected in 1894 and is the earliest monument to be dedicated to the king.

The finest building in Murnau is the Art Nouveau **Münterhaus**, where the artist Wassily Kandinsky lived from 1909 to 1914 with his student and lifetime companion Gabriele Münter. Today it houses a museum dedicated to the famous painter couple, along with works by other members of the Blaue Reiter group.

INSIDER TIP
Hiking in Murnauer Moos
Located to the south of Murnau, Murnauer Moos is an expanse of open moorland ringed by towering peaks. A gentle 12-km (7-mile) marked hiking trail offers stunning views of the Alps.

Münterhaus
Kottmüllerallee 6
(08841) 62 88 80
2–5pm Tue–Sun

13

Ettal

A C5 Ammergauer Str. 8
Oberammergau
W ettal.de

Set in a scenic Alpine valley, this Benedictine abbey was founded by Ludwig IV in 1330. In 1710, when the church was remodelled in the Baroque style, a Gothic rotunda was added. The two-storey façade that Enrico Zucalli intended was not completed until the early 20th century.

The impressive interior decoration is in a pure Rococo style, crowned by the large dome that is visible from afar. The paintings were executed in 1748–50 by Johann Jakob Zeiller, and the stuccowork, one of the great achievements of its time, is by Johann Georg Üblher and Franz Xaver Schmuzer. The high altar has a 14th-century marble statue of the Madonna made in the workshop of Giovanni Pisano. The church is surrounded by various monastic buildings.

Stand-up paddleboarding on the Eibsee lake at the foot of the Zugspitze

The beginnings of the local violin-making trade can be traced back to the 17th century and Matthäus Klotz (1653–1743), a pupil of the famous Nicolo Amati. A violin school was founded in 1853, and in 1930 the **Geigenbaumuseum** (Museum of Violin-Making) was established in the house where Klotz was born.

St-Peter-und-Paul-Kirche was built in 1738–40 by Josef Schmuzer. The late Gothic presbytery survives, and the tower was completed in 1746. The *Lüftlmalerei* on the façade is an outstanding example of this type of decoration). It is by Matthias Günther, who also executed the paintings inside the church. The monument to Matthäus Klotz that stands outside the church was designed by Ferdinand von Miller in 1890.

Geigenbaumuseum

🏠 Ballenhausgasse 3
🕐 10am–5pm Tue–Sun (11am–4pm Jan, mid-Mar–mid-May & mid-Oct–Nov)
🌐 geigenbaumuseum-mittenwald.de

14
Eibsee

🅰 C5 🚌🚆 Garmisch-Partenkirchen

The greenish-blue waters of this lake, surrounded by wooded mountain slopes, lie 974 m (3,195 ft) above sea level. The scenic paths along its shores lead to secluded jetties for yachts and boats.

A regatta, with processions of yachts and great firework displays, takes place here every summer. Above the lake towers Zugspitze, which at 2,963 m (9,718 ft) is the highest peak in the German Alps. The summit can be reached by cablecar or a funicular train, which passes through many tunnels.

STAY

Obermühle
With its spa, pool and mini golf course, Obermühle is well worth a stay. The food is excellent, and breakfast can be enjoyed on the patio in summer.

🅰 C5
🏠 Mühlstr. 2, Garmisch-Partenkirchen
🌐 hotel-obermuehle.de

€€€

15
Mittenwald

🅰 C6 🏠 Dammkarstr. 3
🚌🚆 🌐 alpenwelt-karwendel.de/mittenwald

Situated at the foot of the Karwendel mountain range, this small town stands on what was once the main trade route between Verona and Augsburg. Up until the Thirty Years' War, its wealth was founded on trade but from the 17th century its mainstay was craftsmanship, particularly violin-making.

16
Wallgau

🅰 C5 🏠 Mittenwalderstr. 8
🚌🚆 Mittenwald 🌐 alpenwelt-karwendel.de

This delightful village has small wooden cottages built in the 17th and 18th centuries with *Lüftlmalerei* by Franz Kainer dating from the 1770s. Most of the cottages have been thoroughly modernized and now function as hotels.

The town is popular with the smart Munich set, who come to play golf on the fine local courses.

$\rightarrow$

Building decorated with artwork in Garmisch-Partenkirchen

Garmisch-Partenkirchen is famous for its ski slopes and for hosting international skiing events.

Garmisch-Partenkirchen

C5 Richard-Strauss-Platz 2 W gapa-tourismus.de

Two villages, Garmisch and Partenkirchen, separated by the rivers Loisach and Partnach, were conjoined one year before the 1936 Winter Olympics. Thus came into being one of the best-known winter sports centres in Germany, with a convenient motorway link to Munich. Garmisch-Partenkirchen is famous for its ski slopes and for hosting international skiing events.

Partenkirchen, the older of the two villages, has its roots in the Roman town of Partanum, while Garmisch is first mentioned in a document from the 9th century. Both parts of the town have many houses with characteristically painted façades, some old and others quite modern. The finest churches here include St Anton, in Partenkirchen, a pilgrimage church dating from the first half of the 18th century, with trompe l'oeil painting by Johann Holzer. There are also two churches in Garmisch dedicated to St Martin. One is medieval, with Gothic frescoes in the interior, and the other is Baroque, with stuccowork executed by Josef Schmuzer in 1730–33 and paintings by Matthäus Günther of 1733.

The Olympic stadium in the south part of Partenkirchen was built in 1934. As well as having ski-jumps, it is decorated with larger-than-life sculptures that are typical of Fascist art.

A road south of Partenkirchen leads to the scenic Partnach river gorge (Partnachklamm). Farther along, an uphill walk of several hours leads to Ludwig II's hunting lodge in Schachen, just below the summit of Dreitorspitze. Built in 1870, the lodge has an ornate interior. The king celebrated his birthdays in the lodge, and also came here on multi-day hunting trips.

ZUGSPITZE

At 2,962 m (9,700 ft), Zugspitze is Germany's tallest peak. From the village of Garmisch-Partenkirchen, it can be reached by taking the narrow-gauge railway to Zugspitzplatt or a cable car, which reaches the summit in around ten minutes and offers breathtaking views. Hiking to the top usually takes more than two days, with hikers spending one night in an Alpine guesthouse on the way up.

18

Kochel am See

🗺️ C5 🚉 Bahnhofstr. 23
🚌🚆 🌐 kochel.de

Kochel is a popular resort on Kochelsee. The local church, Michaelskirche, was built in 1688–90, probably by Kaspar Feichtmayr. The frescoes and stuccowork were added in about 1730. Two famous figures are associated with Kochel. One is the blacksmith who became the hero of the Bavarian uprising against Austria in 1705 – a statue of him was erected in 1900. The other is the painter Franz Marc. The house in which he lived is now **Franz Marc Museum**. It is home to his paintings and the works of other artists of the group Der Blaue Reiter *(p33)*.

On the banks of Kochelsee is Walchensee hydro-electric power station. It was built in 1918–24 to a design by Oskar von Miller, who aimed to electrify the Bavarian rail network and to supply electricity to the whole country. Walchensee power station is still one of the largest in Germany today.

Franz Marc Museum

 🚉 Franz-Marc-Parc 8–10
🕐 10am–6pm Tue–Sun & public hols (to 5pm Nov–Mar)
🚫 24 & 31 Dec 🌐 franz-marc-museum.de

19

Freilichtmuseum Glentleiten

🗺️ C5 🚌🚆 Kochel am See, Murnau 🕐 19 Mar–11 Nov: 10am–5pm Tue–Sun (Jun–Sep: also on Mon)
🌐 glentleiten.de

The largest Freilichtmuseum (open-air museum) in Upper Bavaria opened near Großweil in 1976. It recreates the atmosphere of a traditional Bavarian village, with cottages and workshops. The interiors show the way villagers lived. Fields and meadows are cultivated in the traditional way, with grazing cows, horses, sheep and goats.

Did You Know?

The traditional Bavarian farmhouse with exposed beams is called a "bauernhaus".

20

Benediktbeuern

🗺️ C5 🚉 Prälatenstr. 3
🚌🚆 🌐 benediktbeuern.de

The holiday resort of Benediktbeuern, at the foot of the Benediktenwand mountains, is known for its former Benedictine

Fishing village of Walchensee on the shore of the Walchensee

monastery. Founded in 739 as part of the see established by St Boniface, it was one of the first missionary monasteries that he founded in Bavaria.

Work on the present late Baroque church, which stands on the site of a Romanesque church, began in 1682 under the direction of Kaspar Feichtmayr of Wessobrunn. The interior features some fine stuccowork strongly influenced by Italian art. The vaulting over the nave and the side chapels was painted by Hans Georg Asam, father of the renowned Asam brothers, in 1683–7. The monumental altar, built to resemble a triumphal arch, is made out of three different kinds of marble.

By the presbytery, which is fronted by towers, stands the two-storey Anastasiakapelle. It was built in 1750–53 by Johann Michael Fischer and has an oval floor plan. The decoration, by Johann Michael Feichtmayr and Johann Jakob Zeiller, is a masterpiece of Bavarian Rococo style. Also worth visiting are the monastery buildings, now owned by Silesians. Dating from 1669–1732, they are arranged around two courtyards. The Alter Festsaal (Old Banqueting Hall), the Kurfürstensaal (Assembly Hall) and the former library, now a refectory, are particularly worth seeing.

Walchensee

🄰 C5 🏠 Ringstr.1
🚌 🚊 Kochel am See
🌐 zwei-seen-land.de

This lake, which lies in a green valley, is swept by strong winds, and is therefore very popular with windsurfers.

The small church near the lake was built in 1633 and refurbished in 1712–14.

In the nearby town of Zwergern stands the lovely Margarethenkirche, which was built in the 14th century and remodelled in the Baroque style in 1670. Beside it stands a monastery known as the Klösterl. Built in 1686–9, it has striking white walls and a tall, steeply pitched roof.

Near Urfeld stands a small bust of the great 19th-century German writer Johann Wolfgang von Goethe, who stayed in the town when he set off on his famous Italian travels in 1786.

㉒ Schliersee

ⒶD5 **Ⓡ** **ⓘ** Perfallstr. 4;
schliersee.de

Situated east of Tegernsee
and known as its "younger
brother", Schliersee offers
visitors much peace and quiet
and makes for a popular
escape in the summer.
The houses on the northern
lakeshore all have balconies
laden with window boxes.

DRINK

Slyrs Distillery
Visit the famous
Slyrs Distillery to
sample artisanal
Bavarian whisky;
it offers guided tours
and tastings. There's
also a small café with
outdoor seating.

ⒶD5
ⒶBayrischzeller
Strasse 13, Schliersee
ⓦslyrs.com

Did You Know?

Born in Schliersee,
Markus Wasmeier is a
ski racer who won
Olympic gold twice.

The local church of St Sixtus
has frescoes and stuccowork
executed by Johann Baptist
Zimmermann in 1714. The
church also has a distinctive
figure of God the Father with
Christ ascribed to Erasmus
Grasser, and a Madonna
ascribed to Jan Polack. The
interesting **Heimatmuseum**
(local history museum) is
housed in a small 18th-
century hut.

Heimatmuseum
ⒶLautererstr. 6
Ⓒ(08026) 43 97
ⓄMay–Oct: 2–5pm
Tue–Sat

→

Gilded figures
atop a doorway
in Ebersberg's
Sebastianskirche

㉓ Ebersberg

ⒶD4 **Ⓡ** **ⓘ**Marienplatz 1;
ebersberg.de

This little town lies at the
southern end of Germany's
largest expanse of forest. Of
the Augustinian monastery
that was founded here in
934 CE all that remains is
the Sebastianskirche, built
in 1217–31 and remodelled
in 1472–1504 in the Gothic
style. Notable among the
tombs, which span the
14th to the 16th centuries,
is that of the couple who
founded the church. It
features a model of the
church made by Wolfgang
Leb in 1501. On
Marienplatz,
along with
Baroque

↑ Church of St Sixtus overlooking a lake in the Schliersee

and Neo-Classical houses, is the monastery inn, now the town hall.

24

Tegernsee

 D5 🚌🚆 Tegernsee
ℹ Hauptstr. 2; tegern
see.de

For the inhabitants of Munich, Tegernsee, within easy reach of the bustling capital, is an upper-class recreation ground.

The first settlement to be founded in the valley was the Benedictine monastery near Tegernsee, established in the 8th century. The monastery became an important centre of culture, and in the 11th century the Romanesque stained-glass windows made here were renowned. Examples can be seen in Augsburg cathedral. In 1823–4 Leo von Klenze converted the monastery into a summer residence for Maximilian I Joseph. Von Klenze also designed a new façade for the monastery church, built by Enrico Zucalli in the Baroque style.

 25

Bad Tölz

🅰 D5 🚌ℹ Max-Höfler-
Platz 1; bad-toelz.de

Until quite recent times, the inhabitants of Bad Tölz, on the Isar river, made their living through a combination of trade, logging and making and selling their famous painted chests, cases and beds. The rafting and brewery trades also flourished here. When iodine-rich springs were discovered here in 1846, the village became a health spa. The character of the old town has been well preserved around Marktstraße, which leads down to the Isar. Many of the houses, dating from the 17th to the 19th centuries, have characteristic trompe l'oeil wall paintings and striking stuccowork, and distinctive over-hanging eaves.

The Baroque church on Kalvarienberg, one of the most famous in Bavaria, was begun in 1726 and completed at the end of the 19th century. It has two elegant towers, and particularly impressive is the Holy Staircase inside the church. At the festival of St Leonhard, patron saint of horses and cattle, a procession with old-fashioned painted carts and horses (*Leonhardiritt*) ascends Kalvarienberg and is then blessed. A small fair and dancing events are part of the celebration.

↑ Row of historic buildings and street cafés lining Marktstraße in Bad Tölz

↑ Bismarck Tower with the vast Starnberger See in the distance

A DRIVING TOUR
AROUND STARNBERGER SEE

Distance 46 km (28 miles)
Stopping-off points There are restaurants, cafés and hotels in Tutzing and Starnberg

The scenic region around Starnberger See has long enjoyed great popularity. The wealthy citizens of Munich built fine residences here, and the area has become a hotspot for weekend breaks. This tour follows the road around the lake, passing many of the area's finest towns, resorts and lakeside palaces.

Around Starnberger See

UPPER BAVARIA (SOUTH)

Locator Map

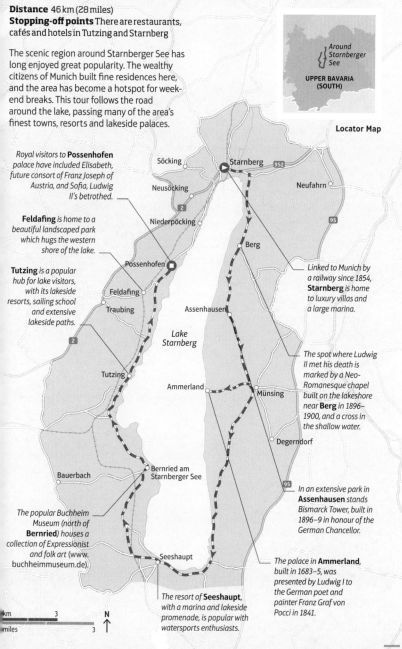

Royal visitors to **Possenhofen** palace have included Elisabeth, future consort of Franz Joseph of Austria, and Sofia, Ludwig II's betrothed.

Feldafing is home to a beautiful landscaped park which hugs the western shore of the lake.

Tutzing is a popular hub for lake visitors, with its lakeside resorts, sailing school and extensive lakeside paths.

The popular Buchheim Museum (north of **Bernried**) houses a collection of Expressionist and folk art (www.buchheimmuseum.de).

Söcking

Neusöcking

Niederpöcking

Possenhofen

Feldafing

Traubing

Tutzing

Bauerbach

Bernried am Starnberger See

Seeshaupt

Starnberg

Neufahrn

Berg

Lake Starnberg

Assenhausen

Ammerland

Münsing

Degerndorf

Linked to Munich by a railway since 1854, **Starnberg** is home to luxury villas and a large marina.

The spot where Ludwig II met his death is marked by a Neo-Romanesque chapel built on the lakeshore near **Berg** in 1896–1900, and a cross in the shallow water.

In an extensive park in **Assenhausen** stands Bismarck Tower, built in 1896–9 in honour of the German Chancellor.

The palace in **Ammerland**, built in 1683–5, was presented by Ludwig I to the German poet and painter Franz Graf von Pocci in 1841.

The resort of **Seeshaupt**, with a marina and lakeside promenade, is popular with watersports enthusiasts.

km   3
miles   3

N
↑

THE ALLGÄU

The Allgäu covers the south of Bavarian Swabia and southeastern Baden-Württemberg, bordered by the Lech Valley and the Bavarian Alps. Throughout its history, the Allgäu has been renowned for its agricultural production, especially its dairy products, and its plethora of folk festivals and traditions. The city of Kempten, which is sometimes claimed to be Germany's oldest town, was originally a Roman military camp, before becoming an imperial city in the medieval period.

One of the least industrialized regions of Bavaria, much of the Allgäu has seen little change over the centuries, though the region's population expanded after World War II with an influx of migrants, many from Sudetenland. The former inhabitants of Gablonz (Jablonec), in the Czech Republic, settled near Kaufbeuren in Neugablonz, bringing with them the traditional trade of jewellery making, which is still practised in the area. The Allgäu is today celebrated for its first-class mountain sports and the extravagant Schloss Neuschwanstein, the grandest of Ludwig II's castles.

THE ALLGÄU

Must Sees

① Memmingen
② Lindau
③ Kempten
④ Schloss Neuschwanstein

Experience More

⑤ Ottobeuren
⑥ Mindelheim
⑦ Babenhausen
⑧ Kirchheim
⑨ Schloss Hohenschwangau
⑩ Maria Steinbach
⑪ Kaufbeuren
⑫ Bad Wörishofen
⑬ Füssen
⑭ Bad Hindelang
⑮ Immenstadt
⑯ Oberstdorf
⑰ Wasserburg

❶
MEMMINGEN

 B4 🚌🚉 **Bahnhofstr.** 🛈 **Marktplatz 3; tourismus-memmingen.de**

Founded in the 12th century, Memmingen stands on the site of an Alemani settlement. In 1803 it became part of Bavaria and has retained the characteristics of a trading centre, while various residential and artisans' districts have developed here. The town is notable for its wide streets and timber-framed Gothic houses.

①
Rathaus

 Marktplatz 1

Originally built in 1488, this Gothic town hall was remodelled and enlarged in the 16th century. Its current appearance dates from 1589. The reconstruction cost was a princely sum of 30,000 guilders. The Rococo stuccowork was added later to the façade in 1765. This elegant Renaissance building has a projecting central axis with oriel windows on the lower storeys culminating in a polygonal tower, and the wings are flanked by side towers.

②
Frauenkirche

 Frauenkirchplatz 4
📞 **(08331) 22 53**

This three-nave basilica was originally a Romanesque building. It was enlarged at the end of the 14th century, and was remodelled in 1456. From 1565 to 1806 the church was shared by Catholics and Protestants. The late Gothic paintings on the walls and ceiling were uncovered in 1893. Their state of preservation and wide thematic range make them among the most significant in southern Germany.

③
Hermansbau

 Zangmeisterstr. 8
⏰ **May–Oct: 11am–5pm Tue–Sun**

This late Baroque patrician palace with an arcaded courtyard was built in 1766 for Benedikt Freiherr von

---

MEMMINGEN'S FISCHERTAG

Every summer Memmingen's Fischertag (Fisherman's Day) takes place. Locals gather in the town's stream to fish out the trouts so that it can be drained and cleaned. It started in medieval times, when tanners washed hides in the stream and people threw rubbish into it. Visitors come to watch or take part in the spectacle, which involves a parade, a lot of cheering when a trout is caught, and the crowning of the fisherman's king (the person who caught the biggest trout).

DRINK

Joesepp's Brauhaus

This beer hall has delicious home-brewed beer, good Bavarian dishes and a pleasant airy interior. It also hosts live performances by local artists.

⌂ Schweizerberg 17
ⓦ joesepps-brauhaus.de

Zur Blauen Traube

Enjoy a glass of wine or a refreshing ale on the terrace of this traditional Bavarian restaurant. There's also a separate kids menu.

⌂ Kramerstr. 8
ⓦ zur-blauen-traube-mm.com

↑ Buildings lining a canal with the Frauenkirche in the distance

Herman. The façade is lavishly decorated with stuccowork, and the central section has a gable with an armorial cartouche.

by crafters from Memmingen in 1501-7. The decorative carvings, with lifelike portraits of the founders, are among the most outstanding examples of late Gothic Swabian art and form a central part of the town's rich artistic history.

④
Martinskirche

⌂ Zangmeisterstr. 13
☏ (08331) 85 69 20

The Protestant Martinskirche was built in the 15th century, replacing a Romanesque basilica, making it one of the oldest churches in Upper Swabia. This church's unique design features a striking quadrilateral tower with a distinctive steeple added later. The 65-m- (213-ft-) tower is the tallest building in the town and can be viewed from a distance.

The interior of the church has notable wall paintings, which date back to the 15th and 16th centuries. The most interesting feature of the interior, however, is the presbytery stalls, made

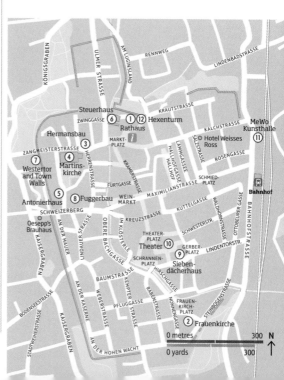

⑤ Antonierhaus

📍 Martin-Luther-Platz 1. Strigeland
AntoniterMuseum
📞 (08331) 85 02 45
🕐 11am–5pm Tue–Sun

This former Antonine monastery and hospital, the oldest established by the order, was built in 1383. It stands on the site of an earlier castle. The four-winged building has internal cloisters with external staircases. Painstakingly rebuilt, since 1996 it has housed a library as well as a café and cultural institutions.

⑥ Steuerhaus

📍 Marktplatz 16

The former customs house was built in 1495 to an elongated rectangular plan. It opens on to Marktplatz with an arcade of 20 arches. The second floor and the shaped gables were added in 1708. The painting on the façade dates from 1906–09. The building currently houses various municipal offices.

⑦ Westertor and Town Walls

The walls of the Old Town were completed before 1181. The outer walls were added in the 13th–15th centuries. In the 19th century they were partially demolished, but significant fragments with bastions and walkways have been preserved. The most noteworthy gate is Westertor, the western gate of Memmingen, which was built as a high span-roofed gateway in the 14th century. It was partially destroyed in the Thirty Years' War,

Did You Know?

Memmingen artist Josef Madlener's Christmas painting, *Der Berggeist*, inspired J.R.R. Tolkien to create Gandalf.

and attained its current octagonal form with a dome after reconstruction in 1660. Another gate worth seeing is the impressive Kemptentor. It was built in 1383 and topped by a tall brick tower.

⑧ Fuggerbau

📍 Schweizerberg 8

The house of the Fugger family *(p289)* was built in 1581–91 for Jakob Fugger. It is a monumental four-winged building with two square stairwells rising from the corners of the courtyards.

↑ Alfresco dining at a street café outside the Steuerhaus in Memmingen

 ←

The Neo-Classical Theater building on Theaterplatz

STAY

Gasthof Zum Schwanen

This traditional guesthouse, close to the train station in the heart of Memmingen, is in a convenient location. It offers rich and hearty Swabian food.

 Kalchstr. 27
w gasthof schwanen.com

€€€

Hotel Weißes Ross

A former brewery, this four-star hotel was built in 1869. It is famed for its customer service. The restaurant is a real highlight; the roast beef served with crispy onions is a popular choice among visitors.

Salzstr. 12
 hotel-weisses-ross.de

€€€

Hotel am Schrannenplatz

A family-run hotel with modern amenities and comfortable beds, Hotel am Schrannenplatz is located on the bustling Schrannenplatz, in the heart of Memmingen. Its central location makes it a preferred option among tourists.

Schrannenplatz 4
 schrannenhotel.de

€€€

 ⑨

Siebendächerhaus

Gerberplatz 7

The "House with Seven Roofs", built in 1601, was specially designed for drying hides and was home to the city's tanners' guild for many centuries. Completely estroyed in April 1945 during World War II before being painstakingly rebuilt, it is one of the town's most distinctive and celebrated historical buildings.

⑩

Theater

Theaterplatz 2
(08331) 94 59 16

The building on what is now Theaterplatz was originally a monastery's barn. Built in 1680, it became an arsenal and then a theatre in 1803, when the Neo-Classical façade was added.

⑪

MeWo Kunsthalle

Bahnhofstr. 1
11am–5pm Tue–Sun
w mewo-kunsthalle.de

Next to the train station, in the red-brick former

Royal Post Office built in 1901, the MeWo Kunsthalle opened as a modern art museum in 2005. Visitors can view the exhibitions for free, under the museum's proud motto "art for everyone". For a small fee, though, children and adults alike can take part in the museum's range of creative workshops held in the ateliers and the pARTiLAB (participation laboratory).

 ⑫

Hexenturm

Schlossergasse

The red-brick Hexenturm, meaning Witches' Tower, is Memmingen's oldest tower, originally dating back to the early 12th century. It was originally used as a prison, and locals believe it may have been used to intern suspected witches. It's no longer open to the public, but the tower's exterior is an impressive sight in historic Memmingen.

The tower is also informally known as the "Leaning Tower of Memmingen" as a result of the tower leaning ever so slightly to one side after its sandy subsoil gave way. Its base is built of porous tuff, while the structure above uses bricks. At the top of the tower is a gable roof.

②

LINDAU

⚐A5 **ℹ** Alfred-Nobel-Platz 1, (08382) 88 99 900
⊡ lindau.de

Lindau is one of the three municipalities on Bodensee (Lake Constance) that belong to Bavaria. The old part of the town is connected to the mainland by a railway and a road bridge. Granted the status of a city in the 13th century, Lindau still retains its medieval plan, which is based around three long parallel streets.

INSIDER TIP
Lake Birds

The third-largest lake in Central Europe, Lake Constance is a popular spot for migrating birds. From Eriskirch Reed Marsh on the northern banks you can see black kites and great crested grebes.

①

Maximilianstraße

The city's main street, Maximilianstraße, is also its widest. Like the parallel streets of In der Grub and Ludwigstraße, it contains houses dating from the 15th to 19th centuries. The small, compact houses with gables facing the street have windows that are often divided by columns, while the façades are broken up by oriels. The arcades and the old hoisting devices of the warehouses in the garrets bear witness to the city's character as a centre of trade.

②

Altes Rathaus

⚐ Bismarckplatz 4

The old town hall, built in 1422–36, was remodelled several times during the 16th century, and again in 1724 and 1865. The programme of rebuilding that took place in 1885–7 was undertaken by Friedrich von Thiersch, who restored the stepped gable that had been removed in 1865 and re-constructed the exterior staircase. The façade was painted in bright colours by Joseph Widmann.

③

Harbour

The harbour built at the southern end of the island in 1811 was modernized in 1856. A marble Lion of Bavaria set on a pedestal 6 m (20 ft) high was added to the tip of the mole at the harbour entrance. A new lighthouse (Neuer Leuchtturm), 33 m (108 ft) high, was built on the tip of the opposite mole.

Lion of Bavaria statue, and *(inset)* the new lighthouse at Lindau harbour

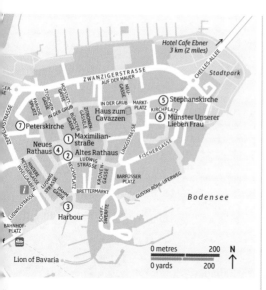

Hotel Cafe Ebner
3 km (2 miles)

Stadtpark

ZWANZIGERSTRASSE
AUF DER MAUER

⑤ Stephanskirche
⑥ Münster Unserer
Lieben Frau

Haus zum
Cavazzen

⑦ Peterskirche

① Maximilian-
straße

Neues
Rathaus
② Altes Rathaus

Bodensee

③
Harbour

Lion of Bavaria

| 0 metres | 200 | N |
| 0 yards | 200 | ↑ |

The promenade beside the harbour, where the former lighthouse, known as the Mangturm, stands, is a popular spot. Built in about 1200, the old lighthouse has a projecting upper storey with a pointed steeple covered in 19th-century glazed tiles.

---

④

Neues Rathaus

⌂ Bismarckplatz 3

The new town hall, built in 1706–17, was also remodelled by Friedrich von Thiersch in 1885. A two-storey building crowned by a tall shaped gable decorated with vases and obelisks, it now houses a cloth shop.

---

⑤

Stephanskirche

Originally a Catholic church, Stephanskirche became a

Protestant church in 1528. The original 12th-century Romanesque building was refurbished several times during the 14th, 15th and 16th centuries. Its present-day form – a three-nave, barrel-vaulted basilica – dates from 1781–3.

---

⑥

Münster Unserer Lieben Frau

⌂ Stiftsplatz 1
ⓒ (08382) 58 50

This church originally belonged to the Benedictine monks who settled here in about 800 CE. Vestiges of the pre-Romanesque church, which was built after 948, are preserved in the west wall. In about 1100 a Romanesque basilica with a transept and a west tower was built. After the fire that devastated the city in 1728, the church was rebuilt to its Romanesque plan. The present airy Baroque church,

lavishly decorated with mouldings and wall paintings, resulted from work carried out in 1748–55 under the direction of Johann Caspar Bagnato.

---

⑦

Peterskirche

This is one of the oldest churches in the Bodensee region. The presbytery and eastern section date from about 1180. The western part was added in the late 15th century. The five-storey tower that stands near the apse, and that was originally in the Romanesque style, was rebuilt in 1425. The interior walls are decorated with frescoes dating from the 13th to 16th centuries. They include works ascribed to Hans Holbein the Elder. Since 1928 the church has functioned as a memorial to war heroes. Beside the church stands the Diebsturm (Thieves' Tower), a circular watchtower built in 1370–80, which was used in conjunction with the Pulverturm (Powder Tower), Ludwigsbastion and Maximilianschanze (Maximilian's Redoubt).

> **Built in about 1200, the old lighthouse has a projecting upper storey with a pointed steeple covered in 19th-century glazed tiles.**

③

KEMPTEN

🅰 B5　🛈 Rathausplatz 24; kempten.de

Originally a Roman town, Kempten was divided into a monastic and a secular district in the Middle Ages. The monastic district was centred around a Benedictine abbey, and in 1712 the monks were granted city rights. Burghalde, the secular district, was a Free City of the Empire from 1289 and accepted the Reformation in 1527. In 1802 the two districts were united into a single entity and incorporated into Bavaria. Today Kempten is the Allgäu's thriving capital, with pretty public squares, vast green parks and a plethora of museums.

①

Rathaus

🄰 Rathausplatz

The late Gothic town hall, built in 1474, has a stepped gable crowned by a small tower. The wooden ceilings of the interior date from about 1460 and originally came from the house of the weavers' guild. Before the town hall stands a copy of a Mannerist fountain of 1601.

②

Rathausplatz

The square on which the town hall stands is lined with patrician palaces and merchants' and guildsmens' houses, which were either remodelled or newly built in the Baroque and Neo-Classical periods. The three-storey Londonerhof at No. 2 has a Rococo façade lavishly covered with stuccowork and featuring a Neo-Baroque doorway of 1899. The Hotel Fürstenhof at No. 8 was built in about 1600. The Ponickauhaus at Nos. 10 and 12 was created in 1740 when two 16th-century houses were knocked together, the first floor being converted into a lavishly decorated Festsaal.

As well as serving as a meeting place and a hub of the town's social life, the square hosts some of Kempten's biggest events, including the Christmas market and the Kempten Jazz Festival, which starts here in early spring.

③

St-Mang-Kirche

🄰 St-Mang-Platz 6

The original church dedicated to St Mang was built in 869. The present church dates from 1426–28, when it was built as the parish church of the Free Imperial City. In 1525 it became a Protestant church, and was

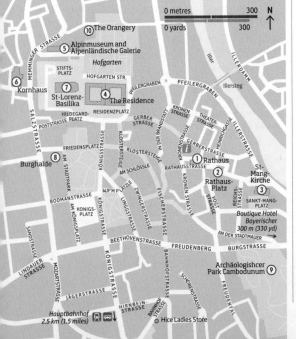

↑ Late Gothic town hall featuring Kempten's coats of arms in the Rathausplatz

Did You Know?

Some archaeologists consider Kempten to be one of Germany's oldest settlements.

remodelled as a three-nave basilica with a tall tower. It was last rebuilt in 1767–68, when the vaulting and late Rococo mouldings were added.

④ ⑤ ⑥

The Residence

⌂ Residenzplatz
☎ (0831) 25 62 51 ⏰ Jan-Mar & Nov: 10am-4pm Sat; Apr-Oct: 10am-4pm Tue-Sun

The Residence was the first Baroque monastery to be built in Germany after the Thirty Years' War. In 1651–74 a group of 11th-century buildings, which were destroyed in 1632, was replaced by a new Baroque monastery. It was also a residence. The monastery consists of buildings grouped around two courtyards. The elegant apartments on the second floor, which were decorated in 1732–42, echo those of the Residenz in Munich (*p82*). The mouldings were executed by stuccoists from Wessobrunn, while the vaulting is by German painter Franz Georg Hermann. The Throne Hall is one of the finest examples of Bavarian and Swabian Rococo interiors.

Today, the Residence is home to Kempten's local and district courts and the State Rooms are managed by the Bayerische Verwaltung der Staatlichen Schlösser, Gärten und Seen (Administration of State Owned Castles, Gardens and Lakes). The State Rooms of the Residence can only be accessed via a guided tour.

↑ Lovely frescoes adorning the ceiling of the St-Lorenz-Basilika

SHOP

Hice Ladies Store

This renowned women's clothing store stocks a great selection of quality German brands such as Armedangels and Birkenstock.

⌂ Bahnhofstr. 18
🌐 hice-ladies.de

Forum Allgäu Kempten

Located in the heart of the city, this spacious mall has three floors of shops and restaurants offering cuisines from all over the world. It's the largest of its kind in the Allgäu region.

⌂ August-Fischer-Platz 1
🌐 forum-allgaeu.de

Thalia Kempten

This well-stocked book-store offers a range of titles, with a small but well-curated selection of translated works as well as some lovely souvenirs.

⌂ Bahnhofstr. 4
🌐 thalia.de

topography and the natural environment, and poetry and painting relating to the mountains. There is also a gallery of regional art.

Kornhaus

⌂ Großer Kornhausplatz 1
📞 (0831) 54 02 120
🕐 10am–4pm Tue-Sun

This former grain warehouse was built in 1700. Today it houses a museum dedicated to the history, culture and art of the city and the region.

St-Lorenz-Basilika

⌂ Landwehrstr. 3

St-Lorenz-Basilika is a three-nave church with two pairs of domed side chapels and an octagonal presbytery crowned by a dome. This arrangement created two separate areas: one for the faithful and one for the friars.

Alpinmuseum and Alpenlandische Galerie

⌂ Landwehrstr. 4
📞 (0831) 25 25 740
🕐 Mar–mid-Nov: 10am–4pm Tue-Sun

The Alpine Museum, in the Residence's former stables, is dedicated primarily to skiing and mountaineering, but also encompasses

St-Lorenz-Basilika is a three-nave church with two pairs of domed side chapels and an octagonal presbytery crowned by a dome.

The interior is breathtaking. The stuccowork in the nave, aisles and presbytery was executed by Giovanni Zuccalli in 1660–70, and the ceilings were painted by Andreas Asper. A comparatively modest twin-towered façade is fronted by a grand staircase. To the east of the presbytery stands the Residence.

Burghalde

⌂ Burgstr.

In 1488 a castle was built on a hill beside the River Iller, where a Roman fort once stood. The castle was incorporated into the city's

fortifications and was then demolished in 1705. Part of the city walls, together with the northern tower and its wooden gatehouse of 1883, survive. Today, Burghalde is an open-air theatre with concerts and a cinema. You can also walk round the city walls.

← Relief of the Roman goddess Epona at the Archäologishcer Park Cambodunum

Archäologischer Park Cambodunum

🏛 Cambodunumweg 3
📞 (0831) 79 731 📅 Mar–Apr & Nov: 10am–4:30pm Tue–Sun; May–Oct: 10am–5pm Tue–Sun

Kempten was once the Roman settlement of Cambodunum. Excavations here have uncovered a Gallic-Roman temple area, a forum, a basilica and baths. The most impressive building was the basilica, which was as large as the present St-Lorenz-Basilika. At the Archäologischer Park, visitors can explore these ancient sites and the ruins, along with a wealth of other discoveries from recent excavations. The shop on-site is home to a curated list of texts on life in the region, and the park has a small café. Children will enjoy playing in the park's Roman-themed adventure playground, which is one of the best in this part of Bavaria (guests do not need a ticket to the park to access the playground).

⑩ The Orangery

The Residence garden once adjoined the Residence on its southern side. The Orangery was built at the north end of the garden in 1780 by Prince Abbot Honorius Roth von Schreckenstein to house delicate plants. Over the centuries, the Orangery has served as a sanctuary for the homeless in Kempten, as an officers' mess and as a youth hostel. It was once home to the municipal library, which still stands today, although a fire in 1966 destroyed large parts. The library's ornate reading room is still open

↑ Late Baroque-style Orangery building set amid the verdant court garden

④ ✧ Ⓜ ▢ 🏛

SCHLOSS NEUSCHWANSTEIN

🗺 B5 🏠 Neuschwansteinstr. 20, Hohenschwangau 🕐 Apr-15 Oct: 9am-6pm daily; 16 Oct-Mar: 10am-4pm daily 🌐 neuschwanstein.de

Built by King Ludwig II as a retreat from public life, the idiosyncratic Neuschwanstein Castle is today one of the most popular palaces in Europe, enticing around 1.5 million visitors per year to make the steep 30-minute walk up from the village of Hohenschwangau.

This monumental castle was built between 1868 and 1892 to plans by the theatre designer Christian Jank, who expressed the king's grand vision inspired by Wagner's operas *Lohengrin* and *Tannhäuser*. The interior decoration was executed by Julius Hoffmann in 1880 – the castle's ornate halls and vast rooms are as lavish as its expansive turreted exterior. Though the castle was never finished, Ludwig saw it as his glowing tribute to the power and beauty of the monarchy. There is a particularly memorable view from Marienbrücke, which giddily spans the rushing waters in the ravine below.

The Throne Room of Neuschwanstein Castle is decorated with gilded mural paintings and mosaics.

→

Singers' Hall, a tribute to medieval knights and the Holy Grail legend

Did You Know?

Neuschwanstein is rumoured to be the inspiration for the castle in Disney's *Cinderella*.

WAGNER AND NEUSCHWANSTEIN

Neuschwanstein was inspired by the mysticism of Richard Wagner's operas. The Byzantine Throne Room captures Ludwig's royal ideals, informed by Wagner's imagery of powerful rulers. The murals in the Singers' Hall depict scenes from the opera *Parsifal*, while the Minstrels' Hall evokes *Tannhäuser*.

←

Schloss Neuschwanstein, former home of the eccentric "Swan King", Ludwig II

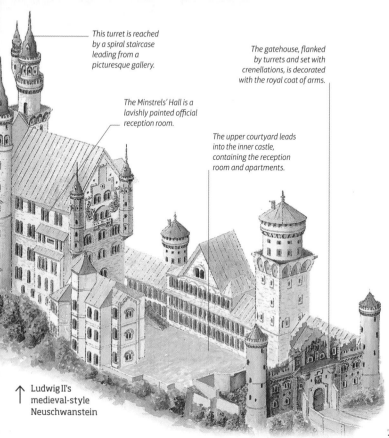

This turret is reached by a spiral staircase leading from a picturesque gallery.

The gatehouse, flanked by turrets and set with crenellations, is decorated with the royal coat of arms.

The Minstrels' Hall is a lavishly painted official reception room.

The upper courtyard leads into the inner castle, containing the reception room and apartments.

↑ Ludwig II's medieval-style Neuschwanstein

EXPERIENCE MORE

⑤ Ottobeuren

🚌🚉 ℹ️ Marktplatz 14; ottobeuren.de

The **Benedictine abbey in Ottobeuren**, dating back to the 8th century, is one of the finest Baroque monasteries in Germany. Nestling in wooded slopes overlooking the River Günz, this fine monumental building is a breathtaking sight. The lavish interior, in a uniform Rococo style, features four domes, the largest of which is 25 m (82 ft) high. The decoration and furnishings are by various artists, including Johann Michael Feichtmayr and Johann Jakob and Franz Anton Zeiller.

Ottobeuren Abbey has been in the hands of Benedictine monks since its foundation. Today the Library, the Abbot's Chapel, the Theatre Hall and the Knights' Hall are open to visitors.

The **Klostermuseum** contains sculpture dating from the 12th to the 18th centuries (by artists who worked in Ottobeuren), as well as clocks and various other artifacts.

The abbey's Kaisersaal is occupied by the **Staatsgalerie**, an interesting art gallery devoted to the works, mostly on religious themes, of Swabian Gothic painters. The gallery forms part of the Bayerische Staatsgemäldesammlungen.

Abtei Ottobeuren Klostermuseum and Staatsgalerie
Ⓢ ☺ 🏠 Sebastian-Kneipp-Str. 1 🕐 Palm Sunday-Oct: 10am–noon & 2–5pm daily; Nov–Mar: by request 🌐 abtei-ottobeuren.de

⑥ Mindelheim

🚌🚉 ℹ️ Maximilianstr. 26; mindelheim.de

During the 15th and 16th centuries Mindelburg, built by Heinrich der Löwe in 1160, belonged to the wealthy Frundsberg family, as did the whole town. The castle was rebuilt in the late 15th to early 16th centuries and again in the late 19th century.

The town's two main streets, Maximilianstraße and Kornstraße, are lined with fine townhouses, remnants of the area's historic wealth. The formerly Jesuit Maria-Verkündigungs-Kirche has fine stuccowork and altars.

Stephanskirche, built in the early 18th century and rebuilt in the early 20th century, contains the tomb of Duke Ulrich von Teck and his two brides. In the former

Altarpieces often take the form of large statues of saints or of one of the Church Fathers.

The Chapel of the Holy Cross is one of the few monastic chapels open only to monks.

The church interior is graced by altars, and the architectural features combine to form a unified whole.

The Library reflects the scientific and cultural aspirations of Bavarian churches.

↑ Belfry clocks on display at the Schwäbisches Turmuhrenmuseum, Mindelheim

church of St Sylvester is the **Schwäbisches Turmuhrenmuseum**, displaying belfry clocks, pocket watches, sundials and other works related to time-keeping and the art of horology.

Schwäbisches Turmuhrenmuseum

🏠 Hungerbachgasse 9 📞 (08 261) 90 97 60 🕐 2–5pm Wed & the last Sun in the month

7

Babenhausen

🅰 B4 🚍🚃 🌐 babenhausen.de

Babenhausen's castle became the property of the von Rechberg family after 1378. In 1539 the castle passed into the hands of the Fuggers *(p289)*, who refurbished it in 1541, adding the west and south wings. In 1955, the small **Fuggermuseum** was founded, with the family retaining ownership of the entire park surrounding the castle.

The town church, which is connected to the castle, was rebuilt in the Baroque style in 1715–30. The interior contains Baroque altars and a pulpit, as well as the tombs of the Rechbergs and Fuggers.

Fuggermuseum

♿ 📞 (08333) 29 31 🕐 Apr–Nov: 10am–noon & 2–5pm Tue–Sat, 10am–noon & 1–6pm Sun

---

8

Kirchheim

🅰 B4 🚍🚃 Mindelheim 🛈 Marktplatz 6; kirchheim-schwaben.de

This small town is bordered to the east by the verdant woodland of Hagenbühl. The main attraction here is the Renaissance castle, owned by the Fugger family since the mid-16th century. The famous Cedar Hall is decorated with wood-carvings on its ceiling and door. The altar of St-Peter-und-Paul-Kirche features a painting of the Holy Family, ascribed to Domenichino, and another of the Assumption, ascribed to Rubens.

The Kaisersaal, or imperial hall, was one of the abbey's countless reception rooms.

The staircase

The ceremonial hall was designed for official gatherings.

↑ Ottobeuren Abbey, one of the largest monastic establishments in Europe

↑ Magnificent furnishings of a room at Schloss Hohenschwangau

STAY

Hotel Wiesbauer
The Wiesbauer is in a great location for exploring Schloss Hohenschwangau and Neuschwanstein; it offers a range of rooms.

B5 🏠Riederwies 112, Füssen 🌐landhotel-wies bauer.de/en

€€€

Hotel Goldener Hirsch
This relaxed hotel in a 16th-century building is only a ten-minute walk from Kaufbeuren train station, making it a convenient stay.

B4 🏠Kaiser-Max-Str. 39–41, Kaufbeuren ☎(08341) 43030

€€€

9

Schloss Hohenschwangau

📍B5 🏠Alpseestr. 12 🕐Apr–15 Oct: 8am–5:30pm daily; 16 Oct–Mar: 9am–3:30pm daily 🌐hohensch wangau.de

This magnificent castle from the 14th century, which was destroyed during the Napoleonic Wars, was acquired by Maximilian II, the king of Bavaria, in 1832. The restoration and rebuilding project executed up to 1837 was primarily the handiwork of renowned German artist and architect Domenico Quaglio.

A bulky building, set with towers and painted yellow, it is situated over a lake against a picturesque backdrop of pristine Alpine scenery.

10

Maria Steinbach

📍A4 🚌🚉Leutkirch

Maria Steinbach is famed for its pilgrimage church, Mariä Schmerzen, which is a masterpiece of Rococo architecture. Situated on a hill in the idyllic rolling landscape of the Iller river valley, the church was built in 1746–54 on the site of earlier Romanesque and Gothic shrines. The building was inspired by the works of Dominikus Zimmermann. The undulating façades, with trompe l'oeil painting, conceal a dazzling interior. The outstanding mouldings and painting by Franz Georg Hermann, the stuccowork of the altars, pulpit, stalls, confessionals and organ loft combine to produce a unified whole.

The figure of the Grieving Madonna, which since 1730

> Situated on a hill in the idyllic rolling landscape of the Iller river valley, the church was built in 1746–54 on the site of earlier Romanesque and Gothic shrines.

has been renowned for its miracle-working powers, was an object of pilgrimage in southern Germany during the 18th century.

The group of presbytery buildings set around a courtyard west of the church dates back to the mid-18th century. The **Wallfahrtsmuseum** contains a large collection of votive gifts made to the Madonna by pilgrims who came to seek her blessings.

Wallfahrtsmuseum
⌂ Kirchhof 4 ☎ (08394) 92 40 ⦿ By appointment

11

Kaufbeuren

⌂ B4 🚌🚆 🛈 Kaiser-Max-Str. 3a; kaufbeuren-tourismus.de

With steep, winding narrow streets lined with colourful houses, the small hilltop town of Kaufbeuren retains much of its medieval character, particularly in the old town.

The old town still has its fortifications from the medieval period, complete with walls and defensive towers. One such tower is the Fünfknopfturm, which was built in about 1420 and functioned as the town's firewatch. After World War II, Neugablonz, a settlement for refugees from Sudetenland, now part of the Czech Republic, was built here.

12

Bad Wörishofen

⌂ B4 🚌🚆 🛈 Hauptstr 16; badwoerishofen.de

This spa resort owes its existence to the priest and influential hydrotherapy advocate Sebastian Kneipp. The town is home to the small but informative Sebastian-Kneipp-Museum, which has over 2,000 exhition pieces documenting the priest's life and ideas. Among the 19th-century guest houses here are the Sebastianeum at Kneippstraße 8 and the Kneippianum at Alfred-Baumgartenstraße 6.

Sebastian-Kneipp-Museum
⌂ Klosterhof 1 ☎ (08247) 39 56 13 ⦿ Feb-mid-Nov: 3–6pm Tue–Sun; 26 Dec–6 Jan: 3–5pm Sun

---

← Pastel-coloured buildings lining a street in Kaufbeuren

Pretty painted façade of the Heilig-Geist-Spitalkirche in Füssen

13
Füssen

B5 ⓘKaiser-Maximilian-Platz 1; fuessen.de

The town's location in the foothills of the Alps, surrounded by lakes and overlooking the River Lech, and its proximity to Schloss Neuschwanstein and Schloss Hohenschwangau, ensure it remains popular with tourists throughout the year.

In Roman times Füssen stood on the road connecting northern Italy with Augsburg. In 1313 it passed into the hands of the bishops of Augsburg, who made it their summer residence. The town's rapid growth was interrupted by the Thirty Years' War and a fire in 1713. After the secularization of the state and its incorporation into Bavaria in 1803, Füssen again enjoyed a period of prosperity, thanks to the interest that the Bavarian kings took in the region.

Füssen has many fine old buildings. The medieval castle has an arcaded façade decorated with trompe l'oeil

Did You Know?

Füssen has been a centre of violin and lute making for centuries.

paintings executed in 1499. Its halls now house the **Filialgalerie der Bayerischen Staatsgemäldesammlungen** (art gallery).

The Benedictine monastery houses the **Museum der Stadt Füssen**, a local history museum, where locally made lutes and violins are displayed. Beside it is St Mang-Kirche, built in 1720–21. The façade of Heilig-Geist-Spitalkirche, painted by Joseph Anton Walch in 1749, is also of note.

Museum der Stadt Füssen

 ⓐLechhalde 3 ⓒ(08362) 90 31 46 ⓒApr–Oct: 11am–4pm Tue–Sun; Nov–Mar: 1–4pm Fri–Sun

Filialgalerie der Bayerischen Staatsgemäldesammlungen

 ⓐMagnusplatz 10 ⓒ(08362) 90 31 46 ⓒApr–Oct: 11am–4pm Tue–Sun; Nov–Mar: 1–4pm Fri–Sun

14
Bad Hindelang

ⓐB5 ⏷ⓡSonthofen ⓘUnterer Buigenweg 2, (08324) 89 20 ⓦbadhindelang.net

This health resort is set in the woodlands in the Ostrach river valley. Visitors can explore it by walking down Marktstraße, starting from the Neo-Gothic church. The 17th-century bishop's palace opposite now houses the town hall. The beautifully restored houses are covered in colourful flowers in summer.

About 1 km (0.6 mile) south of Hindelang is the spa resort of Bad Oberdorf. Hinterstein, 6 km (4 miles) farther on, is popular with mountaineers. The road to Oberjoch, 6.5 km (4.5 miles) northeast, known as the Jochstraße, is the most tortuous section of the Deutsche Alpenstraße.

15
Immenstadt

ⓐB5 ⏷ⓡ ⓘMarienplatz 12; immenstadt.de

Immenstadt has much to offer to watersports enthusiasts and mountaineers, and the town itself is also home to many historic buildings. Nikolauskirche has been rebuilt several times since the Middle Ages. In 1602–20, a palace was built on the market square. One of its apartments has a stuccowork ceiling with hunting scenes and views of German castles. The town hall was built in 1649 and the local history museum is in a mill dating from 1451.

Two km (1.25 mile) north is Bühl, where Stephanskirche contains a chapel built as a replica of the Holy Sepulchre in Jerusalem. The Maria Loreto Chapel with the Cottage of Our Lady of Loreto comprises the Baroque choir of St Annakapelle.

16

Oberstdorf

B6 **🚌🚉🚠** **🛈**Prinzregenten-Platz 1; oberstdorf.de

Oberstdorf, situated in the Iller river valley, is renowned for its health resorts and ski jumps on the slope of Schattenberg. One event in the Four Ski Jumps Tournament is held here. The best-known ski jump here is in the Stillach valley. It was the first large-scale ski jump (*Skiflugschanze*) in the world, and competitors can achieve distances of more than 170 m (550 ft). It was built in 1949–50. The town itself, with its narrow streets and old houses, is extremely attractive. The **Heimatmuseum** has exhibits relating to local history, including the world's largest shoe.

The Breitach river gorge, just 6 km (4 miles) west of Oberstdorf, is a popular attraction. A steep track winds for 2 km (1.25 mile) above the water rushing between cliffs

rising to 100 m (325 ft). To walk the track, a waterproof overgarment and hiking boots are needed.

At the Sturmannshöhle cave outside Fischen, some 200 steps lead to a large cavern with impressive stalactites and stalagmites. The cave's galleries are connected by rushing underground streams that can be heard from the cave mouth.

Heimatmuseum

🏠Oststr. 13 **🕐**10am-noon, 2-5:30pm Tue-Sun & public hols **🚫**3 weeks in Apr & May; Nov-Christmas **🖥**heimat museum-oberstdorf.de

17

Wasserburg

A5 **🚌🚉🚠** **🛈**Lindenplatz 1, (08382) 88 74 74

With a stunningly beautiful location on the tip of a promontory on Bodensee (Lake Constance), Wasserburg is a village of flower-filled streets with views of the lake and hills. Its location makes it a popular place for sailing and other watersports.

In the 10th century, a castle was built to resist Hungarian invaders. It was modernized in the 13th

EAT

Edmund-Probst-Haus

This guesthouse has hearty Bavarian food and a huge terrace overlooking the Alps.

B6 **🚠**Nebelhorn 1, Oberstdorf **🖥**edmund-probst-haus.de

€€€

Zum Wilde Männle

Enjoy rustic Bavarian dishes in an Alpine tavern with views of Oberstdorf's best ski slopes.

B6 **🏠**Oststr. 15, Oberstdorf **🖥**wilde-maennle.de

€€€

century and rebuilt after a fire in 1358. It is a three-winged building. The east wing is a vestige of the medieval structure, while the south wing dates from the 16th century and the west wing from the 18th century. It is now a hotel.

Georgskirche is equally historic. It was founded in the 8th century but was later incorporated into the town's fortifications. The present building is a late Gothic fortified hall dating from the second half of the 15th century.

The square tower was given its onion dome in 1656. The Malhaus (1597), a residence of the Fuggers (*p289*), is now a **museum** with exhibits on the culture of the region and the history of the fishing industry.

Museum im Malhaus

🏠Halbinselstr. 77 **🕐**Mid-Apr-Oct: 10:30am-12:30pm Tue-Sun, 2:30-5pm Wed, Sat & Sun **🖥**museum-im-malhaus.de

↑ Skiers enjoying the spectacular view from the summit of Nebelhorn in Oberstdorf

A DRIVING TOUR
ALPENSTRASSE

Length 450 km (280 miles) **Stopping-off points** The
route takes in many of southern Bavaria's towns and
beauty spots, including Immenstadt and Bayrischzell

In 1927, plans were made for a panoramic road that
was to pass through the most beautiful parts of the
German Alps. This road, the Alpenstraße, starts in
Lindau and heads towards Berchtesgaden, alternating between the High Alps and the foothills lying
between Bodensee and Königssee. It traverses
some of the region's most scenic areas; particularly
impressive are the winding sections of the route, such
as those around Hindelang and Bayrischzell, which
offer breathtaking views.

Locator Map

At 2,962 m (9,718 ft), the
Zugspitze *is the highest
peak in Germany. It is
topped by a cross.*

Jochstraße *is a scenic road that winds
round Hindelang, at altitudes varying as
much as 300 m (985 ft) along a 7 km-
(4 mile-) long route, with views of Ostrachtal.*

Landsberg
am Lech

Ammersee

Kaufbeuren

Schongau

Starnberge
Se

Weilheim in
Oberbayern

Weingarten

Wangen
im Allgäu

Kempten
(Allgäu)

Marktoberdorf

Forggensee

Immenstadt

Jochstrasse

Füssen

Lake
Constance
Lindau

Reutte

*Zugspitze
2,962 m (9,718 ft)*

Dornbirn

Oberstdorf

Ehrwald

Imst

*The picturesque little
town of* **Immenstadt**
*has some fine historic
buildings situated near
the Alpsee.*

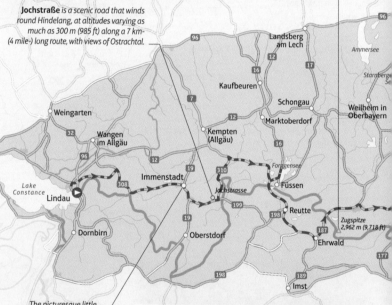

→
Wendelsteinhaus at
the summit of
Wendelstein

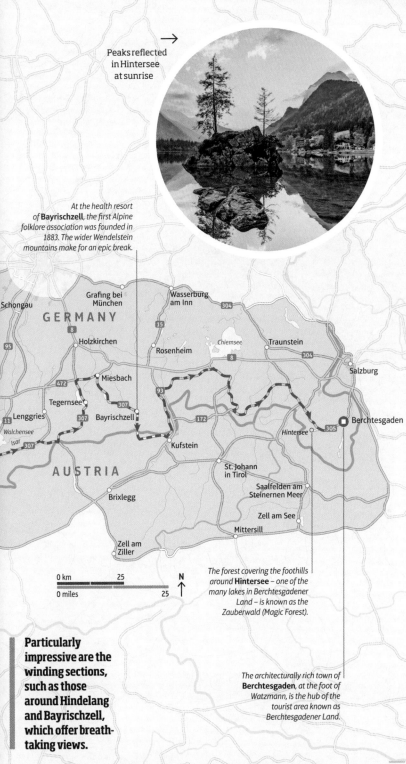

→ Peaks reflected in Hintersee at sunrise

At the health resort of **Bayrischzell**, *the first Alpine folklore association was founded in 1883. The wider Wendelstein mountains make for an epic break.*

GERMANY

Schongau

Grafing bei München

Wasserburg am Inn

Holzkirchen

Rosenheim

Chiemsee

Traunstein

Salzburg

Miesbach

Tegernsee

Lenggries

Walchensee

Isar

Bayrischzell

Kufstein

Berchtesgaden

Hintersee

AUSTRIA

St. Johann in Tirol

Saalfelden am Steinernen Meer

Brixlegg

Zell am See

Mittersill

Zell am Ziller

0 km   25

0 miles   25

N ↑

The forest covering the foothills around **Hintersee** *– one of the many lakes in Berchtesgadener Land – is known as the Zauberwald (Magic Forest).*

Particularly impressive are the winding sections, such as those around Hindelang and Bayrischzell, which offer breathtaking views.

The architecturally rich town of **Berchtesgaden**, *at the foot of Watzmann, is the hub of the tourist area known as Berchtesgadener Land.*

NORTHERN SWABIA

Northern Swabia constitutes the part of historical Swabia that now belongs to Bavaria, hence its German name – Bayerisches Schwaben (Bavarian Swabia). Throughout much of the region's early history, it was divided into numerous small duchies, monastic possessions and Imperial Cities (Reichsstädte). In 1803, Swabia was annexed by Bavaria; the following decades saw the region subjected to integration measures designed to ensure unity between the regions. However, in this transitional area between the German states of Bavaria and Baden-Württemberg, significant differences in language and customs survived.

The historical need for differentiation, self-definition and individuality has made Swabia a state of small towns each with their own character and history. In terms of its politics and its culture as well as its landscapes, Northern Swabia is the most diverse region of Southern Bavaria. Its main attractions for tourists are its historic towns, notably Augsburg, as well as the great Ries Basin and its scenic river valleys.

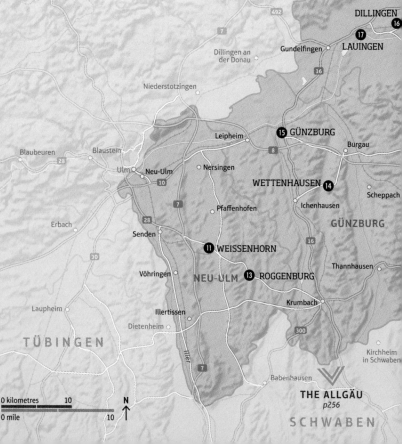

NORTHERN SWABIA

Must Sees
1. Nordlingen
2. Augsburg

Experience More
3. Wallerstein
4. Oettingen
5. Wemding
6. Kaisheim
7. Leitheim
8. Harburg
9. Donauwörth
10. Friedberg
11. Weißenhorn
12. Sielenbach
13. Roggenburg
14. Wettenhausen
15. Günzburg
16. Dillingen
17. Lauingen
18. Höchstädt

Fremdinge

Ellwangen

OSTALBKREIS

Lauchheim

WALLERSTEIN 3

Bopfingen

NÖRDLINGEN 1

Ohmenheim

Neresheim

STUTTGART

HEIDENHEIM

Giengen an der Brenz

Wittislingen

DILLINGEN 16

Dillingen an der Donau

Gundelfingen

LAUINGEN 17

Niederstotzingen

Blaubeuren

Blaustein

Leipheim

GÜNZBURG 15

Burgau

Ulm

Neu-Ulm

Nersingen

Erbach

Pfaffenhofen

WETTENHAUSEN 14

Ichenhausen

Scheppach

GÜNZBURG

Senden

WEISSENHORN 11

Vöhringen

NEU-ULM

ROGGENBURG 13

Thannhausen

Laupheim

Illertissen

Krumbach

Dietenheim

TÜBINGEN

Kirchheim in Schwaben

Babenhausen

THE ALLGÄU
p256

SCHWABEN

0 kilometres   10
0 mile   10

N

NÖRDLINGEN

A B2 **i** Marktplatz 2; noerdlingen.de

Nördlingen, encircled by defensive walls, is the "capital" of the Ries Basin and one of the most picturesque towns in Swabia. The streets that run from the five town gates merge on Marktplatz, the bustling heart of the town. The most attractive aspect of Nördlingen is its houses, a number of which are half-timbered, with colourful, cascading window boxes. Many of the houses are several storeys high, with attic storerooms.

①
Rathaus

A Marktplatz 1

The town hall was built in the 13th century and rebuilt after 1500, acquiring its present form at the beginning of the 17th century. Its most noteworthy feature is the external stone stairway, built from suevite stone by Wolfgang Waldberger. Beneath the staircase landing are the former prison cells.

Commemorating the prison site is a bas-relief depicting a fool, with the ironic inscription *"Nun sind unser zwey"* ("Now it is the two of us"). The wall of the grand Federal Room on the second floor has a painting of the heroic feats of the biblical Judith by Hans Schäufelein.

> **The town hall was built in the 13th century and rebuilt after 1500, acquiring its present form at the beginning of the 17th century.**

②
Georgskirche

A Am Obstmarkt

Georgskirche, built in 1427–1505, stands in the centre of the town. Like many other buildings in the region, it was built with suevite from the Ries Basin. The interior features finely carved late Gothic stalls and a pulpit, a sacrarium of 1522–25 and numerous epitaphs and tombs. The tower, 90 m (295 ft) high, known as the Daniel Tower, can be seen from far away. A flight of 331 stairs leads to the top, where you can enjoy a panoramic view of the Ries Basin. For 300 years a night watchman has called from the top of the Daniel Tower, sometimes every half hour. Today this occurs only between 10pm and midnight.

③
Spital

🏠 **Vordere Gerbergasse 1**

The town's former hospital complex is the largest in Germany. The buildings of the Spitalkrankenhaus and Holzhofstadel that form part of it have been converted into museums. The **Stadtmuseum**, founded in 1960, has a collection of paintings on panel by late Gothic and Renaissance artists, including Friedrich Herlin and Sebastian Daig, as well as a tin figure diorama of the Battle of Nördlingen (1634). The **Rieskrater-Museum** holds moon rocks donated by NASA.

Stadtmuseum

⌖ 🕿 (09081) 84 81 0
🕒 Mid-Mar–4 Nov: 1:30–4:30pm Tue–Sun

Rieskrater-Museum

⌖ 🏠 Eugene-Shoemaker-Platz 1 🕿 (09081) 84 710
🕒 Nov–Apr: 10am–noon, 1:30–4:30pm daily; May–Oct: 10am–4:30pm daily

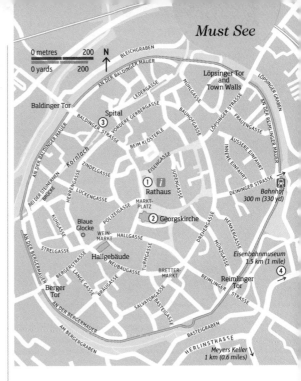

↑ Colourful half-timbered buildings lining a street in the town

④
Eisenbahnmuseum

🏠 **Am Hohen Weg 6a**
🕒 **Hours vary, check website** 🌐 **bayerisches-eisenbahnmuseum.de**

The Bavarian Railway Museum, also known as Bayerisches Eisenbahn-museum (BEM), is housed in the old locomotive depot at Nördlingen train station, which was built in 1849. It holds one of the largest private vehicle collections in Germany and provides visitors with an overview of how railway operations were conducted in Bavaria in earlier times. On display are more than 100 locomotives, from carefully restored steam trains to diesel engines and electric vehicles. The museum hosts regular steam train festivals, where it is possible to see some of the classics in action, watch the railway turntable position the locomotives and book rides on steam trains.

NÖRDLINGER RIES CRATER

Around 15 million years ago, during the Miocene period, a meteorite struck southern Germany, creating the vast Nördlinger Ries crater. The impact of the meteorite on the local graphite deposit produced millions of tiny diamonds. The town of Nördlingen is nestled in the crater's depression, about 6 km (3.7 miles) southwest of its centre. Stones containing the diamonds were used to construct the local buildings that glitter and shimmer today.

Statue of the Emperor
Augustus atop the
fountain on Rathausplatz

②
AUGSBURG

 C3 **i** Rathausplatz 1; augsburg-tourismus.de

Bavaria's third-largest city, Augsburg has a population
of almost 300,000 and is the main university town of
Bavarian Swabia. Founded by the Emperor Augustus
on the final stretch of the trans-Alpine Via Claudia,
it was a bridgehead for Italian culture and is one of
Germany's oldest cities. It stands at the confluence of
the rivers Lech and Wertach, and because of its system
of canals, it has been called the Venice of the North.

①
Schaezlerpalais

Maximilianstr. 46
(0821) 32 44 102
10am-5pm Tue-Sun

This palace, which is the finest
Rococo building in Augsburg,
was built in 1765–70. It
features the famous Festsaal
(ball room), which is decorated
with superb stuccowork, large
paintings and carvings, as
well as chandeliers and can-
delabras. The striking ceiling
was painted by Italian artist
Gregorio Gugliemi.

The palace's art galleries – the
Staatsgalerie and the Deutsche
Barockgalerie – contain works
by such masters as Dürer,
Hans Holbein the Elder, van
Dyck and Tiepolo.

The palace's rococo garden
is free and open to anyone.

②
Stadtmetzg

Metzgplatz 1

This Mannerist building
was built by Elias Holl in
1606–9 for the butchers'

guild. A technological
innovation of the time was
routing one of the town's
canals – the Western Lech –
beneath the cellars of the
Stadtmetzg so that they would
be kept cool for the effective
storage of perishable food.

③
Römisches Museum

Dominikanergasse 15
(0821) 32 44 131
10am-8pm Tue, 10am-
5pm Wed-Sun

The Roman Museum is
housed in the former
Dominican monastery, built
in 1513–15. The two-naved
hall, which is divided by a
row of columns, was rebuilt
in the Baroque style in 1716–
24. The ceiling, which dates
from that time, is decorated
with religious stuccowork
and paintings. The museum
has interesting exhibits
from the Roman as well as
the early medieval periods,
including a gilded horse's
head that once formed
part of a Roman eques-
trian statue.

and 15th centuries. Among the cathedral's many notable features is the world's oldest Romanesque stained glass window, dating from 1140 and depicting figures of the Prophets. Its 11th-century Romanesque bronze doors, with scenes from the Old Testament, are now on display in the Diocesan Museum.

---

⑤ 🖊️ 🖥️ 🛍️

Staatliches Textil- und Industriemuseum

🏠 Provinostr. 46
🕐 9am–6pm Tue–Sun
🌐 timbayern.de

Housed in a former factory, Augsburg's textile industry museum takes visitors through the history of weaving, allowing guests to try their hand at sewing and making yarn using various traditional tools and methods. Even prior to industrialization, Augsburg was at the heart of the European textile industry – the river Lech, which flowed through the city, allowed factory owners to have a bountiful supply of water for power. Thereafter flood-protection measures were installed, and it became an attractive spot for textile and machine

④

Dom Unserer Lieben Frau

🏠 Frauentorstr. 1

The cathedral, whose origins go back to the 9th century, retains the twin towers on the west front that were built in 1150, and two Romanesque crypts. It was remodelled in the Gothic style in the 14th

STAY

Hotel Maximilian's
Situated in the city centre, this upscale 18th-century hotel has long been renowned as the finest place to stay in Augsburg. In addition to elegant rooms, it also has a Michelin-starred gourmet restaurant for the ultimate luxury.

🏠 Maximilianstr. 40
🌐 maximilians-augsburg.de

€€€

factories to set up shop. By the end of the 19th century, over 21 textile factories, with around 10,000 employees, were set up in Augsburg.

The museum also presents current developments in the textile world. The potential future of textiles – from "intelligent clothing" to products made of carbon – is also showcased. The museum's café has a lovely outdoor terrace.

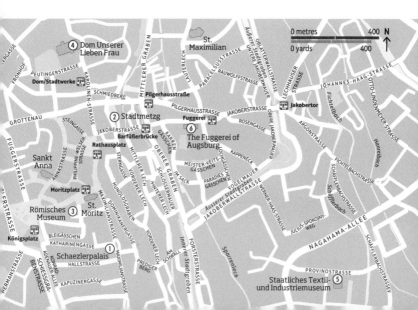

⑥ 🪓 Ⓜ 🍴 ▯

THE FUGGEREI OF AUGSBURG

🕐 Apr-Sep: 8am-8pm daily; Oct-Mar: 9am-6pm daily
🌐 fugger.de

Among Augsburg's main tourist attractions is one of the world's oldest and most striking public housing projects, established by Jakob II Fugger for those in the city who could not afford a private residence.

Built by Thomas Krebs in 1514–23, the estate was named the Fuggerei in honour of its founder. Situated in the Jakobervorstadt, this walled "town within a town" has retained its medieval design; the estate comprised 53 buildings designed to house 106 families. Partly forming a continuous, symmetrical ensemble, the houses have modest façades and steep roofs with stepped gables, and they stand on an uneven plot of land surrounded by a wall with five gates. Each front door still has its bell-pull and iron handle, and the exterior walls still have sandstone plaques with the old house numbers inscribed on them. One of the buildings houses the Fuggereimuseum, dedicated to the social history of the estate.

→

The Fuggerei, Europe's oldest social housing complex

On view at the Fuggereimuseum is an apartment (bedroom and kitchen) furnished in the style of the period.

The Markuskirche was built in 1581 by Johannes Holl, father of Elias Holl. Destroyed in 1944, it was subsequently rebuilt.

↑ Well-preserved bedroom with 18th-century furnishings at the Fuggerei museum

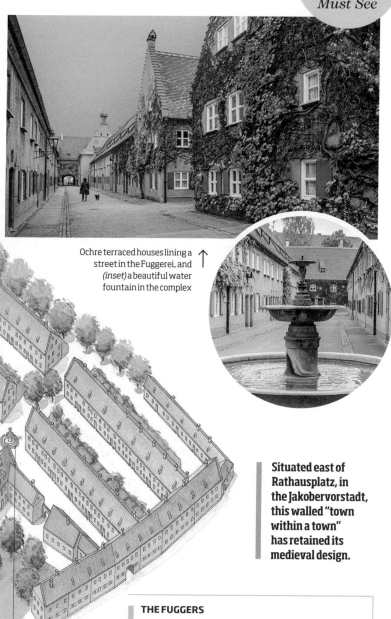

Ochre terraced houses lining a street in the Fuggerei, and *(inset)* a beautiful water fountain in the complex

Situated east of Rathausplatz, in the Jakobervorstadt, this walled "town within a town" has retained its medieval design.

At the point where Herrengasse and Mittlere Gasse meet, forming a small square, stands a modest fountain. It is a favourite meeting place for both local residents and tourists.

THE FUGGERS

The career of the Fuggers began in 1367, when Hans Fugger, a native of Graben, came to Augsburg. Jakob I founded the family of merchants and bankers that still exists today. His sons Ulrich, Georg and particularly Jakob II, "the Rich", acquired unheard-of wealth. Jakob II was banker to emperors, kings and popes. He was also known as a patron of the arts, and thanks partly to him Renaissance art took root in Germany. He also founded social institutions. Once the owners of 100 villages, the Fuggers still own several castles in Bavaria.

A SHORT WALK
AUGSBURG

Distance 1 km (0.5 miles) **Time** 15 minutes
Nearest station Rathausplatz

Augsburg is known for its secular
buildings. Although many of them
were destroyed by air raids in 1944,
they were rebuilt after World War II.
The city's appearance was largely
defined in the early 17th century by
Elias Holl, the architect of many of
the buildings here, most notably the
Mannerist town hall. This leisurely
walk winds along Augsburg's main
street, Maximilianstraße, from
the Rathausplatz, showcasing the
city's eclectic architectural styles
and periods along the way.

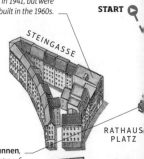

Period houses
on *Steingasse were
destroyed by air raids
in 1941, but were
rebuilt in the 1960s.*

START

STEINGASSE

RATHAUS
PLATZ

Augustusbrunnen,
*the statue of
Emperor Augustus
on the fountain on
Rathausplatz, is a
copy. The original,
cast in bronze in
1588, is in Augsburg's
Town Hall.*

PHILIPPINE-WELSER-STR.

Annakirche, *the chapel
of the Fugger family, is an
architectural jewel. It is
the earliest Renaissance
building in Germany.*

ANNASTR.

Built in 1543–46, the
Maximilianmuseum *is
located in two of the city's
finest patrician palaces.*

BGM.-FISCHER-S

The **Zeughaus**
*(old arsenal), which
was begun in 1607
by Elias Holl, features
a beautiful frontage built
in the Mannerist style
by Josef Heintz.*

KÖNIGS-
PLATZ

ZEUGGAS

←

Richly decorated altar of
the Annakirche, chapel
of the Fugger family

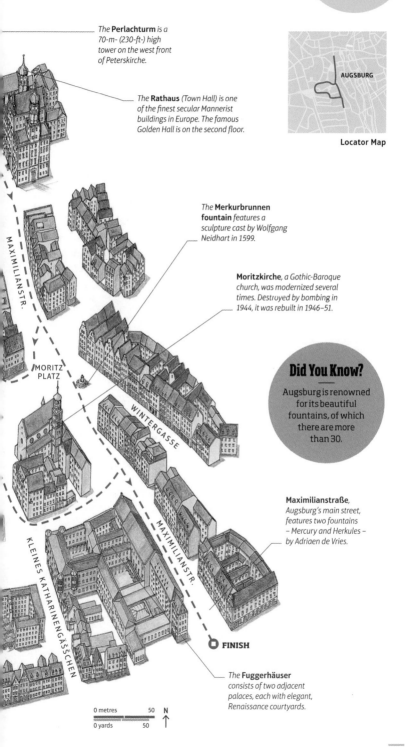

The **Perlachturm** is a 70-m- (230-ft-) high tower on the west front of Peterskirche.

The **Rathaus** (Town Hall) is one of the finest secular Mannerist buildings in Europe. The famous Golden Hall is on the second floor.

The **Merkurbrunnen fountain** features a sculpture cast by Wolfgang Neidhart in 1599.

Moritzkirche, a Gothic-Baroque church, was modernized several times. Destroyed by bombing in 1944, it was rebuilt in 1946–51.

Maximilianstraße, Augsburg's main street, features two fountains – Mercury and Herkules – by Adriaen de Vries.

The **Fuggerhäuser** consists of two adjacent palaces, each with elegant, Renaissance courtyards.

FINISH

MAXIMILIANSTR. · MORITZPLATZ · WINTERGASSE · KLEINES KATHARINENGÄSSCHEN

0 metres 50 / 0 yards 50 · N

Locator Map — AUGSBURG

Did You Know?
Augsburg is renowned for its beautiful fountains, of which there are more than 30.

EXPERIENCE MORE

3
Wallerstein

 B2 🚌🚉 *i* Weinstr. 19;
markt-wallerstein.de

Wallerstein is a small town at the foot of a hill on which stands a castle with a fine view of the Ries Basin. On the hilltop are the remains of 12th-century fortifications as well as a restaurant and a ducal brewery. **Fürst Wallerstein Brauhaus** has been brewing beer since 1598, using locally sourced Spalter hops.

Albanskirche was built in 1242 in the Gothic style. The plague column commemorates the Marseilles plague of 1722–25, and is crowned with figures of St Mary and the Holy Trinity.

**Fürst Wallerstein
Brauhaus**
⊛ 🏠 Berg 78 📞 (09081) 80 52 62 0

4
Oettingen

 B2 🚌🚉 *i* Schlossstr. 36;
oettingen.de

This town, with an oval outline, was surrounded by a wall in the late 13th century. The town gates on the south side – the Unteres Tor and the Königsturm, which was built in the 16th century – still stand.

Schlossstraße, the main street, is lined with half-timbered town houses. The 15th-century Gothic town hall contains the local history museum. Surpassing them in elegance is Residenzschloss, the resplendent Baroque residence of the Dukes of Oettingen-Spielberg, built in 1679–83. To the west the palace looks out over landscaped gardens, peopled with statues of dwarfs and a Hercules of 1678. The palace, whose interior is decorated with stuccowork and murals, is now the Staatliches Museum für Völkerkunde. Visitors can see the apartments and reception rooms and admire the collections of 18th-century pewter, porcelain and faience. The palace courtyard is surrounded by outbuildings and has a fountain dating from 1720–28 in the centre.

The Jakobskirche nearby was remodelled in the Baroque style after 1680 and decorated with stuccowork by Matthias Schmuzer the Younger. Inside is an interesting pulpit and baptismal font from the 17th century, and numerous tombstones as well as plaques from the 15th to 18th centuries.

INSIDER TIP
Oettingen Walks

A great way to explore Oettingen's hidden lanes is by taking a guided Night Watchman tour. These 90-minute walks start at the town hall and can be booked through the tourist information office.

5
Wemding

 B2 🚌🚉 *i* Mangoldstr. 5;
wemding.info

Set on the rim of the Ries Basin, this charming little town has often been used as a location by filmmakers. The main square is lined with Renaissance and Baroque houses with typically Bavarian decorated gables. Prominent among these is the Renaissance town hall. On Wallfahrtstraße, near the gate tower, is a typical mid-16th-century house with a corner oriel, now the Gasthaus zum Weißen Hahn inn. The tower of Emmeramskirche

dominates the skyline. The church dates from the 11th century, but it was rebuilt in its current Baroque form in the 17th century.

It is worth taking a walk along the defensive walls, built in the first half of the 14th century and particularly well preserved on the north side of the town.

On the road leading out towards Oettingen, the small pilgrimage chapel of Maria Brünnlein can be seen in the distance. The interior is decorated with Rococo mouldings and frescoes by Johann Baptist Zimmermann.

↑ Beautifully landscaped garden in the Burg Harburg complex

Kaisheim

🅰C2 🏛Münsterplatz 5
🚌🚉 🌐kaisheim.de

The extensive complex of the former Cistercian monastery houses the 14th-century Gothic Mariä Himmelfahrtskirche as well as the monastery itself. The monastery was converted into a prison in the 1800s. The exquisite Kaisersaal (Imperial Hall), with ornate stuccowork, was completed in about 1720.

The church has a Baroque organ loft, whose carvings are ascribed to Andreas Thamasch. In the nave is a sarcophagus with a statue of the founder of the original Romanesque church, showing him holding a model of the church.

Leitheim

🅰C3 🏛Münsterplatz 5, Kaisheim 🚌🚉Kaisheim
📞(09099) 96 600

Set high on a bank of the Danube, **Schloss Leitheim** and a chapel were built in 1685 to

←
Charming half-timbered houses line the streets of the old city of Oettingen

designs by Wölfl as a summer residence for Cistercian monks from the monastery at Kaisheim. For centuries the monks tended vineyards on the sunny slopes around the residence. Indeed, Leitheim was one of the centres of wine-making in the Danube region.

The chapel was decorated in the late 17th century by artists from Wessobrunn. In the mid-18th century an additional storey and a mansard roof were added to the palace. The stuccowork and paintings in the state rooms are among the finest examples of Bavarian-Swabian Rococo. After 1835 the palace passed into the hands of the Tucher von Simmeldorf family. The owners organize highly popular chamber concerts here.

Schloss Leitheim
🏛Schlossstr. 1 🕐May–Sep: by prior arrangement only
🌐schloss-leitheim.de

Harburg

🅰B2 Schlossstr. 1
🚌🚉 🌐stadt-harburg-schwaben.de

This quaint town is nestled on the banks of the river Wörnitz and retains a delightful medieval layout. The town is most famous for

one of the oldest and best-preserved castles in southern Germany, Burg Harburg. The castle was built by the Hohenstaufens around 1150, before it was acquired by the counts of Oettingen. Since 1731 it has been in the possession of the Oettingen-Wallerstein family.

Dramatically situated on a high rocky hill overlooking the Wörnitz river valley, the castle dominates the entire area. In the 14th and 15th centuries it was surrounded by walls set with towers. It has an outer and an inner gate on the west side, with a gatehouse dating from 1703; within these walls stands Michaelskirche, the castle church.

9

Donauwörth

C3 🚌🚆 **ℹ** Rathausgasse 1; donauwoerth.de

Donauwörth is one of the largest towns in Swabian Bavaria. It is located at the confluence of the Wörnitz and the Danube, and its development was shaped largely by its position at the point where major trade routes crossed the Danube.

Reichsstraße, the main street, is lined with colourful gabled houses and is one of the finest streets in southern Germany. It stretches from Zu Unserer Lieben Frau, the church built in 1444–67 and decorated with 15th- and 16th-century frescoes, to the town hall, remodelled in the Neo-Gothic style in 1854.

The west end of the town is dominated by a former Benedictine monastery, of which the Kreuzkirche, built by Josef Schmuzer in 1717–20, formed a part. Not to be missed is a walk along the town walls, which run parallel to an arm of the Wörnitz. The Rieder Tor, one of the two town gates, houses a museum dedicated to the town's history. Also worth visiting are the **Heimatmuseum** of local history and the **Käthe-Kruse-Puppen-Museum**, with a collection of dolls.

Heimatmuseum

🏠 Insel Ried, Museumsplatz 2 📞 (0906) 78 91 70 🕐 2–5pm Tue–Sun (Nov–Apr: Wed, Sat & Sun only)

HIDDEN GEM
Sweet Treats

The Edel boiled sweets factory (edel-bonbon. de) in Donauwörth produces about 250 flavours of sweets and sells them globally. You can buy in the factory or from tourist information in Donauwörth.

↑ Impressive Rieder Tor, one of the two entrances to Donauwörth

Käthe-Kruse-Puppen-Museum

🏠 Pflegstr. 21a 📞 (0906) 78 91 70 🕐 Apr & Oct: 2–5pm Tue–Sun; May–Sep: 11am–6pm Tue–Sun; Nov–Mar: 2–5pm Wed, Sat–Sun & public hols; 25 Dec–6 Jan: 2–5pm daily

10

Friedberg

C3 🚌🚆 **ℹ** Marienplatz 5; friedberg.de

During the Middle Ages this town was a fortress meant to protect the region from attacks by the inhabitants of Augsburg. In about 1490 defensive walls set with semicircular towers were added. The medieval castle in the north of the town was destroyed during the Thirty Years' War and rebuilt in 1559. It now houses a local history museum, the **Museum Wittelsbacher Schloss**.

The streets are lined with houses dating from the 17th and 18th centuries. In the centre of the main square stands the town hall, built in 1673 and decorated in the style of Elias Holl. Jakobskirche, which has an unusual design, was built in 1871 in imitation of the Romanesque cathedral of St Zeno in Verona.

The finest building in Friedberg is Herrgottsruh, a pilgrimage church located in the east of the town. In the Middle Ages it was built as a rotunda resembling the Church of the Holy Sepulchre in Jerusalem. Fragments of the building were uncovered beneath the presbytery of the present church.

The latter, built in 1731–51 by Johann Benedikt Ettl, has a tall tower and an imposing domed rotunda. The paintings in the presbytery and the dome are by Cosmas Damian Asam, while those in the nave are by Matthäus Günther. The Rococo mouldings are by Franz Xaver Feichtmayer and Johann Michael Feichtmayr. The silver antependium of the high altar was made by Johann Georg Herkomer of Augsburg. The altar in the south aisle contains a 15th-century group of figures of the Sorrowing Christ to which miraculous powers are ascribed. Votive images fill the aisles.

Museum Wittelsbacher Schloss

🏠 Schlossstr. 21 📞 (0821) 600 26 84 🕐 10am–5pm Tue–Sun & public hols

11

Weißenhorn

B3 🚌🚆 **ℹ** Schlossplatz 1; weissenhorn.de

Neat, quaint and tidy, Weißenhorn is a quintessential small Swabian town. Its historic character is preserved virtually intact. The main thoroughfare, the Hauptstraße, runs from a large, irregular square where the church and palace stand

to the Unteres Tor (Lower Gate). The 15th-century Oberes Tor (Upper Gate), flanked by circular towers, opens on to the square. Adjoining the gate is the former weigh-house, dating from the 16th century, and the Neues Rathaus, built in the 18th century.

The Altes Schloss, dating from 1460–70, and Neues Schloss, built by the Fuggers (p289) in the 16th century, are interconnected. The dominant building in the town is Mariä-Himmelfahrt-Kirche, built in 1864–71, one of the finest examples of the revivalist trend in Swabia's religious architecture.

Sielenbach

C3 🚌🚉 Weißenhorn
🛈 Schwaigstr. 16; sielenbach.de

The pilgrimage church of Unserer Lieben Frau im Birnbaum (Mary in the Pear Tree) is located at the southern end of the town. It is an exceptional work of 17th-century Bavarian architecture. It was built in 1661–68 by Konstantin Bader to a design by Jakob von Kaltenthal, a

ROMANTISCHE STRASSE

Many visitors to this part of southern Bavaria, particularly Donauwörth, follow the Romantic Road (romantischestrasse.de). This beautiful route traces the path of the Roman Via Claudia. Beginning in Franconian Würzburg, it also passes through Nördlingen, Augsburg, Landsberg, Schongau, Steingaden and Füssen, in southern Bavaria, and ends at Schloss Neuschwanstein, Ludwig II's famous castle. The best known of the tourist routes in Germany, it is particularly popular with American tourists.

Commander of the Teutonic Knights. It consists of five circular, semicircular and oval rooms. The towers and onion domes are particularly unique, and are particularly reminiscent of an Eastern Orthodox church.

The interior, which is lit by large oval windows and decorated with stuccowork, is far more unified and in keeping with Bavarian religious architecture. The object of worship is a late Gothic Pietà dating from the early 16th century, to which miraculous powers are ascribed. It stands on the high altar in a pear tree. The tree and the name of the church commemorate the miraculous survival of the figure in 1632, during the Thirty Years' War, when in the course of the Swedish invasion the figure survived thanks to its being hidden in a pear tree.

→
Exquisite stuccowork on the domed ceiling of the Church of Maria Birnbaum in Sielenbach, and (inset) its Baroque exterior

Roggenburg

B4 🚌🚊 **ℹ** Vohringen. Prälatenhof 2; roggenburg.de

On e of the main attractions in Roggenburg is the Mariä-Himmelfahrt-Kirche, a former Premonstratensian monastery built in the late 18th century. The cavernous interior of the church produces an impression of levity, even though the windows are concealed behind columns. The most interesting objects here are the two reliquaries with painted images of St Severinus and St Laurentius in fine costume of the period. The monastery, built from 1732 to 1766, houses local government offices, although parts are open to the public.

⑭ Wettenhausen

B3 🚌🚊 **ℹ** Günzburg. Abbey: Kammeltal, Dossenberger-str. 46; (08223) 40 040

The old Augustinian monastery in Wettenhausen dominates the surrounding landscape. Mariä-Himmelfahrt-Kirche, originally a Romanesque church, was rebuilt in the late Gothic style in the 16th century and remodelled in the Baroque style in 1670. The frescoes and the highly decorative altars and pulpit, dating from the 17th century, create a unified interior. The altar in the south chapel features a fine late Gothic Coronation of the Virgin.

Parts of the abbey are open to the public. The rooms in the cloister – including one that has a figure of Christ seated on a donkey – are visible through a decorative wrought-iron grille.

→

The enchanting world of LEGO® Mythica at Legoland in Günzburg

Günzburg

B3 🚌🚊 **ℹ** Schloßplatz 1; guenzburg.de

The origins of this sizeable town at the confluence of the rivers Günz and Danube go back to Roman times. The main square, closed off by the 14th-century Unteres Tor (Lower Gate), is surrounded by Baroque houses with typically Swabian gables. These houses recall the days when the town was at its height. Notable is Brentanohaus at No. 8, built in 1747 with a tiled mansard roof and Rococo mouldings on its elegant façade. Beside the old Franciscan monastery stands the Frauenkirche, built in 1736–41 by Dominikus Zimmermann. Substantial fragments of the 15th-century town walls, defensive towers and gateways survive.

The attraction that draws many tourists to this town, however, is Legoland, located a short distance to the south.

Did You Know?

There are many "Barfußpfade," or barefoot trails, in Bavaria. Just take off your shoes and stroll.

⑯ Dillingen

B3 🚌🚊 **ℹ** Königstr. 37–38; dillingen-donau.de

For centuries Dillingen, the spiritual capital of Swabia and a town dubbed the "Rome of Swabia", was the seat of the bishops of Augsburg and a major university town. The main street, Königstraße, lined with patrician townhouses, defines the town's character. Königstraße leads into Kardinal von Waldburgstraße, on which the elongated Baroque façade of the Jesuit University rises. The highlight of the town is the formerly Jesuit Mariä-Himmelfahrt-

Kirche. The early Baroque architecture of the building and its Rococo stuccowork, painting and furnishings combine to produce a splendid ensemble. The stately 13th-century castle has preserved its defensive character despite being rebuilt several times over the centuries. Fragments of the town walls, set with towers and pierced by the Mitteltor (Middle Gate), can still be seen today.

17 Lauingen

B3 Herzog-Georg-Str. 17; lauingen.de

Set on a high bank overlooking the Danube, this town has largely preserved its medieval character.

The outlines of two tall towers that dominate the town can be seen from afar. The more distinctive of the two is the former watchtower. Exceptionally tall and narrow, it was built in 1457–78 together with the adjacent arcades containing market stalls, and was extended in 1571.

The Neo-Classical town hall, built in 1782, was erected on the orders of the Elector Karl Theodor despite strong opposition from the townspeople.

Martinskirche is one of the last Gothic hall-churches to have been built in southern Germany. Its triple-nave interior with web vaulting is unparalleled in height and the walls and ceilings are decorated with frescoes.

In the suburb of Faimingen, the remains of Roman buildings can be seen. The partially reconstructed Temple of Apollo Grannus, the Roman deity who also came to be worshipped by the Celts, bears witness to Lauingen's long history.

18 Höchstädt

B3 Herzog Philipp-Ludwig-Str. 10; hoechstaedt.de

This little town on the banks of the Danube is flanked by its church and its castle. The late Gothic Mariä-Himmelfahrt-Kirche, which was completed in about 1520, is decorated with frescoes in contrasting styles. The town's finest historic building is the turret-shaped Gothic sacristy.

The **Heimatmuseum** has numerous collections of objects relating to local history.

On a hill overlooking the town stands the Renaissance castle, built in about 1589 to replace the medieval seat of Duke Philip Ludwig, the Palatine of Neuburg. Well restored, it is now used as the museum's headquarters.

Heimatmuseum
Marktplatz 7 (09074) 4412 Apr-Oct: 2-5pm Sun; Nov-Mar: 2-4pm 1st Sun of month and by appointment

EAT

Wetzel Karlsbader Oblaten
This popular spot is known for its traditional Bavarian waffles, baked treats and sweet, crispy delicacies.

B3 Austr. 5, Dillingen wetzel-oblaten.de

€€€

Zur Glocke
In the heart of Höchstädt, this modern hotel serves fantastic food in a wood-panelled room.

B3 Friedrich-von-Teck-Str. 12, Höchstädt glocke.one

€€€

NEED TO KNOW

A train at Marienplatz U-Bahn Station

BEFORE YOU GO

Things change, so plan ahead to make the most of your trip. Be prepared for all eventualities by considering the following points before you travel.

AT A GLANCE

CURRENCY
Euro

AVERAGE DAILY SPEND

ON A BUDGET	MODERATE SPENDER	SPLASH OUT
€50	€100	€300+

BOTTLED WATER	COFFEE	BEER	DINNER FOR TWO
€2.00	€3.50	€4.00	€80

ESSENTIAL PHRASES

Hello	Guten Tag
Goodbye	Auf Wiedersehen
Please	Bitte
Thank You	Danke
Do you speak English?	Sprechen Sie Englisch?
I don't understand	Ich verstehe nicht

ELECTRICITY SUPPLY

Power sockets are type F, fitting two-pronged plugs. Standard voltage is 220–230v.

Passports and Visas

For entry requirements, including visas, consult your nearest German embassy or check the **German Federal Foreign Office** website. Citizens of the UK, US, Canada, Australia and New Zealand do not need a visa for stays of up to three months but in future must apply in advance for the **European Travel Information and Authorization System** (ETIAS); roll-out has been postponed so check website for details.
ETIAS
W travel-europe.europa.eu/etias_en
German Federal Foreign Office
W auswaertiges-amt.de/en

Government Advice

It is a good idea to consult both your and the German government's advice before travelling. The **UK Foreign, Commonwealth and Development Office**, the **US State Department**, the **Australian Department of Foreign Affairs and Trade**, and the German Federal Foreign Office (above) offer the latest information on security, health and local regulations.
Australian Department of Foreign Affairs and Trade
W smartraveller.gov.au
UK Foreign, Commonwealth and Development Office (FCDO)
W gov.uk/foreign-travel-advice
US State Department
W travel.state.gov

Customs Information

You can find information on laws relating to goods taken in or out of Germany on Germany's **Central Customs Authority** website.
Central Customs Authority
W zoll.de/EN

Insurance

We recommend taking out a comprehensive insurance policy covering medical care, theft, loss of belongings, cancellations and delays, and

reading the small print carefully. UK citizens are eligible for free emergency medical care in Germany provided they have a valid European Health Insurance Card (EHIC) or **UK Global Health Insurance Card** (GHIC).
GHIC
w ghic.org.uk

Vaccinations

No inoculations are required to visit Germany.

Booking Accommodation

Bavaria offers a wide range of accommodation, from five-star hotels to campsites. Lodgings tend to fill up quickly in the summer and during Oktoberfest, as do the ski resorts in winter, so it's worth booking ahead.

Money

Germany's currency is the euro. Major credit and debit cards are accepted by most businesses, while prepaid currency cards and American Express are accepted in some. Contactless payments are increasingly common, but it's always a good idea to carry some cash for smaller items, just in case.

Cash machines (ATMs) can be found everywhere. It is customary to tip between 5-10 per cent, and when buying a beer at a bar, by rounding up to the nearest euro.

Travellers With Specific Requirements

In Munich and Bavaria's larger cities, many museums and sights are wheelchair accessible. Most museums and galleries also offer audio tours and induction loops for those with impaired sight and hearing.

Buses and trams cater to travellers using wheelchairs, though some intercity trains are poorly catered to travellers with disabilities. Many hotels have lifts or accessible ground-floor rooms with specially adapted bathrooms.

Wheelchair accessibility is improving across the Bavarian Alps, with many attractions now offering services for those with limited mobility, even those in remote rural areas. Note, however, that many sites require pre-booking to ensure

adequate provisions are in place. Schloss Neuschwanstein offers accessible tours, and the ferries at Chiemsee are fully accessible. **Bavaria Tourism**'s website has useful information for all accessible trips.
Bavaria Tourism
w bavaria.travel/accessible-holidays

Language

The official language is German. The standard of English among younger Germans is excellent. Bavarian is spoken in villages and among the older generation, a dialect that even Germans from other parts of the country struggle with.

Opening Hours

Situations can change quickly and unexpectedly. Always check before visiting attractions and hospitality venues for up-to-date opening hours and booking requirements.

Sundays Many rural shops are closed, and public transport services are reduced.
Monday Many museums and tourist attractions and some restaurants are closed for the day.
Public holidays Schools, post offices, shops and banks are closed.

PUBLIC HOLIDAYS

1 Jan	New Year
6 Jan	Epiphany
Mar/Apr	Good Friday
Mar/Apr	Easter Monday
1 May	Labour Day
9 June	Whit Monday
16 June	Corpus Christi
3 Oct	German Unity Day
1 Nov	All Saints Day
25 Dec	Christmas Day
26 Dec	St Stephen's Day

GETTING
AROUND

Whether you're planning on a hiking trip, a cycling tour, a city break or all of the above, here's all you need to know to navigate Munich and Bavaria.

AT A GLANCE

PUBLIC TRANSPORT COSTS

SINGLE JOURNEY

€2.90

Inner city Munich

TRAVEL CARD

€6.70

Inner Zone
on bus, tram and metro

DAILY TRAVEL CARD

€9.20

M-Zone
on bus and trains

TOP TIP
Avoid on-the-spot fines – be sure to present your e-ticket on request.

SPEED LIMIT

RURAL AREAS
100 km/h (60m/h)

URBAN AREAS
50 km/h (30m/h)

AUTOBAHN
130 km/h (80m/h)

TOWING A TRAILER
80 km/h (50m/h)

Arriving by Air

Munich's Franz Josef Strauß International Airport is Germany's second-busiest airport after Frankfurt am Main. Main airlines with links between the UK and Munich include British Airways and Lufthansa, Germany's national airline; both operate regular flights from London direct to Munich. Direct journeys to Germany are also available from major US cities, including New York (JFK).

Munich's international airport is located 28 km (17 miles) outside the centre, but you can reach the city by bus or S-Bahn in under 45 minutes (see p304).

Nuremberg also has an international airport, the second largest in Bavaria. If travelling domestically in Germany, however, it's worth noting that flying is rarely faster than taking the high-speed trains.

Train Travel

Both Munich and wider Bavaria have a vast and efficient railway network, though the country's reputation for punctual rail services isn't always accurate, especially during the peak season. In any case, travelling by train is a great way to get around Munich and southern Bavaria.

Domestic Train Travel

Munich is home to an extensive and efficient rail system with three main train stations: München Hauptbahnhof (Hbf), München Ost and München-Pasing. München Hbf, about 1 mile (1.6 km) from the city centre, is one of the country's busiest stations and the city's primary transportation hub, with local, intercity and regional connections. Since the high-speed rail route opened between Munich and Berlin, it takes just 3 hours 45 minutes to travel between the two cities.

The state-owned Deutsche Bahn (DB) is Germany's national railway company, and operates the vast majority of services in Germany. The country's fastest trains – InterCity Express (ICE) – connect the largest cities, and can travel at more than 200 km/h (125 mph). Bavaria itself has a vast rail network with fast

and reliable trains. You can buy tickets and plan your journey on the **Deutsche Bahn** website.
Deutsche Bahn
🆆 int.bahn.de/en

International Train Travel

Munich has direct connections with most major European cities. The most popular route from the UK is to travel to Brussels by **Eurostar** and pick up a connection to Germany from there. Buy tickets and passes for multiple international journeys via **Eurail** or **Interrail**; you may still need to pay a reservation fee for certain trains. Always check that your ticket is valid in advance.
Eurail
🆆 eurail.com
Eurostar
🆆 eurostar.com
Interrail
🆆 interrail.eu

Long-Distance Bus Travel

Most visitors will typically travel to and from Munich by high-speed train, but there are also inexpensive long-distance coach services from within and beyond Germany, most of which arrive at Munich's central bus station (ZOB) at Hackerbrücke. Other cities in the Bavarian Alps can also be reached by local coach companies, though the roads can be busy in the high season.

Travel by coach can be a fair amount cheaper than rail travel, though travel times are longer. There are an array of European coach companies who operate long-distance services to Munich including **Flixbus** and **Omio**.
Flixbus
🆆 flixbus.co.uk
Omio
🆆 omio.co.uk

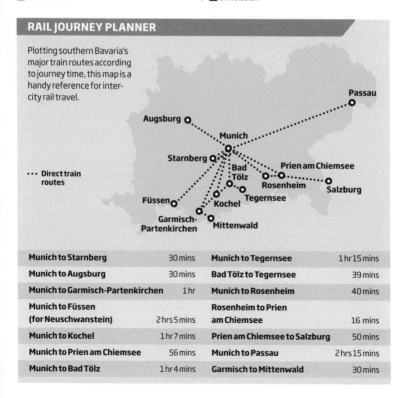

RAIL JOURNEY PLANNER

Plotting southern Bavaria's major train routes according to journey time, this map is a handy reference for inter-city rail travel.

••• Direct train routes

Munich to Starnberg	30 mins	**Munich to Tegernsee**	1 hr 15 mins
Munich to Augsburg	30 mins	**Bad Tölz to Tegernsee**	39 mins
Munich to Garmisch-Partenkirchen	1 hr	**Munich to Rosenheim**	40 mins
Munich to Füssen (for Neuschwanstein)	2 hrs 5 mins	**Rosenheim to Prien am Chiemsee**	16 mins
Munich to Kochel	1 hr 7 mins	**Prien am Chiemsee to Salzburg**	50 mins
Munich to Prien am Chiemsee	56 mins	**Munich to Passau**	2 hrs 15 mins
Munich to Bad Tölz	1 hr 4 mins	**Garmisch to Mittenwald**	30 mins

Munich Public Transport

Munich has a highly developed and functional urban transport system run by the Munich Transportation Corporation (MVG). The city's public transport is comprised of four integrated pillars: U-Bahn, S-Bahn, tram and bus.

Tickets for Munich's public transport network are the same across every mode of transport, with all routes falling within the Munich Transport and Tariff Association (or MVV) area. Prices range from €2.90 for a single ticket covering one zone, and from €6.70 for a one-day travelcard around the inner city. Tickets, timetables and safety information can be found on the **MVV** wesbite. It's highly recommended that you download the **MVGO** app, which allows you to buy, use and display digital tickets.

MVGO
Ⓦ mvg.de
MVV
Ⓦ mvvmuenchen.de

S-Bahn

The S-Bahn (short for "Stadtschnellbahn") has eight lines and 150 stations covering the entire metropolitan area. The core route runs through the city centre with regular trains (up to every 10 minutes in rush hour; every 20 minutes outside rush hour). You can transfer from Munich Airport to the city centre with the S-Bahn lines S1 and S8. S-Bahn stations are marked with a capital "S" on a green background.

U-Bahn

Munich's subway system consists of around 100 stations. The network of eight U-Bahn lines is interconnected with the S-Bahn, with each line numbered. U-Bahn stations are marked with a capital "U" on a blue background.

Buses

Though the S-Bahn and U-Bahn form the core of Munich's public transport, there is also an extensive and reliable bus network. Scheduled bus services are operated across the city's metropolitan area, with special lines operating at night (the city's night buses are marked with an "N" in front of the line number). Many tourists make particular use of bus line 100, which passes by all of the city's major museums and many main galleries.

Trams

Munich's tramway dates back to 1876, when the network's vehicles were drawn by horse. The city's fully electric trams now run along 13 daytime train lines and 4 night lines, with a total of 165 stops throughout Munich. Special night lines operate at night (marked with an "N" in front of the line number).

Bavarian Public Transport

Public transport throughout southern Bavaria is generally efficient and reliable. For information on tickets and schedules within Upper Bavaria, visit the **Oberbayern** website, or for transport in and around Kempten and the Allgäu region, visit the **Kempten Tourism** website. You can also find out more information about schedules and integrated regional tickets on the Deutsche Bahn website (*p304*).

Kempten Tourism
Ⓦ kempten-tourismus.de
Oberbayern
Ⓦ oberbayern.de

Buses

Almost all Bavarian towns and villages are connected by a local bus network, particularly in places where there is no railway station. Most towns have a Zentraler Omnibus Bahnhof (ZOB) close to the train station. It is here that most bus services originate and where tickets can be purchased, and service timetables and other information can be obtained. Stops are frequent in rural areas, and buses will stop on request.

Boats and Ferries

Bavaria's many rivers and large lakes make boat trips a great way of getting around, and many attractions are only accessible by water. Local providers offer services on all of Bavaria's main lakes – Starnberger See, Ammersee, Tegernsee, Chiemsee and Königssee – and on rivers such as the Danube. **Bayerische Seenschifffahrt** (the Bavarian Lake Shipping Company) operates a passenger shipping service on the Upper Bavarian lakes Königssee, Tegernsee, Starnberger See and Ammersee. The company runs a fleet of over 30 ships, making it one of the largest inland shipping companies in Germany.

On the state's smaller lakes, boats can be hired with or without a captain. Longer cruises are available on the Danube from Passau to Vienna, and can be combined with a tour of the historic sights along the Danube valley. To the north of Munich, kayaking and canoeing are popular ways of navigating the waterways in the Altmühl Naturpark.

Bayerische Seenschifffahrt
Ⓦ seenschifffahrt.de

Driving

Visiting Bavaria by car is relatively straight-forward, and Alpine road trips are an incredibly popular way of admiring the region. Just an hour's drive southeast of Munich, some jaw-dropping Alpine scenery beckons, with longer roads like the Deutsche Alpenstraße attracting motorists from all over the world.

Driving to Bavaria

Many travellers throughout Europe choose to visit Bavaria by car. As such, in the summer months and over public holidays considerable queues can build up at crossings into Germany, especially from the Czech Republic. During Oktoberfest, routes to and from Italy through Switzerland are also congested.

Driving in Bavaria

The swiftest and most popular way to tour Bavaria tends to be by car, making use of the excellent Autobahn, or national motorway. Secondary roads are usually of great quality, too. Note, however, that during the holiday season, roads in the Bavarian Alps swell with motorists. To avoid a tiresome traffic jam, check the holiday calendar in advance or avoid the motorways altogether. Although slower, travelling off the main motorways gives you a more intimate view of the countryside.

Note if driving within Munich that traffic can be very slow at rush hour, and parking is generally difficult to find. Don't assume your hotel will have on site parking.

Car Hire

Car-hire firms can be found at airports and railway stations. **Europcar** have branches throughout the city. Drivers need to produce their passport, driving licence and a credit card with enough capacity to cover the excess. Most hire agencies require drivers to be over the age of 21 and to have an international licence.
Europcar
w europcar.com

Rules of the Road

The minimum driving age in Germany is 18, even if your licence qualifies you to drive at a younger age in your home country. Motorists in Germany drive on the right and overtake on the left. Traffic approaching from the right has priority at crossroads and junctions unless otherwise indicated. In heavy motorway traffic, vehicles are permitted to overtake on either side – just don't use the hard shoulder to do so. Do not indicate when entering a roundabout, only when you see your exit.

At all times, drivers must carry a valid driver's licence, registration and insurance documents. The wearing of seat belts is compulsory for both drivers and passengers, lights must be used in tunnels and the use of a mobile phone while driving is prohibited, with the exception of a hands-free system. All drivers must have third-party insurance. Drivers will be fined for speeding, tailgating and for committing parking offences. The drink-drive limit is strictly enforced. Only overtake trams on the right. There must be a first-aid kit in your car.

Cycling

Munich is widely known as Germany's most bike-friendly city, though a number of the country's cities now challenge that claim. Munich's vast network of dedicated bike routes exceeds the total length of the city's road network; it's an ambitious, safe and successful example of cycling infrastructure, with cyclists entirely protected from vehicles on much of the route. Bicycles can be taken on the U-Bahn and S-Bahn in the last carriage marked with a cycle logo, except at rush hour.

Outside Munich, southern Bavaria is an idyllic cycling destination, offering great road, gravel and mountain riding. With 120 cycle routes across 8,800 km (5,400 miles) of track, wider Bavaria's cycleways take in the region's greatest sights; particularly popular routes include those around lakes like Chiemsee, the forested routes in the Bayerischer Wald and the longer Danube Cycle Path which crosses into Austria (p214). Despite this superb network, Germany still doesn't attract quite as much attention as cycling destinations in France or Italy, so the best routes are rarely congested.

Bike Hire

MVG Bike is a bike hire scheme which operates around 4,500 silver-blue hire bikes throughout Munich and its outer districts. Fees are calculated by duration of ride, though you are usually entitled to free minutes upon first use. Bikes can be located and booked using the MVGO app.

Outside of Munich, there are numerous reputable bike hire companies situated in many of the state's most beautiful cycling regions. Many cyclists opt to take a guided cycling tour through Bavaria, with Munich's **Mike's Bike Tours** offering tour guides and extended hire for longer excursions.
Mike's Bike Tours
w mikesbiketours.com

Walking and Hiking

Exploring Munich on foot is always a rewarding experience. Much of the Old Town is closed to traffic, and most of the main tourist attractions in the Old Town are within 20 minutes' walk of each other. Farther afield, strolling through the city's outlying districts can be a pleasant experience in itself.

Wider Bavaria is a great place for hiking, with many trails and routes for all abilities that showcase the region's natural beauty. The Bavarian Alps offer a variety of walks and treks, including waymarked day hikes and *Fernwanderwege* (long-distance, multi-day hiking routes).

PRACTICAL
INFORMATION

A little know-how can go a long way in Munich and Bavaria. Here you can find all the essential advice and information you might need during your stay.

AT A GLANCE

EMERGENCY NUMBERS

GENERAL EMERGENCY	AMBULANCE
112	**112**

FIRE SERVICE	POLICE
112	**110**

TIME ZONE

CET/CEST
Central European Summer Time runs from late March to late October.

TAP WATER

Unless stated otherwise, tap water in Germany is safe to drink.

WEBSITES

www.handbookgermany.de
A complete A–Z of life in Germany, available in multiple languages

www.germany.travel
National Tourist Board website

www.munich.travel
Simply Munich offers tips on events and activities across the city.

Personal Security

Bavaria is generally a safe place for visitors, but it is always a good idea to take sensible precautions and be aware of your surroundings. Pickpockets are known to operate in busy tourist areas, particularly on public transport in Munich and larger towns and cities.

If you have anything stolen, report the crime as soon as possible to the nearest police station. Get a copy of the crime report in order to claim on your insurance. Contact your embassy if you have your passport stolen, or in the event of a serious crime or accident.

Germans are generally accepting of all people, regardless of their race, gender or sexuality. Although long celebrated as a liberal and tolerant country, homosexuality was only officially legalized in Germany in 1994. In Munich, many LGBTQ+ events and venues were and still are based in the Glockenbachviertel district, though you can find safe spaces across the city. Despite all the freedoms that the LGBTQ+ community enjoy, acceptance is not always a given, especially in more rural areas where locals may be unaccustomed to tourists. Rural Bavarians in particular are noted for their traditional outlook, but this rarely gives rise to hostility. If you do at any point feel unsafe, the **Safe Space Alliance** pinpoints your nearest place of refuge.
Safe Space Alliance
w safespacealliance.com

Health

Germany has a world-class health service. EU citizens are eligible to receive emergency medical treatment in Germany free of charge. If you have an EHIC or GHIC present this as soon as possible. For visitors from outside the EU, payment of medical expenses is the patient's responsibility. It is important to arrange comprehensive medical insurance before travelling. Pharmacies (*Apotheke*) are indicated by a red stylized letter "A" and can be used for help with minor ailments or prescriptions. You may need a doctor's prescription to obtain

certain pharmaceuticals, and the pharmacist can inform you of the closest doctor's practice. Pharmacies are usually open 8am–6pm, and details of the nearest 24-hour service are posted in all pharmacy windows or can be found online. For a serious illness or injury, visit a hospital (*Krankenhaus*) or call an ambulance. All emergency rooms are part of the public health system, so your EHIC, GHIC or insurance will cover you.

Smoking, Alcohol and Drugs

Germany has a smoking ban in all public places, including bars, cafés, restaurants and hotels. However, many establishments circumvent these laws by naming themselves a *Raucher-kneipe*, or smoking pub. The possession of narcotics is prohibited and could result in prosecution and a prison sentence. Unless stated otherwise, it is permitted to drink alcohol on the streets and in public parks and gardens. Germany has a strict limit of 0.05 per cent BAC (blood alcohol content) for drivers.

ID

There is no requirement for visitors to carry ID, but in the event of a routine check you may be asked to show your passport. If you don't have it with you, the police may escort you to wherever your passport is being kept.

Local Customs

Germany has strict laws on hate speech and symbols linked to the Nazis. Disrespectful behaviour in public places can warrant a fine, or even prosecution. Pay close attention to signage indicating when photos aren't allowed and think carefully about how you compose your shots. Visitors have come under serious criticism for posting inappropriate photos taken at sites of national significance on social media.

Responsible Travel

Overtourism is having a stark impact on many of Bavaria's most scenic spots, with crowds of domestic and international tourists flocking to the lakes and slopes. This, coupled with the effects of climate change, can have serious environmental consequences. Ensure you stick to marked routes and refrain from swimming in forbidden spots. To offset the region's heavy traffic in summer, make use of the excellent public transport options and cycling paths. When hiking, always deposit rubbish in the available receptacles, or take it with you.

Mobile Phones and Wi-Fi

Visitors travelling to Germany with EU tariffs can use their mobile phones abroad without being affected by data roaming charges; instead they will be charged the same rates for data, SMS and voice calls as they would pay at home. Visitors from other countries should check their contracts before using their phone in Germany in order to avoid unexpected charges.

Post

German post offices and post boxes are easy to spot with their distinctive yellow Deutsche Post signs. Stamps (*Briefmarken*) can be bought in post offices, newsagents, tobacconists and most supermarkets. There are usually self-service stamp machines placed outside post offices.

Taxes and Refunds

VAT is 19 per cent in Germany. Non-EU residents are entitled to a tax refund subject to certain conditions. In order to obtain this, you must request a tax receipt and export papers (*Ausfuhrbescheinigung*) when you purchase your goods. When leaving the country, present these papers, along with the receipt and your ID, at customs to receive your refund.

Discount Cards

There are a number of discount cards in Munich which may make your stay cheaper and more enjoyable. The Munich Card offers a wide range of reductions and discounts on entrance fees to museums, exhibitions, sights and attractions. City tours can also be booked at a reduced price. The Munich City Pass includes public transport tickets and admission to museums. More info can be found at **Simply Munich**.
Simply Munich
w munich.travel/en

INDEX

Page numbers in **bold** refer to main entries.

M

PHRASE BOOK

IN AN EMERGENCY

Where is the telephone?	**Wo ist das telefon?**	*voh ist duss tele-fon?*
Help!	**Hilfe!**	**hilf**-*uh*
Please call a doctor	**Bitte rufen Sie einen Arzt**	**bitt**-*uh* **roof**'*n zee ine-en artst*
Please call the police	**Bitte rufen Sie die Polizei**	**bitt**-*uh* **roof**'*n zee dee poli*-**tsy**
Please call the fire brigade	**Bitte rufen Sie die Feuerwehr**	**bitt**-*uh roof'n zee dee* **foyer**-*vayr*
Stop!	**Halt!**	**hult**

COMMUNICATION ESSENTIALS

Yes	**Ja**	**yah**
No	**Nein**	**nine**
Please	**Bitte**	**bitt**-*uh*
Thank you	**Danke**	*dunk-uh*
Excuse me	**Verzeihung**	*fair*-**tsy**-*hoong*
Hello (good day)	**Guten Tag**	**goot**-*en tahk*
Goodbye	**Auf Wiedersehen**	*owf*-**veed**-*er-zay-ern*
Good evening	**Guten Abend**	*goot'n* **ah***b'nt*
Good night	**Gute Nacht**	*goot-uh* **nukht**
Until tomorrow	**Bis morgen**	*biss* **morg**'*n*
See you	**Tschüss**	*chooss*
What is that?	**Was ist das?**	*voss ist duss*
Why?	**Warum?**	*var*-**room**
Where?	**Wo?**	**voh**
When?	**Wann?**	**vunn**
today	**heute**	**hoyt**-*uh*
tomorrow	**morgen**	**morg**'*n*
month	**Monat**	**mohn**-*aht*
night	**Nacht**	**nukht**
afternoon	**Nachmittag**	**nahkh**-*mit-tahk*
morning	**Morgen**	**morg**'*n*
year	**Jahr**	*yar*
there	**dort**	**dort**
here	**hier**	**hear**
week	**Woche**	**vokh**-*uh*
yesterday	**gestern**	**gest**'*n*
evening	**Abend**	**ah***b'nt*

USEFUL PHRASES

How are you? (informal)	**Wie geht's?**	*vee gayts*
Fine, thanks	**Danke, es geht mir gut**	*dunk-uh, es gayt meer goot*
Until later	**Bis später**	*biss* **shpay**-*ter*
Where is/are?	**Wo ist/sind...?**	*voh ist/sind*
How far is it to...?	**Wie weit ist es...?**	*vee* **vite** *ist ess*
Do you speak English?	**Sprechen Sie Englisch?**	*shpresh'n zee* **eng**-*glish*
I don't understand	**Ich verstehe nicht**	*ish fair*-**shtay**-*uh nisht*
Could you speak more slowly?	**Könnten Sie langsamer sprechen?**	**kurnt**-*en zee* **lung**-*zam-er* **shpresh**'*n*

USEFUL WORDS

large	**gross**	**grohss**
small	**klein**	**kline**
hot	**heiss**	**hyce**
cold	**kalt**	**kult**
good	**gut**	**goot**
bad	**böse/schlecht**	**burss**-*uh*/**shlesht**
open	**geöffnet**	*g'***urff**-*nett*
closed	**geschlossen**	*g'***shloss**'*n*
left	**links**	**links**
right	**rechts**	**reshts**
straight ahead	**geradeaus**	*g'***rah**-*der*-**owss**

MAKING A TELEPHONE CALL

I would like to make a phone call	**Ich möchte telefonieren**	*ish mer-shtuh tel-e-fon*-**eer**'*n*
I'll try again later	**Ich versuche es später noch einmal**	*ish fair-zookh-uh es* **shpay**-*ter nokh ine-mull*
Can I leave a message?	**Kann ich eine Nachricht hinterlassen?**	*kan ish* **ine**-*uh nakh-risht hint-er*-**lahss**-*en*
answer phone	**Anrufbeantworter**	*an-roof-be*-**ahnt**-*vort-er*
telephone card	**Telefonkarte**	*tel-e*-**fohn**-*kart-uh*
receiver	**Hörer**	**hur**-*er*
mobile	**Handy**	*han-dee*
engaged (busy)	**besetzt**	*b'zetst*
wrong number	**Falsche verbindung**	*falsh-uh fair*-**bin**-*doong*

SIGHTSEEING

library	**Bibliothek**	*bib-leo*-**tek**
entrance ticket	**Eintrittskarte**	*ine-tritz*-**kart**-*uh*
cemetery	**Friedhof**	**freed**-*hofe*
train station	**Bahnhof**	**barn**-*hofe*
gallery	**Galerie**	**gall**-*er-ree*
information	**Auskunft**	**owss**-*koonft*
church	**Kirche**	**keersh**-*uh*
garden	**Garten**	**gart**'*n*
palace/castle	**Palast/Schloss**	*pallast/shloss*
place (square)	**Platz**	**plats**
bus stop	**Haltestelle**	**hal**-*te-shtel-uh*
national holiday	**Nationalfeiertag**	*nats-yon*-**ahl**-*fire-tahk*
theatre	**Theater**	*tay*-**aht**-*er*
free admission	**Eintritt frei**	*ine-tritt fry*

SHOPPING

Do you have/Is there...?	**Gibt es...?**	*geept ess*
How much does it cost?	**Was kostet das?**	*voss* **kost**'*t duss?*
When do you open/ close?	**Wann öffnen Sie? schliessen Sie?**	*vunn* **off**'*n zee* **shlees**'*n zee*
this	**das**	*duss*
expensive	**teuer**	**toy**-*er*
cheap	**preiswert**	**price**-*vurt*
size	**Grösse**	**gruhs**-*uh*
number	**Nummer**	**noom**-*er*
colour	**Farbe**	**farb**-*uh*
brown	**braun**	*brown*
black	**schwarz**	**shvarts**
red	**rot**	**roht**
blue	**blau**	**blau**
green	**grün**	**groon**
yellow	**gelb**	**gelp**

TYPES OF SHOP

antique shop	**Antiquariat**	*antik*-**var**-*yat*
chemist (pharmacy)	**Apotheke**	*appo*-**tay**-*kuh*
bank	**Bank**	**bunk**
market	**Markt**	**markt**
travel agency	**Reisebüro**	**rye-z***er-boo-roe*
department store	**Warenhaus**	**vahr**'*n-hows*
chemist's/drugstore	**Drogerie**	*droog-er*-**ree**
hairdresser	**Friseur**	*freezz*-**er**
newspaper kiosk	**Zeitungskiosk**	*tsytoongs-kee-osk*
bookshop	**Buchhandlung**	**bookh**-*hant-loong*
bakery	**Bäckerei**	*beck-er*-**eye**
post office	**Post**	*posst*
shop/store	**Geschäft/Laden**	*gush*-**eft/lard**'*n*
film processing shop	**Fotogeschäft**	**fo**-*to-gush*-**eft**
self-service shop	**Selbstbedienungs-laden**	*selpst-bed*-**ee**-*nungs-lard'n*
shoe shop	**Schuhladen**	*shoo-lard'n*
clothes shop	**Kleiderladen/ Boutique**	*klyder-lard'n* *boo*-**teek**-*uh*
food shop	**Lebensmittel-geschäft**	**lay**-*bens-mittel-gush-eft*
glass, porcelain	**Glas, Porzellan**	**glars, port-sell-ahn**

STAYING IN A HOTEL

Do you have any vacancies?	**Haben Sie noch Zimmer frei?**	*harb'n zee nokh* **tsimm**-*er-fry*
with twin beds?	**mit zwei Betten?**	*mitt tsvy bett'n*
with a double bed?	**mit einem Doppelbett?**	*mitt ine'm* **dopp**'*l-bet*
with a bath?	**mit Bad?**	*mitt* **bart**
with a shower?	**mit Dusche?**	*mitt* **doosh**-*uh*
I have a reservation	**Ich habe eine Reservierung**	*ish* **harb**-*uh ine-uh rez-er*-**veer**-*oong*
key	**Schlüssel**	*shlooss'l*
porter	**Pförtner**	**pfert**-*ner*

EATING OUT

Do you have a table for...?	**Haben Sie einen Tisch für...?**	*harb'n zee tish foor*
I would like to reserve a table	**Ich möchte eine Reservierung machen**	*ish* **mer**-*shtuh ine-uh rezer*-**veer**-*oong makh'n*
I'm a vegetarian	**Ich bin Vegetarier**	*ish bin vegg-er*-**tah**-*ree-er*
Waiter!	**Herr Ober!**	*hair* **oh**-*barel*
The bill (check), please	**Die Rechnung, bitte**	*dee* **resh**-*noong bitt-uh*
breakfast	**Frühstück**	**froo**-*shtock*
lunch	**Mittagessen**	**mit**-*targ-ess'n*
dinner	**Abendessen**	**arb**'*nt-ess'n*
bottle	**Flasche**	**flush**-*uh*
dish of the day	**Tagesgericht**	**tahg**-*es-gur-isht*
main dish	**Hauptgericht**	**howpt**-*gur-isht*
dessert	**Nachtisch**	**nahkh**-*tish*
cup	**Tasse**	**tass**-*uh*
wine list	**Weinkarte**	*vine-kart-uh*

tankard	Krug	khroog
glass	Glas	glars
spoon	Löffel	lerff'l
teaspoon	Teelöffel	tay-lerff'l
tip	Trinkgeld	trink-gelt
knife	Messer	mess-er
starter (appetizer)	Vorspeise	for-shpize-uh
the bill	Rechnung	resh-noong
plate	Teller	tell-er
fork	Gabel	gahb'l

MENU DECODER

Aal	arl	eel
Apfel	upf'l	apple
Apfelschorle	upf'l-shoorl-uh	apple juice with sparkling mineral water
Apfelsine	upf'l-seen-uh	orange
Aprikose	upri-kawz-uh	apricot
Artischocke	arti-shokh-uh-	artichoke
Aubergine	or-ber-jeen-uh	aubergine (eggplant)
Banane	bar-narn-uh	banana
Beefsteak	beef-stayk	steak
Bier	beer	beer
Bockwurst	bokh-voorst	a type of sausage
Bohnensuppe	burn-en-zoop-uh	bean soup
Branntwein	brant-vine	spirits
Bratkartoffeln	brat-kar-toff'ln	fried potatoes
Bratwurst	brat-voorst	fried sausage
Brot	brot	bread
Brötchen	bret-tchen	bread roll
Brühe	bruh-uh	broth
Butter	boot-ter	butter
Champignon	shum-pin-yong	mushroom
Currywurst	kha-ree-voorst	sausage with curry sauce
Dill	dill	dill
Ei	eye	egg
Eis	ice	ice/ice cream
Ente	ent-uh	duck
Erdbeeren	ayrt-beer'n	strawberries
Fisch	fish	fish
Forelle	for-ell-uh	trout
Frikadelle	Frika-dayl-uh	rissole/hamburger
Gans	ganns	goose
Garnele	gar-nayl-uh	prawn/shrimp
gebraten	g'braat'n	fried
gegrillt	g'grilt	grilled
gekocht	g'kokht	boiled
geräuchert	g'rowk-ert	smoked
Geflügel	g'floog'l	poultry
Gemüse	g'mooz-uh	vegetables
Grütze	grurt-ser	groats, gruel
Gulasch	goo-lush	goulash
Gurke	goork-uh	gherkin
Hammelbraten	hamm'l-braat'n	roast mutton
Hähnchen	haynsh'n	chicken
Hering	hair-ing	herring
Himbeeren	him-beer'n	raspberries
Honig	hoe-nikh	honey
Kaffee	kaf-fay	coffee
Kalbfleisch	kalp-flysh	veal
Kaninchen	ka-neensh'n	rabbit
Karpfen	karpf'n	carp
Kartoffelpüree	kar-toff'l-poor-ay	mashed potatoes
Käse	kayz-uh	cheese
Kaviar	kar-vee-ar	caviar
Knoblauch	k'nob-lowkh	garlic
Knödel	k'nerd'l	noodle
Kohl	koal	cabbage
Kopfsalat	kopf-zal-aat	lettuce
Krebs	krayps	crab
Kuchen	kookh'n	cake
Lachs	lahkhs	salmon
Leber	lay-ber	liver
mariniert	mari-neert	marinated
Marmelade	marmer-lard-uh	marmalade, jam
Meerrettich	may-re-tish	horseradish
Milch	milsh	milk
Mineralwasser	minn-er-arl-vuss-er	mineral water
Möhre	mer-uh	carrot
Nuss	nooss	nut
Öl	erl	oil
Olive	o-leev-uh	olive
Petersilie	payt-er-zee-li-uh	parsley
Pfeffer	pfeff-er	pepper
Pfirsich	pfir-zish	peach
Pflaumen	pflow-men	plum
Pommes frites	pomm-fritt	chips/ French fries

Quark	kvark	soft cheese
Radieschen	ra-deesh'n	radish
Rinderbraten	rind-er-brat'n	joint of beef
Rinderroulade	rind-er-roo-lard-uh	beef olive
Rindfleisch	rint-flysh	beef
Rotkohl	roht-koal	red cabbage
Rüben	rhoob'n	turnip
Rührei	rhoo-er-eye	scrambled eggs
Saft	zuft	juice
Salat	zal-aat	salad
Salz	zults	salt
Salzkartoffeln	zults-kar-toff'l	boiled potatoes
Sauerkirschen	zow-er-keersh'n	cherries
Sekt	zekt	sparkling wine
Senf	zenf	mustard
scharf	sharf	spicy
Schlagsahne	shlahgg-zarn-uh	whipped cream
Schnittlauch	shnit-lowkh	chives
Schnitzel	shnitz'l	veal or pork cutlet
Schweinefleisch	shvine-flysh	pork
Spargel	shparg'l	asparagus
Spiegelei	shpeeg'l-eye	fried egg
Spinat	shpin-art	spinach
Tee	tay	tea
Tomate	tom-art-uh	tomato
Wein	vine	wine
Weintrauben	vine-trowb'n	grapes
Wiener Würstchen	veen-er voorst-sh'n	frankfurter
Zander	tsan-der	pike-perch
Zitrone	tsi-trohn-uh	lemon
Zucker	tsook-er	sugar
Zwieback	tsvee-bak	rusk
Zwiebel	tsveeb'l	onion

NUMBERS

0	null	nool
1	eins	eye'ns
2	zwei	tsvy
3	drei	dry
4	vier	feer
5	fünf	foonf
6	sechs	zex
7	sieben	zeeb'n
8	acht	uhkht
9	neun	noyn
10	zehn	tsayn
11	elf	elf
12	zwölf	tserlf
13	dreizehn	dry-tsayn
14	vierzehn	feer-tsayn
15	fünfzehn	foonf-tsayn
16	sechzehn	zex-tsayn
17	siebzehn	zeep-tsayn
18	achtzehn	uhkht-tsayn
19	neunzehn	noyn-tsayn
20	zwanzig	tsvunn-tsig
21	einundzwanzig	ine-oont-tsvunn-tsig
30	dreissig	dry-sig
40	vierzig	feer-sig
50	fünfzig	foonf-tsig
60	sechzig	zex-tsig
70	siebzig	zeep-tsig
80	achtzig	uhkht-tsig
90	neunzig	noyn-tsig
100	hundert	hoond't
1,000	tausend	towz'nt
1,000,000	eine Million	ine-uh mill-yon

DATES

Monday	Montag	mohn-targ
Tuesday	Dienstag	deens-targ
Wednesday	Mittwoch	mitt-vokh
Thursday	Donnerstag	donn-ers-targ
Friday	Freitag	fry-targ
Saturday	Samstag/	zums-targ
	Sonnabend	zonn-ah-bent
Sunday	Sonntag	zon-targ
January	Januar	yan-ooar
February	Februar	fay-brooar
March	März	mairts
April	April	april
May	Mai	my
June	Juni	yoo-ni
July	Juli	yoo-lee
August	August	ow-goost
September	September	zep-tem-ber
October	Oktober	ok-toh-ber
November	November	no-vem-ber
December	Dezember	day-tsem-ber

ACKNOWLEDGMENTS

The publisher would like to thank the following for their kind permission to reproduce their photographs:

(Key: a-above; b-below/bottom; c-centre; f-far; l-left; r-right; t-top)

123RF.com: Preve Beatrice 154-155b, boedefeld 11br
4Corners: Reinhard Schmid 182-183t

Alamy Stock Photo: AA World Travel Library 270bc, Alimdi.net / Reinhold Ratzer 295bl, allfive 18cr, allOver images / TPH 166tl, 234, Associated Press 47cb, Azoor Photo 43cr, Azoor Photo Collection 139bl, B.O'Kane 116-117t, Carol Barrington 16crb, Bildagentur-online / Joko 73, Bildarchiv Monheim GmbH / Peter Eberts 220b, blickwinkel 215tr, blickwinkel / allOver / TPH 254, blickwinkel / DuM Sheldon 11cr, BTEU / AUSMUM 43cb, Cavan Images / Niedring / Drentwett 30bl, Sunny Celeste 42crb, 243tr, Connect Images / JLPH 28-29b, Ian Dagnall 152bl, Walter Bibikow / DanitaDelimont 27cl, Armin Weigel / dpa 41cra, Felix Hörhager / dpa 38-39t, 145, Lino Mirgeler / dpa 105b, Peter Kneffel / dpa 189, Sven Hoppe / dpa 38bl, 39br, 40cra, 41tl, Sergey Dzyuba 264b, filmfoto-02 231tr, Peter Forsberg 142-143b, GL Archive 45tr, 45clb, Glasshouse Images / JT Vintage 46tl, Manfred Glueck 139t, Diego Grandi 122cl, Paul Grove 120bc, Greg Guy 138, Bibikow Walter / Hemis.fr 96bl, 143t, Johann Hinrichs 72, 90-91b, Paul Hobart 24bl, Heinz Tschanz-Hofmann 274, Ulf Huebner 264crb, Image Professionals GmbH / Andreas Strauss 34tl, Image Professionals GmbH / Franz Marc Frei 159b, 242tr, Image Professionals GmbH / LOOK-foto 41tr, 160-161t, 183br, 185t, 187b, 198-199t, 233br, 293, Image Professionals GmbH / Thomas Peter Widmann 209br, Image Professionals GmbH / TravelCollection 28tr, 91tl, 156, 211tr, Imagebroker / Arco / Joko 8clb, 110bl, 119tl, Imagebroker / Arco / K. Kreder 262, 273tl, imageBROKER / Guenter Graefenhain 84cla, imageBROKER / Kurt Amthor 211tl, imageBROKER / Manfred Bail 66-67b, 105t, 121br, 140-141b, 147br, 188t, 295br, imageBROKER / Martin Siepmann 12t, imageBROKER / Michael Rucker 241tr, imageBROKER / Moritz Wolf 48-49, 53t, 78, 106-107t, 158, imageBROKER / Patrick Frischknecht 205ca, imageBROKER / Raimund Kutter 252br, imageBROKER / Stefan Arendt 224-225b, imageBROKER / Werner Dieterich 86-87, imageBROKER.com GmbH & Co. KG / J.W.Alker 31cr, imageBROKER.com GmbH & Co. KG / Manfred Bail 76bl, 127br, 140tl, 185cla, 228-229t, imageBROKER.

com GmbH & Co. KG / Mara Brandl 25br, 53bl, 98, imageBROKER.com GmbH & Co. KG / Maria Breuer 179cl, imageBROKER.com GmbH & Co. KG / Martin Siepmann 32bl, 106crb, 202, 224t, imageBROKER. com GmbH & Co. KG / Raimund Kutter 187clb, 253br, imageBROKER.com GmbH & Co. KG / Stefan Auth 160bl, imageBROKER.com GmbH & Co. KG / Thomas Robbin 263, Imago 41clb, IMAGO / Rolf Poss 26tl, INTERFOTO / Fine Arts 84br, 117crb, 124tl, 132clb, INTERFOTO / History 43bl, INTERFOTO / Personalities 43tr, 44tl, 44cb, 132br, 185br, Ivy Close Images 42bc, 133clb, @diana_jarvis 35cl, Jayskyland Images 18bl, Jon Arnold Images Ltd 10clb, Jon Arnold Images Ltd / Doug Pearson 294, Keystone Press 241br, Jason Knott 52, 56, Art Kowalsky 68bl, Lanmas 43cla, mauritius images GmbH / Ernst Wrba 197br, 210, 212tl, mauritius images GmbH / Günter Gräfenhain 24-25t, mauritius images GmbH / H. Schmidbauer 227b, mauritius images GmbH / Josefine Clasen 150-151t, mauritius images GmbH / Steve Vidler 10ca, 40crb, mauritius images GmbH / Torsten Krüger 93cra, mauritius images GmbH / Volker Preusser 36-37t, 174-175b, Paul Mayall 229br, Martina Melzer 20-21ca, multimaps360 285crb, Sonja Novak 298-299, Cum Okolo 214br, Werner Otto 269t, PA Images / Bradley Collyer 47br, Prisma Archivo 132bc, 175tr, Andreas Prott 40cr, Frederic Reglain 152crb, Robertharding / Hans-Peter Merten 13br, Ageev Rostislav 104, rudi1976 200, Wibowo Rusli 93t, Riccardo Sala 55, 83cra, 148, Maurice Savage 88, 126cl, 152bc, 288bl, Peter Schatz 34-35b, 40cla, Peter Schickert 240-241b, Guido Schiefer 269b, Robert Schneider 172, Schoening 173t, Shotshop GmbH / Classic Collection 275tr, Wolfgang Simlinger 41cla, Alfred Haase / Süddeutsche Zeitung Photo 208bl, Claus Schunk / Süddeutsche Zeitung Photo 144, Scherl / Süddeutsche Zeitung Photo 46-47tc, Stephan Rumpf / Süddeutsche Zeitung Photo 107cla, Süddeutsche Zeitung Photo 46cb, 46br, SuperStock 133crb, 134, Robbie Taylor 226cra, The Print Collector / Heritage Images 44br, Ivan Vdovin 133br, Steve Vidler 35tr, volkerpreusser 25cl, 178, 205cla, 230-231, Westend61 GmbH / Kerstin Bittner 111tl, Westend61 GmbH / Werner Dieterich 94-95b, World History Archive 45br, Ernst Wrba 31bl, Robert Wyatt 203, Zoonar / Wolfilser 132cra

Alte Pinakothek: Severin Schweiger 33crb

AWL Images: ClickAlps 151cra, Cahir Davitt 248, ImageBROKER 40clb, Markus Lange 206-207b, 277, Stefano Politi Markovina 286-287t, Christian Mueringer 250-251, 252-253t

DK | Penguin Random House

Main Contributors Izabella Galicka, Katarzyna Michalska, Rachel Preece, Marc Di Duca

Senior Editors Zoë Rutland, Dipika Dasgupta

Senior Designer Vinita Venugopal

Project Editors Alex Pathe, Anuroop Sanwalia

Editors Vineet Singh, Nandini Desiraju

Proofreader Kathryn Glendenning

Indexer Helen Peters

Picture Research Nishwan Rasool, Virien Chopra, Manpreet Kaur, Priya Singh

Illustrators Lena Maminajszwili, Bohdan Wróblewski, Piotr Zubrzycki

Publishing Assistant Simona Velikova

Jacket Designer Vinita Venugopal

Jacket Picture Researcher Laura O'Brien

Senior Cartographic Editors James Macdonald, Mohammad Hassan

Cartography Manager Suresh Kumar

DTP Designer Rohit Rojal

Image Retouching Vijay Kandwal

Senior Production Controller Samantha Cross

Managing Editors Beverly Smart, Hollie Teague

Managing Art Editor Gemma Doyle

Senior Managing Art Editor Priyanka Thakur

Art Director Maxine Pedliham

Publishing Director Georgina Dee

MIX
Paper | Supporting
responsible forestry
FSC
www.fsc.org   FSC™ C018179

This book was made with Forest Stewardship Council™ certified paper – one small step in DK's commitment to a sustainable future. Learn more at **www.dk.com/uk/ information/sustainability**

A NOTE FROM DK

The rate at which the world is changing is constantly keeping the DK team on our toes. While we've worked hard to ensure that this edition of Munich and the Bavarian Alps is accurate and up-to-date, we know that opening hours alter, standards shift, prices fluctuate, places close and new ones pop up in their stead. So, if you notice we've got something wrong or left something out, we want to hear about it. Please get in touch at travelguides@dk.com

First edition 2002

Published in Great Britain by
Dorling Kindersley Limited,
20 Vauxhall Bridge Road, London SW1V 2SA

The authorised representative in the EEA is
Dorling Kindersley Verlag GmbH. Arnulfstr.
124, 80636 Munich, Germany

Published in the United States by DK Publishing,
1745 Broadway, 20th Floor, New York, NY 10019, USA

Copyright © 2022, 2025 Dorling Kindersley Limited
A Penguin Random House Company

24 25 26 27 10 9 8 7 6 5 4 3 2 1

A CIP catalog record for this book
is available from the British Library.

A catalog record for this book is available
from the Library of Congress.

ISSN: 1542 1554
ISBN: 978 0 2417 1722 6

Printed and bound in China.

www.dk.com